lonely planet

RIO DE JANEIRO

Joel Balsam, Ana Duék, Marisa Megan Paska

FROM LEFT: XINHUA/ALAMY, BRAZIL PHOTO PRESS/ALAMY

Samba dancer, Carnaval Parade, Sambódromo da Marquês de Sapucaí (p188)

Contents

Plan Your Trip

Praia da Urca (p125)

The Guide

Toolkit

Storybook

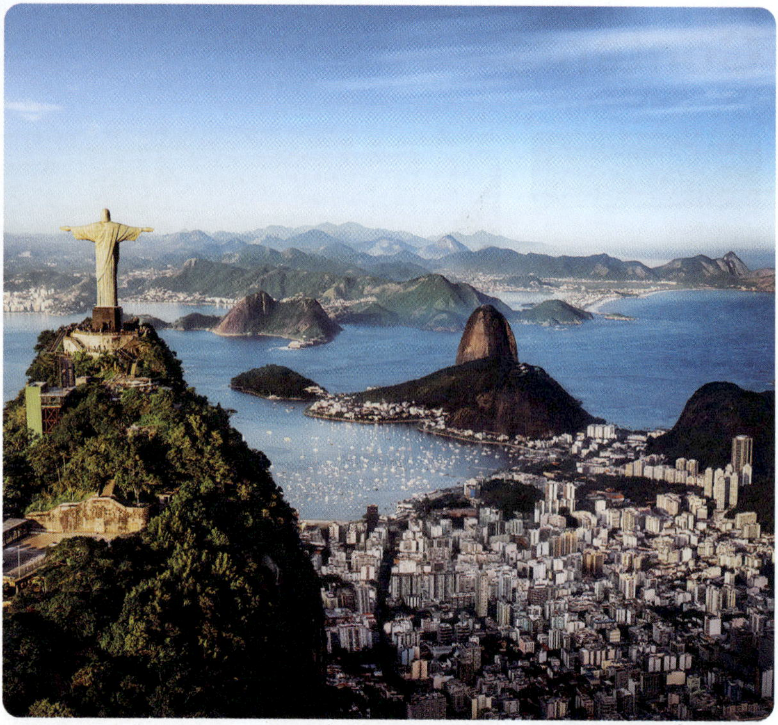

DIEGO GRANDI/SHUTTERSTOCK

Cristo Redentor (p66)

RIO DE JANEIRO

THE JOURNEY BEGINS HERE

Imagine a place where breathtaking granite peaks cascade into the ocean, making this Marvelous City that sits inside a verdant jungle, all lined with white-sand beaches. A place where joy resonates in the air, and singing and dancing are a part of day-to-day life and smiles are contagious. A place where people of all races mix together – in bars, on the beaches, around barbeque grills or samba circles – all with the same goal: to enjoy this giant, messy thing we call life. Rio asks you to fall in love with it – it's a subtle seduction, where beauty, adventure, creativity and connection all play a part – and if you're anything like I was the first time I visited, you might find yourself already enamored on the drive from the airport to your hotel.

Marisa Megan Paska

@_marisamegan

Marisa writes about travel, culture and conservation whenever she's not out surfing.

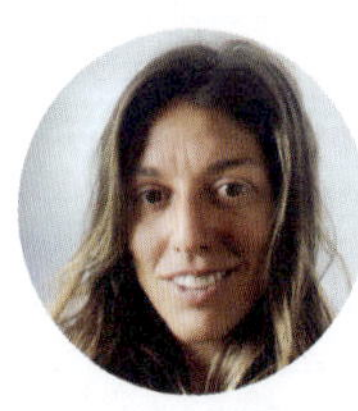

My favorite experience is Rio in the morning, before the crowds. The world is quiet, the beaches are empty and the natural beauty of the city resonates to its fullest.

WHO GOES WHERE

Our writers chose the places that, for them, define Rio de Janeiro.

JOEL BALSAM/LONELY PLANET

I've traveled to more than 60 countries, and have no doubt that **Rio de Janeiro** is the best city in the world – for me anyhow.

Joel Balsam

@joelbalsam

Joel Balsam is a Canadian freelance journalist based in Rio de Janeiro. He wrote the Copacabana & Leme; Botafogo, Urca & Humaitá; Flamengo, Laranjeiras, Catete & Glória; and Santa Teresa & Lapa chapters.

PRADEEP SUBRAMANIAN/ALAMY

Pequena África (p185), in Rio's port district, holds a special place in my heart – a powerful site of memory as one of the world's largest landing points for enslaved Africans, and today a vibrant cultural hub. It's the soul of samba and countless other rhythms, pulsing with history and creativity. A must-visit for any traveler.

Ana Duék

@viajarverde

Ana Duék is an award-winning Brazilian travel journalist and marketer, who is passionate about exploring new cultures and connecting with people. She wrote the Meet the Cariocas chapter.

EAT YOUR ART OUT

This exceptionally creative city isn't just the Hollywood of Brazil – the heartbeat of the country's film and TV industry – Rio is also a hotbed for artistic creation. The city is plastered with murals and graffiti art; lined with galleries and home to some of the coolest and most unique museums, exhibitions and art events around. Get under the skin of the art scene if you really want to know the Marvelous City.

FROM LEFT: AGIF/ALAMY, BIR FOTOS/STOCKIMO/ALAMY, BERNARD BARROSO/SHUTTERSTOCK

ArtRio

This massive annual fine-art fair has played an important role in keeping the city's art scene moving since 2011.

Galleries Galore

Artists tend to flock to certain neighborhoods – such as Gávea, in Zona Sul, and Santa Teresa (pictured above) – and galleries sprout behind them.

EAV Parque Lage

Rio is also home to a renowned art school, EAV Parque Lage, located in a unique Italian-style palazzo on the edge of the Atlantic rainforest.

Fábrica Bhering (p187)

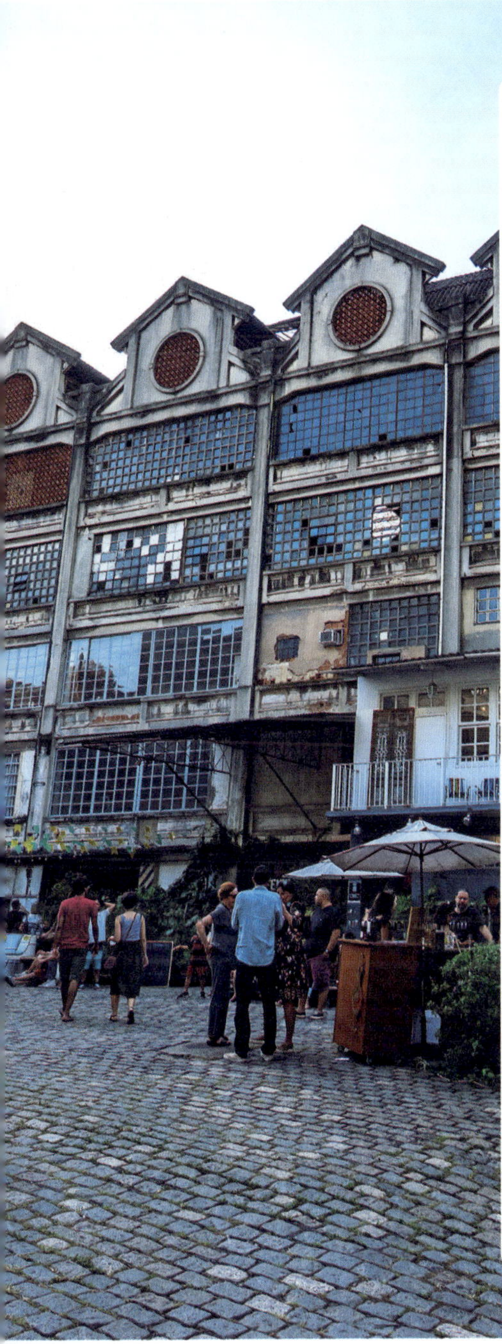

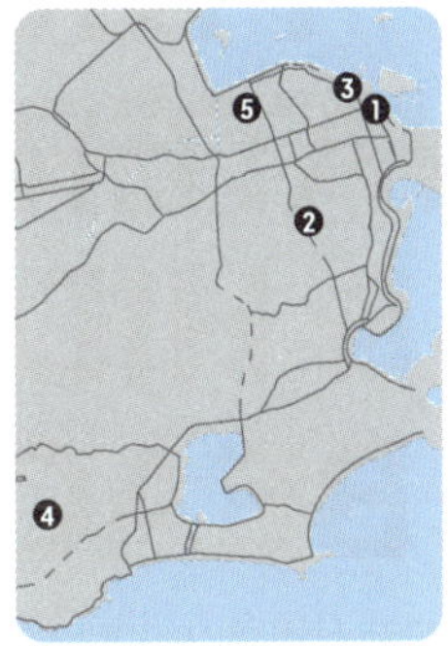

BEST ART EXPERIENCES

One of the most visited museums in the world, the ❶ **Centro Cultural Banco do Brasil** (p176) hosts a number of the city's best international exhibitions.

Walk around the streets of ❷ **Santa Teresa** (p156) and marvel at the colorful murals and graffiti art around every turn.

The ❸ **Museu de Arte do Rio** (p182) is the only museum in the city dedicated to exhibiting *carioca* artists and artwork.

Inside a rainforest park in a circa-1800 former family home you'll find ❹ **Museu Histórico da Cidade** (p56) with contemporary and photographic exhibitions.

❺ **Fábrica Bhering** (p187), a gritty former candy factory near the city's center, was repurposed as artists' ateliers, transforming it into a hub for artistic creation.

PARKS, WATERFALLS & HIDDEN BEACHES

Cariocas (Rio's residents) act like they're always on holiday, and it's no wonder when you live in a place where you can hike through the rainforest in the morning, swim in a crystal-clear waterfall then spend the afternoon on a white-sand beach. While it may be a gritty city, Rio has the largest urban rainforest – and one of the largest urban parks – in the world, so there's plenty of nature to explore.

FROM LEFT: JS NETO FOTOGRAFIA/SHUTTERSTOCK, DERSON SANTANA/SHUTTERSTOCK, VITORMARIGO/SHUTTERSTOCK

Endless Trails

The **Tijuca National Park** (pictured above; p74) has around 200km of trails for exploring, taking you through caverns, waterfalls, viewpoints and mountaintops.

Beat the Crowds

Beaches like Copacabana and Ipanema may be the best known, but to get away from it all, head out west to beaches like **Praia da Barra da Tijuca** (pictured above; p211).

View from the Top

There are plenty of easy hikes, like Pedra Bonita and the Mirante da Lagoa, giving a bird's-eye view of Rio's beauty.

Hiking to Pico da Tijuca, Parque National da Tijuca (p74)

BEST NATURE EXPERIENCES

Entering through the gates of the ❶ **Parque National da Tijuca** (p74) feels like passing through a portal into another, much greener, world.

There's no better way to escape the crowds and beat the heat than a swim in one of Horto's freshwater waterfalls – ❷ **Cachoeiras do Horto** (p63).

Dramatic cliffs hide a tiny beach – ❸ **Praia da Joatinga** (p201) – with turquoise water where the crowds don't go.

❹ **Aterro do Flamengo** (p136) – a 120-hectare oceanfront park is one of landscape artist Burle Marx's most lovely legacies, and an easy place to escape to nature.

❺ **Praia dos Amores** (p204) is a tiny white-sand beach that is only visible at low tide and feels like a piece of the Caribbean.

ARCHITECTURE LOVERS

Rio is renowned for its contrasts, in its landscape and people, but also its architecture. Constructions in the city range from European-influenced historic buildings and art-deco apartment blocks to massive, modernist marvels and neo-futuristic creations – as well as the informal architecture that lines the city's hillsides.

BEST ARCHITECTURE EXPERIENCES

❶ **Theatro Municipal** (p179), inspired by the Paris Opera House, was one of the first buildings built when Brazil became a republic.

The jewel of the Praça Mauá, Rio's LEED-certified science museum, ❷ **Museu do Amanhã** (p182), was designed by Spanish neo-futuristic architect Santiago Calatrava.

An ornate Neo-Manueline-style Portuguese library, ❸ **Real Gabinete Português de Leitura** (p176) is a cultural center from the late 1800s with lavish details.

❹ **Museu de Arte Moderna** (p152) is a modernist concrete museum building, with a 3370-sq-meter gallery space completely free of pillars.

One of Brazil's mega-famous architect Oscar Niemeyer's most notable buildings, ❺ **Museu de Arte Contemporânea** (p220) in Niteroi has amazing views of the Marvelous City.

A Carioca Legend

Brazil's most famous architect was *carioca* Oscar Niemeyer, whose famous constructions include the Palácio Itamaraty (pictured above) and the UN building in New York.

Designing Landscapes

Alongside its structures, many of Rio's landscapes and gardens were also careful curated, primarily by renowned *carioca* landscape architect Roberto Burle Marx (p218).

Catedral Metropolitana de São Sebastião

The Saint Sebastian Metropolitan Cathedral, a grandiose brutalist-style modern cathedral in Rio's center, draws attention from afar due to its unique conical shape.

FROM LEFT: ALEJANDRO ZAMBRANA/SHUTTERSTOCK, LUAN REZENDE/SHUTTERSTOCK LAZYLLAMA/SHUTTERSTOCK

Surfing, Arpoador Beach (p88)

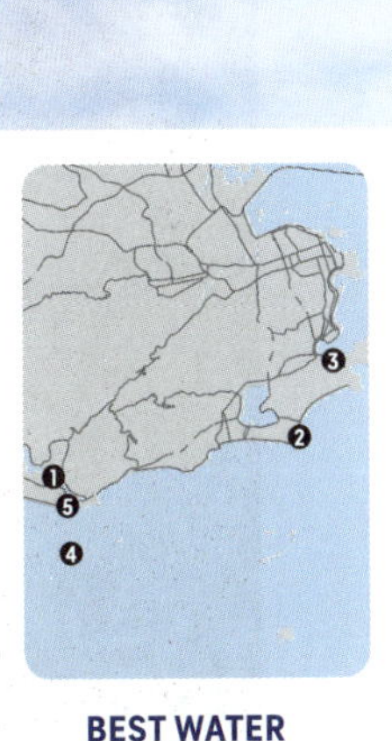

BEST WATER EXPERIENCES

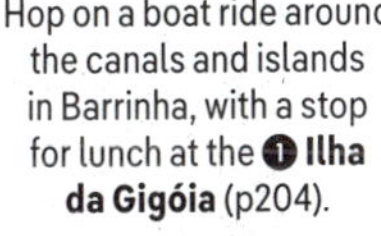

Hop on a boat ride around the canals and islands in Barrinha, with a stop for lunch at the ❶ **Ilha da Gigóia** (p204).

Head to ❷ **Posto 6** (p105) in Copacabana to watch one of the most beautiful sunrises in the world from the water.

From June to August, the humpback whales migrate along Rio's coast, and there's nothing like taking a day trip with ❸ **Sail in Rio** (p150) to see them.

Just 2km from shore, ❹ **Ilhas Tijucas** (p208) are tiny islands reachable by paddleboard, boat, Jet Ski or even swimming.

Imagine gliding along a glassy wave with one of Rio's mountains as your backdrop. Grab a board and go surfing with ❺ **Gaia Surf Feminino** (p206).

ON THE WATER

The Marvelous City is surrounded by water. You're face-to-face with the Baía de Guanabara and the Atlantic Ocean, while lakes, rivers, canals and waterfalls appear all across town. Many of the city's residents make the best of this fortuitous location, waking up early to surf, paddle, sail or swim.

Coastal Living

Rio has nearly 250km of coastline running around the Baía de Guanabara and the Atlantic Ocean (in the state, there's more than 600km of shoreline).

Sailing the World

One Brazilian family spent more than 10 years living and traveling the world on a sailboat, and told their story in the 2007 documentary *O Mundo em Duas Voltas*.

SHAKIN' & GROOVIN'

Rio is a rhythm, and dancing is a part of everyone's life, meaning there are plenty of places to get your groove on in the Marvelous City. Even if you're not a dancer, you'll love enjoying live music in one of Rio's informal street settings. While some of the spots are *carioca* classics, others bring together rhythm and beats from across Brazil – or even the world.

Afro Beats

One of Rio's popular Carnaval groups, the Tambores de Olokun (pictured above), take their hypnotic, rhythmic drumming and African dancing to the streets throughout the year.

The King of Choro

Statue of Pixinguinha (pictured above), who was considered to be the king of *choro* (instrumental samba-adjacent music). A lifelong musician, he composed his first song, 'Lata de leite', at 11 years old.

Study Up

Samba is best when you know all the words; singing them out during the song is a big part of the experience.

FROM LEFT: YASUYOSHI CHIBA/GETTY IMAGES, BRAZIL PHOTOS/GETTY IMAGES, MAURITIUS IMAGES GMBH/ALAMY

Pedra do Sal (p186)

BEST MUSIC EXPERIENCES

Get your samba on the spot where the music was born – at ❶ **Pedra do Sal** (p186), where Monday is samba night.

Head to the ❷ **Feira de Laranjeiras** (p140) on Saturday mornings to hear this instrumental music style born on the streets of Rio.

Feel like dancing? Hit up the ❸ **Feira de São Cristóvão** (p191) for some lively *forró* – a partner dance from Brazil 's Northeast.

Jazz rings out across the night at ❹ **The Maze** (p145): a unique, hand-decorated spot overlooking Catete.

The low-ceiling sweatbox, ❺ **Vaca Atolada** (p168) in Lapa plays traditional samba nearly every night of the week.

FROM LEFT: MARCO AURELIO JR/SHUTTERSTOCK, SEUNGKI LEE/SHUTTERSTOCK, TAUANYALVESS/SHUTTERSTOCK

Sunset, Pedra do Arpoador (p88)

CARIOCA CLASSICS

There are so many amazing under-the-radar things to do in Rio – yet so many of the city's classic sights are still exceptional. The postcards of Rio de Janeiro are nothing if not more breathtaking in person, and there are some sights and experiences in the city that simply can't be missed.

Tourist Central

Rio de Janeiro is the number-one tourist destination in the southern hemisphere – and, trust us, there is a reason that everyone keeps coming back for more.

Take the Train

The distinctive Santa Teresa *bondinho*, a yellow tramcar, runs a tourist route that takes you over the Lapa Arches up to the hilltop.

BEST CLASSIC RIO EXPERIENCES

❶ **Maracanã Football Stadium** (p194) is the largest football stadium in Brazil and akin to church for many.

Whether you hike it, climb it, or ride the cable car up, sunset from the top of the ❷ **Pão de Açúcar** (p128) is unbeatable.

Visiting a giant statue of ❸ **Cristo Redentor** (p66) in Corcovado isn't as corny as it sounds. The views are otherworldly.

Spend at least a few days on the sands of ❹ **Ipanema Beach** (p82) for a true cultural immersion.

Applaud when the sun goes down in ❺ **Pedra do Arpoador** (p88). We promise, you won't forget it.

ADRENALINE JUNKIES

Rio isn't just a city for outdoor lovers, it's a magnet for sport enthusiasts of all kinds. The granite peaks spread across the city offer world-class climbing, consistent winds make for great flying, while the Atlantic Ocean offers everything else an adrenaline junkie might be up for trying.

Long-Haul Flights

Rio's skies are so ideal for paragliding that one hobby flier once made it 165km in the air, flying from Saquarema to Angra dos Reis.

Historical Climbs

The first registered climbs up Pedra da Gávea (pictured above; p206) took place in 1828, although sport climbing would only make it to Rio in 1970.

Windsurfing

Windsurfing, practiced at beaches across the city, gained popularity in Rio after Brazilian athletes Carlos Rossi, Marc Erzberger and Felipe Barreto competed in the modality in the 1984 Olympics.

BEST ADRENALINE EXPERIENCES

Fly like a bird on a para- or hang-gliding flight - you'll jump from ❶ **Pedra Bonita** (p200) to land on the sandy beach below.

If you're looking for an alternative way to summit the ❷ **Pão de Açúcar** (p128), climb your way up by Via Feratta.

For an exciting mountaintop adventure, the four-to-six-hour round-trip ❸ **Pedra da Gávea** (p206) climb will do just fine.

Take a two-wheeled adventure up to the top of ❹ **Corcovado** (p66).

Harness the wind and ride the waves along the windswept coastline of ❺ **Praia da Barra da Tijuca** (p211).

FOR FREE

While living in the city can be expensive, you don't have to be rich to enjoy everything that Rio has to offer. There are a host of free outdoor activities that anyone can easily partake in, along with plenty of no-cost cultural offerings on order as well. A number of the city's most popular museums offer free entry at least once a week, and free events are constantly taking place around town.

FROM LEFT: PISANSTOCK/SHUTTERSTOCK, CELSO PUPO/SHUTTERSTOCK, FELIPE PETROLINI NUNES/SHUTTERSTOCK

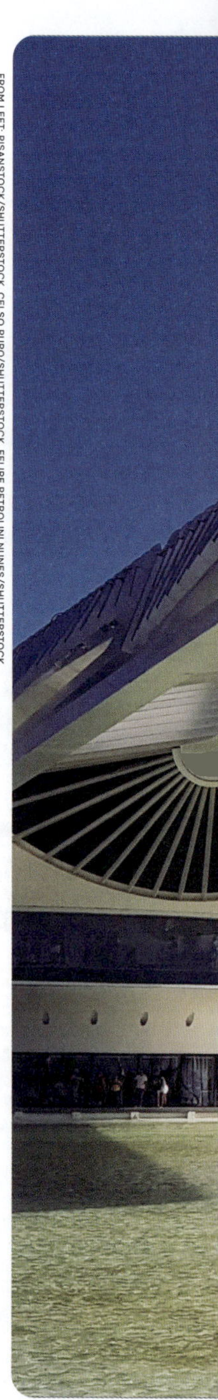

0800

In Rio, something that's free is called '0800' (*zero-oito-centos*, zero eight hundred), which is the dial code for a no-cost telephone call.

Follow Along

There are plenty of tips online and accounts on Instagram will update you on events in town: *@atrilhadoamor*, *@diariodorio* and *@ahseeuvo*.

Market Culture

Rio has a culture of *feiras* (outdoor markets) around the city. Some are food focused, others involve amazing cultural offerings.

Museu do Amanhã (p182)

BEST FREE EXPERIENCES

Instead of paying the expensive cable-car fare for the Sugarloaf Mountain, you can hike up ❶ **Morro da Urca** (p129).

Museums, such as the ❷ **Museu do Amanhã** (p182) and the Museu de Arte do Rio (p182), offer free entry for all on Tuesdays.

Every Sunday the streets of ❸ **Glória** (p148) transform into a huge outdoor street market, where food, clothes and samba shine.

Although you'll have to pay transport there and back, the (free) views from the ❹ **Mirante Dona Marta** (p144) are otherworldly.

Some of Rio's best live music is free – like *choro* at Serginhos, Jazz at Armazém de Cardosão or *forró* at the ❺ **Praça São Salvador** (p142).

UNDER THE RADAR

Rio is a city for those in the know – in this sprawling metropolis there is always something to discover; be it a cool event, a new bar opening or a secret beach you simply never knew was there. The more you look around, the more the city opens up to you, and you'll find that the wonders of the Marvelous City are nearly endless.

Island Getaways

There are more than 100 islands off Rio's shores, like the **Ilhas Tijucas** (pictured above; p208) – reachable by paddleboard – or the **Ilha de Paquetá** (p196), a destination in its own right.

Foreign Names

While many names in Rio come from the Tupiniquim language, Copacabana (pictured above) is actually a Quechua word, meaning 'view of the blue'.

Good Reads

Rio's Biblioteca Nacional now holds more than 15,000 volumes, making it the eighth-largest library in the world.

FROM LEFT: SPACE-TRAVELER/SHUTTERSTOCK, JOEL BALSAM/LONELY PLANET, RACH V/SHUTTERSTOCK

Waterfront, Ilha de Paquetá (p196)

BEST UNDER-THE-RADAR EXPERIENCES

In Rio, there are beautiful views around every corner, but ❶ **Mirante do Pedrão** (p144) hosts epic samba nights; ones that can't be beat.

Courses, workshops, a gallery, theater and live-music nights fill the agenda at ❷ **Retrato Cultural** (p151), an industrial-style cultural center in Glória.

❸ **Nau Cultural** (p157) is a gorgeous shop in Santa Teresa selling unique folk art and artisanal works by artists from around Brazil.

Hop on the ferry to a quaint island in the middle of the Baía de Guanabara called ❹ **Ilha de Paquetá** (p196), where motorized vehicles aren't allowed.

❺ **Quilombo de Sacopã** (p60) is a hidden-away *quilombo* (community of runaway slaves) along Zona Sul's Lagoa, hosting family-friendly *feijoada* and samba events, keeping Afro-Brazilian culture alive.

WITH KIDS

Cariocas – and Brazilians in general – have a very family-oriented culture. Kids are welcome nearly anywhere you go, and are always included in activities and conversations, no matter their age. The city has a number of spots that are geared towards children; however, there are also plenty of activities in the city that are genuinely fun for the whole family.

Snacks on the Go

Keep the kids cooled and fueled with *açaí* (berry smoothie), juice-bar sandwiches and *pão de queijo* (cheesy bread) are easily found everywhere and loved by all.

Rainy Days

Rain in Rio isn't ideal – bookstores, museums, shopping malls and Evolution's indoor climbing wall are favorite rainy day haunts for kids.

Beat the Heat

Rio summer heat is often unbearable, so aim for outdoor activities in the early morning and late afternoon.

FROM LEFT: FLORENCIA MAISONNAVE/SHUTTERSTOCK, SAMOILA IONUT/SHUTTERSTOCK, DENI WILLIAMS/SHUTTERSTOCK

AquaRio (p184)

BEST EXPERIENCES WITH KIDS

❶ **AquaRio** (p184) is a mega-kid attraction, although walking through the plexiglass tunnel is awe-inspiring for kids of any age.

❷ **Parque Lage** (p72) is an amazing forest-backed park that's perfect for picnics, indigenous arts and exploring the mansion, forest and caves on the grounds.

The 40-minute hike up ❸ **Pedra Bonita** (p200) is easy enough for most kids 5+, and rewards you with monkey spotting and exceptional views.

❹ **Parque da Catacumba** (p60), a hidden park near the Lagoa, has picnic areas and playgrounds; climbing walls and ropes courses; and an easy hike to a lovely lookout point.

Riding Rio's distinctive yellow tram car, the ❺ **Bonde** (p156), over the Lapa Arches and through the hilltop hamlet of Santa Teresa is an amazing adventure for kids of all ages

Perfect Days

While there's enough to do in the Marvelous City for three weeks straight, here is a starter kit for spending three perfect days in Rio de Janeiro.

Theatro Municipal (p179)

JC FOTOGRAFIA/SHUTTERSTOCK

DAY 1

Ipanema & Leblon

Wake up early and head to the beach before the crowds roll in. Fitness buffs can head for a workout at the outdoor, Flintstones-style **Arpoador Gym** (p88); opt for a surf class or book a rooftop yoga class at the Aporador Hotel. Or, simply enjoy your favorite book in the morning sun, followed by a refreshing dip in the ocean.

Lunch Stop at **ARP Bar** (p89) for brunch with an ocean view.

Jardim Botânico

After, make your way to **Jardim Botânico** (p68) for a tropical plant immersion and a delicious pastry at the nearby **La Bicyclette** (p65). Then, hike up to the Horto Waterfalls for a fresh-water swim. Later, wander around **Parque Lage** (p72).

Dinner Head to the quirky **Rio Scenarium** (p169), an eclectic, vintage-style dinner and samba club.

Lapa

Head to Lapa for a night on the town, starting with *petiscos* (snacks) and drinks at **Suru** (p169) to line your stomach. Then, it's off to the **Bar da Cachaça** (p168) to taste Brazil's national spirit before heading to the dance floor. **Beco do Rato** (p169) and **Vaca Atolada** (p168) are two traditional samba spots for die-hard fans.

DAY 2

Santa Teresa

Wake up in Santa Teresa for a loaded breakfast at **Cafe do Alto** (p162) before heading off for an **art walking tour** (p165) of the neighborhood. Peruse the numerous cool **bohemian shops** (p156), then head over to the **Parque Glória Maria** (p162) to marvel at the views. When you've had your fill, saunter down the colorful **Escadaria Selaron** (p166) towards Centro – just don't forget to turn around and look uphill to enjoy the view.

Lunch Grab lunch at **Lilia** (p177) restaurant.

Centro

Take yourself on a **walking tour of the historic buildings** (p178) around Cinelândia (the **Theatro Municipal** is a jewel), then continue on to the **Real Gabinete Português de Leitura** (p176) before making your way to the Praça Mauá, where **Museu do Amanhã** (p182) awaits you.

Dinner Start off with a chic Italian-style meal at **Sult** (p120).

Botafogo

The place to be in the city these days is Botafogo, where the streets are lined with bars and restaurants galore. Grab a drink at **Bar Tero** (p124) before heading off to **Treme Treme** (p118) for beers and mingling. End the night with a dance fest at **Quartinho** (p124).

DAY 3

Zona Oeste

It's time to head west, starting with a hike up **Pedra Bonita** (p200) for stunning views of the city. If you're game, you can even opt to **para-** or **hang-glide** (p200) down. Then, hop in a car and head far out west to **Prainha** (p212), one of Rio's most beautiful and pristine beaches, or a bit further to the undeveloped **Praia de Grumari** (p216) – also home to Rio's only nudist-friendly bit of sand.

Lunch Enjoy a traditional seafood lunch at one of Barra de Guaratiba's caiçara restaurants, such as **Bira** (p217).

Zona Oeste

When you've finished lounging in the sand, you can opt to hike along the **Praias Selvagens** (p215) trail, up to the top of Telegraph Rock.

Dinner Grab a decadent sunset meal at **Ocyá** (p205) on Ilha de Primeira (reservations required).

Zona Oeste

On your way back, stop for a boat ride around the islands of **Barrinha** (p204). When you're back on the mainland, head to **Av Olegário Maciel** (p207) in Jardim Oceânico for drinks and dancing, and if you're still going strong, head off to one of **Barra's nightclubs** (p211) for an all-night dance fest.

WHEN TO GO

Rio de Janeiro is a year-round city, with a reason to go for every season.

The Marvelous City is marvelous all year-round; however, when you choose to visit depends on what type of traveler you are. Crowds flock to the city in the summertime, when New Year and Carnaval fill the streets with revelers of all ages. It's the most exciting time to be in Rio – but also the most expensive, and the downright hottest. If you're not the festival type, and crowds, heat and lines aren't your thing, then opt to plan your trip between April and October (although do your best to avoid Easter week.)

Off-Season Deals

Prices can be significantly higher in the summer, and off the charts for New Year or Carnaval. If you're looking to save some money, visit in the spring autumn or winter, or book a room that's further from the beach.

I LIVE HERE

SUMMER OFFERS ENDLESS OPTIONS

Willy Reuter (@willyreuter) is an architect and visual artist.

It's no wonder that summers in Rio attract people from all over the world: you can climb a mountain or hike through the forest in the morning, relax on the beaches of Ipanema or Copacabana in the afternoon, then head out for music or a party on a warm summer's night. This fusion between lush nature and fast-paced urban life makes Rio de Janeiro so special.

Dois Irmãos, seen from Ipanema Beach (p82)

FROM LEFT: MAURITIUS IMAGES GMBH/ALAMY, IULIA TIMOFEEVA/SHUTTERSTOCK

RAIN IN RIO

Rio isn't well designed for rain, and *cariocas* hate the stuff. Beyond the fact that many of the city's best activities are outdoors, the streets tend to flood, and events are canceled when water falls from the sky.

Weather Through the Year

JANUARY	FEBRUARY	MARCH	APRIL	MAY	JUNE
Avg. daytime max: **30°C**	Avg. daytime max: **32°C**	Avg. daytime max: **30°C**	Avg. daytime max: **28°C**	Avg. daytime max: **26°C**	Avg. daytime max: **25°C**
Days of rainfall: **10**	Days of rainfall: **9**	Days of rainfall: **6**	Days of rainfall: **4**	Days of rainfall: **10**	Days of rainfall: **8**

BEAT THE HEAT

One of Rio's finer nicknames is *Rio 40 graus*, meaning Rio 40 degrees, referring to the city's aggressive heat. It's not an exaggeration, either. In the summer, parts of the city can hit higher than 40°C, so plan your sun covering and activities accordingly.

Summer Festivals

Summer in Rio is one big party, however there are two festivals that simply can't be beat.

The first isn't technically a festival, but New Year's Eve celebrated in Rio is as good a party as you can find anywhere. Hordes of revelers dressed in white descend on Copacabana Beach to watch an otherworldly fireworks display – and hop over seven waves in the sea to get good luck for the coming year.

Hot on its toes comes Carnaval in February (sometimes March), one of the biggest and most awaited festivals in the world. Carnaval in Rio attracts people from all over the globe and, for *cariocas* (Rio's residents), it's more than a way of life – it's a reason for being.

After Carnaval ends, the year can officially begin; however in April, Semana Santa, or Easter Week, gives us one last reason to celebrate before summer ends.

Winter Festivals

Winter in Rio is a very merry season, when everyone dresses up like countryside folk, lights bonfires, drinks spiced wine and dances *quadrilha* at the ever-popular Festas Juninas, a series of festivals in honor of the saints days of Santo Antônio, São João and São Pedro.

These parties – which in the northeast of Brazil are more celebrated than Carnaval – mostly take place in June, but frequently continue on through July as well.

In August, music lovers flock to the city's Festival de Inverno (Winter Fest), which brings together huge names in Brazilian music, while the sporting types fly in from around the country for Rio's annual Marathon.

Rather hang out inside? Check out Rio's Semana de Cinema in September, when flicks at theaters across the city are half price – both new releases and Brazilian classics.

I LIVE HERE

AUTUMN LIGHT

Laura Guazelli is the head chef and owner of Laurices (@universolaurices), a gluten-free baked-goods brand.

Autumn sunsets are alive with earthy orange tones. The sepia light sometimes gives me the feeling that I've time-traveled back to an older, less globalized, more authentic Rio. Autumn is also a time of year when the city has more locals and fewer tourists, making you feel a bit more at home. You know the names of the waiters at your favorite bar, and they know yours.

Copacabana Beach (p104)

SWEATER WEATHER

In the winter Rio does cool down, with lows from July to August sometimes hitting the single digits overnight. While it is a rare occurrence, *cariocas* don't usually know what to do, as many of them don't even own clothes for this sort of weather.

JULY
Avg. daytime max: **25°C**
Days of rainfall: **8**

AUGUST
Avg. daytime max: **23°C**
Days of rainfall: **7**

SEPTEMBER
Avg. daytime max: **26°C**
Days of rainfall: **5**

OCTOBER
Avg. daytime max: **27°C**
Days of rainfall: **7**

NOVEMBER
Avg. daytime max: **28°C**
Days of rainfall: **10**

DECEMBER
Avg. daytime max: **30°C**
Days of rainfall: **9**

FROM LEFT: LAZYLLAMA/SHUTTERSTOCK, PHOTO 12/ALAMY

Ipanema Beach (p82)

GET PREPARED FOR RIO DE JANEIRO

Useful things to load in your bag, your ears and your brain.

Clothes

Less is more: They say if you want to fit in, you've got to look the part, and nothing is truer on the beachy streets of the Marvelous City. *Carioca*-style is laid-back, to say the least – shorts, tank tops and Havaianas are the uniform; however, outfits are also unpretentiously chic enough to go from the beach to the bar without skipping a beat.

What to pack: Summer dresses, shorts, tank tops and T-shirts are all women will need, while men should opt for boardshorts and T-shirts over more formal attire. Even on nights out, err towards dressing down if you don't want to look out of place.

Manners

Cariocas Rio's residents) are generally friendly and outgoing and love talking to strangers, so be prepared for chats, whether you're sitting side by side at a restaurant or sharing an elevator. While it may be strange for people from more closed-off cultures, remember that it's all good-natured – having full conversations with people you just met on the street is pretty normal in Rio.

Cold happens: If you're traveling during Rio's winter, don't forget to include a jacket, pair of pants and some closed-toed shoes for the infrequent but still existent cold spells that do fall over the city.

READ

Memórias Póstumas de Brás Cubas (Machado de Assis; 1881) Assis' most famous work recounts the fictional life of Brás Cubas.

A Alma Encantadora Das Ruas: The Enchanting Soul Of The Streets (João Rio; 1904–07) Collection of essays about the streets of Rio.

How to be a Carioca (Priscilla Ann Goslin; 1991) Lighthearted, fun and funny alternative tourist guide about life in Rio.

A Hora da Estrela (Clarice Linspector; 1977) A novel about a Northeastern Brazilian woman who moves to Rio de Janeiro.

Words

Água Water

Água de coco Coconut water

Amigo/a Friend, also a polite way to refer to anyone whose name you don't know

Bom dia Good morning (used until noon)

Boa tarde Good afternoon (used from noon until sundown)

Boa noite Good night (used after dark)

De boa it's all good

Desculpa I'm sorry – used if you accidentally bump into someone

Liçensa Excuse me – used to ask to pass someone on the sidewalk, for instance

Moço/Moça Young man or woman, also a polite way to call the attention of a waiter or waitress

Obrigado/a Thank you; meaning 'I am obliged to you' – if you identify as female, always say *obrigada*; if you identify as male or don't identify with any gender, *obrigado* is both the masculine and neutral version

Onde está Where is. Used for asking directions

Por favor Please

Posso pedir May I ask for... a more polite way to ask for something you'd like

Praia Beach

Quero A simple way to ask for something you'd like

Sem problemas No worries or no problems

Suco Juice

Tudo bom? Tudo bem? Both mean 'Is it good?' and are used as both the question and the response to 'how are you doing?'

WATCH

Coisa Mais Linda (Giuliano Cedroni & Heather Roth; 2019) Fun TV series set in Rio's bossa-nova era; drenched in *carioca* culture.

Que Horas Ela Volta? (pictured above; Anna Muylaert; 2015) Poignant dramedy giving insights into the culture of household help in Brazil.

City of God (Kátia Lund & Fernando Meirelles; 2002) Classic film about young kids growing up in one of Rio's most dangerous favelas.

Amarelo – É Tudo pra Ontem (Fred Ouro Preto; 2020) Documentary by Brazilian Rapper Emicida explains/celebrates Afro-Brazilian culture.

LISTEN

Zero (Liniker; 2015) The song that put Liniker, Brazil's most prominent trans-woman composer and singer, on the map.

Várias Queixas (Gilsons; 2021) An EP by the famous pop-music trio comprising three of musical icon Gilberto Gil's children.

A Tábua de Esmeralda (Jorge Ben Jor; 1974) Arguably the best album by one of Rio's (and Brazil's) top musical artists.

Transa (Caetano Veloso; 1972) One of this Brazilian singer's most popular albums was composed during his political exile in London.

FROM LEFT: AD-FOTO/SHUTTERSTOCK, KENCHIRO168/SHUTTERSTOCK

Taxis

GETTING THERE

Whether you're arriving at Galeão–Antonio Tom Jobim international Airport (GIG), or to Santos-Dumont (SDU) on a connecting flight from São Paulo, there are a few easy ways to get to your hotel from the airport.

Public Bus

There's an air-conditioned bus service that runs from the GIG airport to Zona Sul or to Barra, and costs only R$24.84. The bus, nicknamed the Frescão, runs every hour from 5am to 10pm, seven days a week. The Zona Sul line follows the beach and ends at Praça Antero de Quental in Leblon. The Barra da Tijuca line (Galeão x Alvorada) is circular, but stops at both the Windsor Barra Hotel and the Jardim Oceânico Metro Station. There are official stops, although you can ask to be let out close to your street. Exit the airport at door C, cross the crosswalk and look for a rather indiscreet sign saying 'Bus'.

Taxis

There are three types of taxis leaving GIG. Official airport taxis (Táxi Oficial or Rádio Táxi), which charge a fixed up-front fee to your destination neighborhood, are the most expensive, but the least hassle. Option two is the prepaid self-service terminal selling fixed-rate vouchers for normal taxis (Táxi Común). Purchase, then simply take your voucher and stand in the taxi line. Option three is to head outside and get a normal metered taxi; however, beware of scams.

Rideshare

Rideshare cars, popular in Rio, are available from the airport, as long as you can connect to the Wi-Fi, which the airport does have, although it doesn't always work. At SDU, the Uber waiting area is well signposted; while at GIG, you'll need to go to the bottom floor, out the door to the left and walk until you see the Uber sign.

FROM THE AIRPORT TO THE CITY CENTER

From GIG Airport to Copacabana

All taxi and rideshare car costs are approximate and subject to change, depending on the time of day, time of year and current demand. All ride durations are subject to change depending on traffic, which can greatly affect ride time.

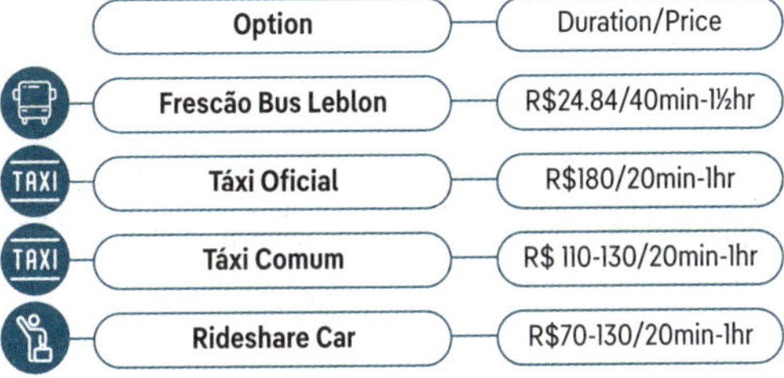

Option	Duration/Price
Frescão Bus Leblon	R$24.84/40min-1½hr
Táxi Oficial	R$180/20min-1hr
Táxi Comum	R$ 110-130/20min-1hr
Rideshare Car	R$70-130/20min-1hr

From SDU Airport to Copacabana

All taxi and rideshare car costs are approximate and subject to change depending on the time of day, time of year and current demand. All ride durations are subject to change depending on traffic, which can greatly affect ride time.

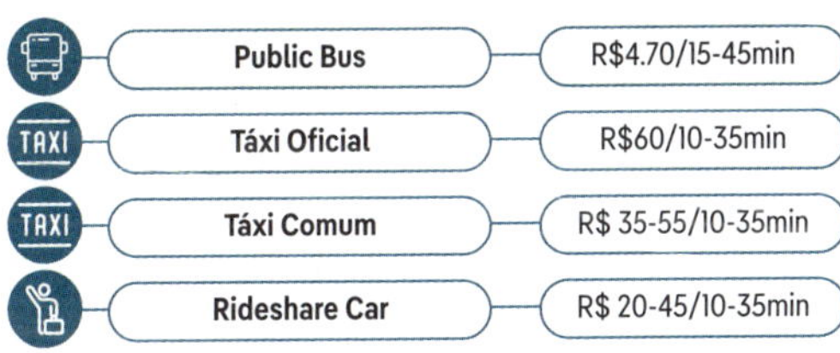

Option	Duration/Price
Public Bus	R$4.70/15-45min
Táxi Oficial	R$60/10-35min
Táxi Comum	R$ 35-55/10-35min
Rideshare Car	R$ 20-45/10-35min

GETTING CONNECTED: SIM CARDS

You can purchase a local SIM card at any newspaper kiosk in the city, however you'll need a **local tax number** (called a CPF; p238) to activate it. If you can't find someone to do it for you, then head to an official cell-phone service provider – such as Vivo, Claro or TIM – where there are options to activate a line with your passport number.

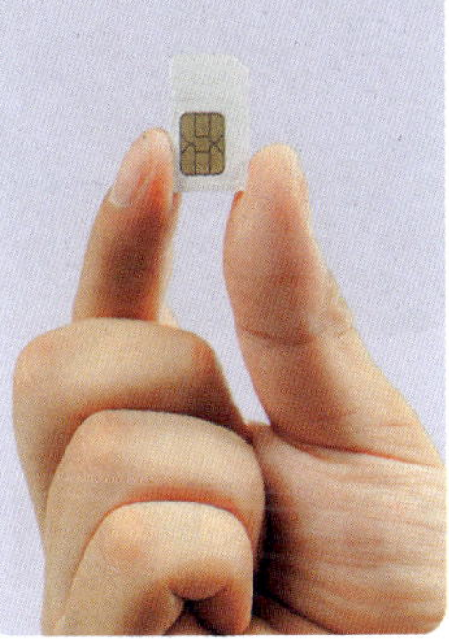

OTHER POINTS OF ENTRY

InterCity Bus

If reaching Rio by bus from another city, you'll arrive at the Rodoviária Novo Rio bus terminal in Santo Cristo, in the city's center. There is a BRT station at Terminal Gentileza, a short, 300m walk from the bus terminal, that will take you to Leblon; or you can opt to get a city bus or a rideshare car all the way to your destination, or to the nearest metro station at Uruguaiana.

Transfer Service

There are a number of transfer van services that will take you to/from popular destinations around Rio. 'In Búzios' is a popular transport service to the paradisiacal peninsula, while Paraty Tours is one of the top options if you're heading south to the quaint colonial town. Services typically run door-to-door, and are perfect if you're not up to facing public transport in Portuguese.

Car

If you're driving into Rio de Janeiro from another city, beware of your arrival times so you don't hit some of the city's monumental traffic. Avoid rush hour at all costs, but also be aware of late Sunday afternoons, especially after a holiday weekend or a particularly nice beach day.

FROM LEFT: TOM-5400/SHUTTERSTOCK, WAGNER CAMPELO/SHUTTERSTOCK

Catete Metro Station

GETTING AROUND

There are a number of ways to get around the Marvelous City – be it by public transport, rideshare car or the power of your own two legs.

Metro

Rio's metro only has two lines. Line one runs from Uruguai station in Tijuca to Jardim Oceânico at the beginning of Barra da Tijuca, while line two runs from Pavuna to Botafogo. You can transfer between lines at any of the stations between Central do Brasil and Botafogo by simply hopping over to the other platform. Trains run from 5am to midnight Monday to Saturday, and 7am to 11pm on Sundays and holidays. It costs R$7.50 for a one-way fare.

TIP

During rush hour, there are designated women-only cars on the metro trains, which can help solo-women travelers to avoid any uncomfortable situations when the trains are packed to the brim.

Buses

Buses run 24 hours a day, although between midnight and 5am you may have longer waits. It's R$4.30 per ride with a Rio transport card or any tap-and-pay device. Note: any bus schedules you may find (Moovit, Google Maps, etc), probably won't be kept to.

VLT

The Veículo Leve Sobre Trilhas (VLT), aka Rio's new electric tramcars, function in and around the city's Centro neighborhood, running from Santos Dumont airport through Centro, Praça Mauá, Saúde, Gamboa and Santo Cristo. They're open 5am to 11pm; R$4.30 one way by cash, card or RioCard (change isn't available).

BRT

The BRT are modern, extended, express buses that function as an above-ground metro. Lines run from Jardim Oceânico to Recreio, through Zona Norte, and from Zona Norte to Barra. It's R$4.30 per ride, payable with transport cards or your digital wallet.

TIP

The bike lanes aren't exclusively used by cyclers, so keep alert. They're also used by commuters, so be polite and keep to your far right to allow others to pass if you're slowing.

Cycling

While the network of cycling lanes in Rio is limited, the existing bike lanes run along the most beautiful parts of the city, offering postcard views of the Pão de Açúcar, Cristo Redentor, Dois Irmãos and more. Rio's bike-sharing system Itaú (*bikeitau.com.br/rio*) offers more than 5000 bright orange bicycles – both normal and electric – for public use, with nearly 400 stations in the city. With a SIM card you

PUBLIC TRANSPORT ESSENTIALS

Buying Tickets

There are different types of transport cards in Rio: Giro card is primarily used for the metro, while Riocard+ works on all forms of transportation, and gives you discounts on integrated travel (ie metro+bus). If all you're looking for is a one-way ride, simply use your digital wallet to tap and pay on the metro or bus.

If you do opt to buy a transport card, they're available at the kiosks inside metro or BRT stations. There is a fixed one-time R$4.30 cost for the card, plus a minimum recharge of R$5. There are no discounted round-trip fares, so simply load up your card with the amount of rides you expect to take, and recharge it at the same terminals when you run out of credit. Bus terminals also sell transport cards, however bus stops do not.

Free Rides

On the metro and public buses, children under age six ride for free, and you can typically just walk through the turnstile with them in front of you as you swipe your card (although in rare cases, someone might ask their age). Travelers over the age of 65 with a Brazilian tax number are also eligible to receive a ride-for-free metro pass, although you'll need to organize it at the 'Posto de Gratuidades' prior to riding.

Etiquette

All seats on the metro are considered preferential; if you see a person with a disability, an elderly or pregnant person, or a parent with small children without a chair, correct etiquette stipulates that you should give up your seat. Although it can be a bit tricky at rush-hour, Brazilians typically adhere to these social norms – even on buses, where there are designated preferential seats.

Bus Routes

Figuring out bus routes can be a bit tricky, although both the Google Maps and Moovit apps offer generally solid options for buses to take to get to/from your destination. The only caveat is the actual schedules – bus schedules are hardly ever kept to; however, if you wait patiently at the station, your bus is sure to arrive in time.

LAZYLLAMA/SHUTTERSTOCK

can download the app and pay per ride (although the monthly pass, at R$39.99, is a much better deal).

Walking

Rio may be spread out, however most neighborhoods are very walkable, and walking around Rio can be a joy. Walking through the streets of Zona Sul or Zona Oeste during the day is typically safe, even on your own; while in Centro and Zona Norte, walking is preferable in pairs or groups. Taking transport is still recommended at night.

Taxi/Rideshare

Both taxis and rideshares are widely available around the city, and you're able to pay fares with cash or credit card. Taxi fares are metered, while rideshare fares are agreed upon via the app prior to departure. Apps like TaxiRio, 99 and Uber all work well in the city.

Ferry Boats

At Praça XV's ferry boat terminal, you'll find boats to take you across the Baía de Guanabara to Niterói, or to a number of the city's islands. The ferry boat is inexpensive,

ACCESSIBILITY

Many of the city's metro stations offer elevators and ramps for wheelchairs or those with mobility issues – a complete list can be found on its website *(metrorio.com.br/GuiaDoCliente/Acessibilidade)*.

All of the stations have textured floors, as well as signs and maps in braille to help passengers with visibility challenges reach their trains. Nearly all city buses have wheelchair lifts, although the equipment may not be well maintained. If you're looking for a reliable accessible lift, ordering a wheelchair-friendly taxi in advance.

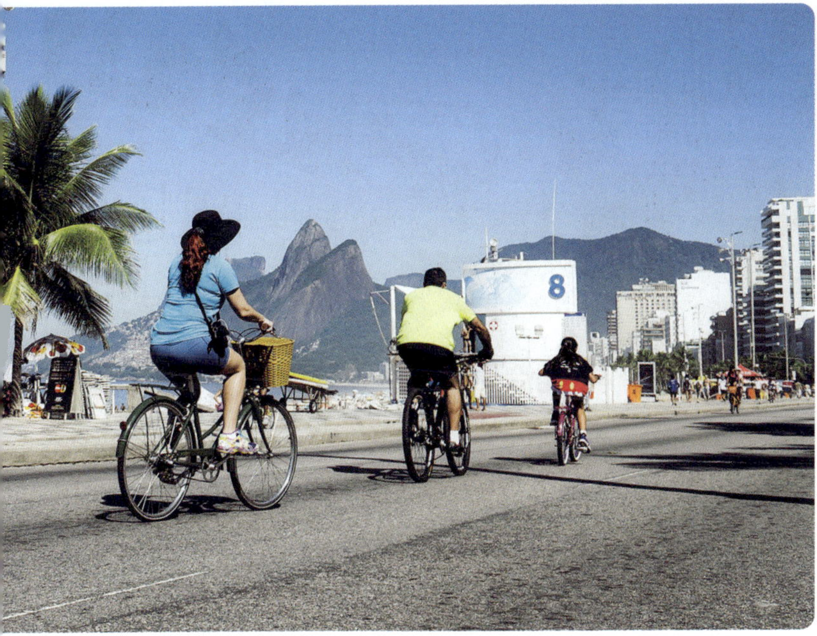

Ipanema Beach (p82)

fast and offers beautiful views – and in the case of Paquetá, it's the only way to arrive. Boats run from 6am to 11pm, and a one-way ticket on the CCR Barcas line to either Niterói or Paquetá costs R$7.70

Mototaxi

Rideshare apps in Rio also offer motorcycle taxis. Fares are significantly cheaper, avoid traffic and in places like Santa Teresa, they're often the easiest way to arrive. Riding a motorcycle in Rio, however, isn't for the faint of heart.

Driving & Parking

In the city itself, driving can be a frustrating experience even if you know your way around. Traffic snarls and parking problems do not make for an enjoyable holiday.

Be aware that Rio has extremely strict drink-driving laws (the Lei Seca, or 'dry law'), with a fine of around R$2000 for those with a blood-alcohol content of over 0.06%.

Police checkpoints are set up nightly around the city in changing locations.

JOEL BALSAM/LONELY PLANET

Bar, Santa Teresa (p156)

DINING OUT

The food scene in Rio de Janeiro is on the rise, with new and creative restaurants popping up all over town.

Rio's culinary scene has grown leaps and bounds in the last few years, with innovative chefs launching creative new projects across the city – some of which are now decorated with Michelin stars.

You'll find everything in the city, from high-end cuisine to mouthwatering bar snacks made from farm-fresh ingredients, to artisanal food offerings served at lively outdoor markets.

Variety comes in many forms in Rio, which is unsurprising, given the large immigrant population. Lebanese, Japanese, Spanish, German, French and Italian cuisines are among the standouts, though there's an equally broad selection of regional Brazilian restaurants, along with some exceptional Indian, Thai and Korean-fusion options popping up among the crowd.

Despite top-notch chefs, ethnically diverse cuisine and a rich bounty from farm, forest and sea, Rio hasn't earned much of a culinary reputation abroad. Within Brazil, it's a different story, with most *cariocas* (Rio's residents) convinced that there's no place quite like home for sitting down to a first-rate meal.

Juice Bars

Most *cariocas* start their morning with a stop at the local juice bar, informal counter joints where you can get an *açaí* (berry smoothie), toast with eggs and an infinite number of freshly squeezed tropical fruit juices.

Unique flavors to try include *cupuaçu* (Amazonian fruit), *caju* (fruit from the cashew-nut tree), *acerola* (tropical cherry),

Best Rio Snacks

MILHO
Fresh steamed corn – on the cob or in a bowl.

JOELHO
Savory rolled-up bread filled with ham and cheese.

PÃO DE QUEIJO
Cheesy-bread made with tapioca flour (gluten free).

TAPIOCA
Manioc-flour crepe stuffed with sweet or savory fillings.

carambola (star fruit), *graviola* (custard apple), *fruta do conde* (sugar apple) and *cacau* (made from the creamy pulp of the cocoa pod; nothing like cocoa) – not to mention the more traditional fruits, such as *maracujá* (passion fruit), *manga* (mango), *goiaba* (guava) and *tangerina* (tangerine). To order yours without sugar, request '*sem açúcar*.'

Feiras

The *feiras* (outdoor food markets) pop up in different locations throughout the week, and nothing beats wandering through a market and taking in the action. *Feiras* are the best places to shop for juicy mangoes, papayas, pineapples and other fruits; along with a whole range of produce, eggs, freshly caught fish, cured meat and cheeses, and even fresh meat, depending on the market.

While you're there, grab a freshly fried *pastel-da-feira* (fried meat/cheese-filled dough) with a glass of *caldo de cana* (sugar-cane juice) on the side – it's a well-loved Brazilian tradition. The best time to go is from 8am to noon; the *feiras* end by 2pm or 3pm.

Vegans & Vegetarians

Brazil may have a meat-heavy culture, but in the cultural capital of the country, it's actually pretty easy to find vegetarian or vegan cuisine.

There's a strong movement in the city for well-being and healthy eating, and these days there are excellent vegetarian and vegan *por-kilo* (per-kilo) venues, *botecos* (small open-air bars) and even high-end restaurants in the city – along with a number of veg-friendly options on most menus. *Banana da terra* (plantains), *jaca* (jackfruit) and *caju* (cashew nut) are some of the local ingredients favored in Rio's vegan fare. There is even an entire ice-cream shop, **Hoba**, serving only cashew-nut-based products.

Prato Feito

A traditional dish in Brazil – that you'll find on lunch tables across the country – nearly always has the same elements. Start with rice and beans (black beans, if you're in Rio); then add a protein like chicken, eggs, fish or meat; a lettuce and tomato salad; french fries and *farofa* (toasted cassava flour used as a food topper). When you order it at a corner restaurant, this

Stuffed tapioca crepes
JULIA-BOGDANOVA/SHUTTERSTOCK

FOOD FESTIVALS

Rio Gastronomia *(@riogastronomia)* All the city's restaurants get together for a star-studded event across two to three weekends.

Comida di Buteco *(comidadibuteco.com.br)* Rio's best *botecos* go head-to-head in battle to see who has the best bar food.

Festival Comida de Favela *(@comidade favela)* Gastronomic establishments from the city's favelas come together once a year in Maré to show off their culinary prowess.

Rio Wine & Food Festival *(@riowineand foodfestival)* Barra da Tijuca–based festival brings together hundreds of food and especially wine vendors for a week every autumn.

Restaurant Week *(restaurantweek.com.br)* A week to discover all the gastronomy the city has on offer.

KIBE
Deep-fried Middle Eastern snack with a whole-wheat crust and ground-beef filling.

COXINHAS
Pear-shaped cornmeal balls that are filled with shredded chicken.

ACARAJÉ
Deep-fried bean balls topped with spicy pastes and shrimp.

ESFIRRA
Triangle-shaped pastry stuffed with meat, spinach or cheese.

Mô Café (p161)
ALEXANDRE ROTENBERG/ALAMY

BEST CAFES IN THE CITY

Cirandaia (p131) Modern specialty coffee shop in Humaitá with simple but delicious breakfast options.

Mô Café (p161) The best place in Santa Teresa for an espresso coffee and some good conversation.

La Bicyclette (p68) An exceedingly popular French-style cafe situated in front of Globo TV Studios.

Café da Carol (p65) Breads, sweets and full-on brunches served in a charming, corner red-brick building.

Slow Bakery (p65) *Carioca*-born local chain of artisanal bakeries, with bread and pastries to die for.

Nusa Leblon (p93) One of the best spots in the neighborhood for a healthy breakfast or brunch.

Okanossa (p93) Vegetarian and vegan breakfasts with a side of freshly ground specialty coffee.

complete, inexpensive meal is called a *prato feito* (or PF), which simply means 'made plate,' and it's a perfect, easy solution to lunchtime hunger.

Por-Kilo Restaurants

Another lunchtime option is the pay-by-weight restaurant, which can range from simple, working-class affairs to sumptuous buffets lined with fresh salads, grilled meats, pastas, seafood dishes and copious desserts. These *por-kilos* are found all across the city, and are a great way to sample a wide variety of Brazilian dishes – and to get a meal that's exactly the size you want to eat.

Most places charge around R$60 to R$100 per kg, with a sizable plate of food costing about R$50 to R$70.

Botecos

Rio has a culture of *botecos*, which are the equivalent of a bar/restaurant that serves plates, beers and bar snacks. They're typically very informal – the least fancy ones are nicknamed *pé-sujos*, which means dirty feet, referring to the fact that you'll be served no matter how wet, sandy or dirty you are. *Botecos* often will have a number of rice, bean and protein plates, as well as traditional bar snacks like *pastel* (freshly fried dough pockets stuffed with cheese, meat, shrimp and beyond) or *bolinhos de bacalhau* (fried codfish balls). Some *botecos* are known for their creative cuisine, and there is even an annual, city-wide festival (called Comida di Buteco) to name *botecos* with the best bar food in Rio.

Local Dishes

There are a number of local dishes from across the country served in the Marvelous City, which you'll have plenty of opportunity to taste test as you eat your way across

RIO FOOD WEBSITES

VEJA RIO: COMER E BEBER
vejario.abril.com.br/comer-e-beber
Monthly magazine on all things *carioca*. Its Eat & Drink section is considered a food bible by many in the city.

GLOBO GASTRONOMIA
oglobo.globo.com/rioshow/gastronomia
Food and drink section of Rio's largest newspaper keeps you up-to-date on restaurant openings and events.

ONDE COMER NO RIO
@ondecomernorio
Obsessively followed Instagram of *carioca* digital influencers Suzanne Malta and Bárbara Guedes.

BLOG COMIE AI
@blogcomieai
Carioca Hannah Vaz's Instagram shows off her love of food and the Marvelous City.

Rio. Sample rich, shrimp-filled *moqueca* (seafood stew cooked in coconut milk) from Bahia or tender *carne seca* (jerked meat) covered in *farofa* (manioc flour), a staple in Minas Gerais. Daring palates can venture north into Amazonia, enjoying savory *tacacá* (manioc paste, lip-numbing leaves of the vegetable *jambú* and dried shrimp) or *tambaqui* (a large Amazonian fish) and other meaty fishes from the mighty Amazon. Cowboys and the *gaúcho* from the south bring the city its *churrascarias* (Brazil's famous all-you-can-eat barbecue restaurants), where crisply dressed waiters bring piping-hot spits of freshly roasted meats to your table.

However, there is no dish as distinctively *carioca* as a *feijoada*. A *feijoada* is a bean and meat stew, consisting of black beans slowly cooked with a variety of meat – such as dried tongue and pork offcuts – seasoned with salt, garlic, onion and oil. The stew is served with rice and finely shredded, cooked kale, then topped with fried *farofa* (manioc flour), plus some pieces of orange on the side (for digestion). It's a popular Sunday meal that often starts with a caipirinha (the national lime-based cocktail) and ends with a long afternoon nap.

Dining Etiquette

Most restaurants accept reservations for both lunch and dinner, so call ahead to avoid a wait. Reservations are essential at high-end restaurants, and the answering host will usually speak English.

Cariocas are quite casual when it comes to dress, and dining out is no exception. Even at the nicest places, a pair of smart jeans and a collared shirt or blouse will do just fine.

A 10% tip is usually included in restaurant bills. When it isn't included, it's customary to leave 10%, although some higher-end restaurants recommend a 12–13% gratuity. Tipping at informal venues, such as juice bars and *por-kilo* restaurants, isn't customary.

CESAR LIMA/SHUTTERSTOCK

***Acarajé* (deep-fried bean balls topped with spicy pastes and shrimp)**

LUIZSOUZA/SHUTTERSTOCK

Armazem Senado, Lapa (p166)

BAR OPEN

Rio's nightlife is exciting, incredibly varied and, in many cases, will keep you up until sunrise.

Going out in Rio starts early – often enough your first caipirinha will be during sunset on the beach. While most do try to head home to shower and change before a night out, one thing does so easily roll into another, and you might just find yourself heading from the beach to a *boteco*, then a bar, and maybe even a dance party later on.

Many music events start at 6pm or 7pm during the week (as there is an enforced 1am closing time on weekdays for bars in residential zones). From Thursday through the weekend, bars are often already packed by 8pm or 9pm. Even some of the best electronic dance parties will start in the late afternoon (and keep going all night long), as much to enjoy the afternoon as to make the best of the city's exceptional scenery.

Although it may not be as wildly varied as São Paulo, or as 24/7 as New York, there is always something going on for nightlife lovers in Rio.

Find Your Tribe

As in most places in the world, there are a few different subcultures within the nightlife circuit, and although there's plenty of crossover between groups, you'll want to know where to go to find your tribe.

The well-heeled from the Zona Sul tends to favor high-end bars along **Dias Ferreira** (p90) and **Baixo Gávea** (p56), while the hip crowds head to popular watering holes in **Botafogo** (p124) or the alternative bars in **Glória** (p151).

Those from Zona Oeste head to **Av Olegário Maciel** (p207) for a night on

Lonely Planet's Top Bars

SURU Lapa's gastro-bar has craft beers and pork belly sandwiches.

BECO DO RATO One of the most storied, hole-in-the-wall samba clubs in the city.

BOTAFOGO Hands down the best neighborhood (p118) for bar-hopping.

FATCHIA Cool bar in Glória, mixing fresh, hot pizza slices with funky live DJ sets.

the town, while Santa Teresa has its own lively bar scene for the more artsy crowd, centered around the **Largo dos Guimarães** (p160).

Lapa and Centro both have a unique mix of bars, clubs and dance halls that attract a range of people from all backgrounds, whose main thing in common is their love of music – especially samba.

Craft Beer & Brewhouses

Over the last few years, the craft-beer scene in Brazil has expanded exponentially. To follow the trend, new bars have opened across Rio featuring local microbrews from within the city, state and beyond. Brewteco is one such *carioca* brand with multiple locations across the city, each with more than 30 craft brews on the menu, including a large number of house-made options on tap. Local craft beer brands like Three Monkeys Beer and Praya can be found at bars around the city – even Zona Norte *boteco* **Bar da Frente** (p193) is on the craft-beer train. Recently, Rio's government even invested in a development project in Centro called the **Rua de Cerveja** (or beer street; p176), which is turning Rua *carioca* into a pedestrian street lined with craft-beer bars.

STOCK-BORIS/SHUTTERSTOCK

Get Your Groove On

Rio has some exceptional places to shake your booty – unsurprising, as it's one of the things Brazilians do best. The music scene is lively, with DJs regularly coming in from São Paulo, New York and London to perform at clubs such as **D-EDGE** (p176), festivals

Beach bar, Copacabana Beach (p104)
BOBNOAH/SHUTTERSTOCK

NEED TO KNOW

Opening Hours

Bars open from 6pm to 1am Monday to Friday, and noon to 2am or 3am Saturday and Sunday (although some, like Jobi, stay open till 4am).

Nightclubs open from 11pm to 5am Friday to Sunday.

Drink Prices

A beer costs R$12–17, while cocktails run R$15 to R$25, or up to R$40.

Most bars add a 10% service charge.

Getting in

Dress codes aren't strict in Rio. Styled beachwear is fine for bars, and for laid-back *botecos* you can go straight from the sand. Shorts and sneakers will still get you into clubs, although Havaianas (flip-flops) and swimsuits will not. Go before midnight to beat the crowds – and remember to get your ticket online before arrival.

D-EDGE	VIADUTO DE MADUREIRA	BAR DA CACHAÇA	LIZ COCKTAIL & CO
São Paulo's storied electronic-music nightclub now has a Rio de Janeiro outpost.	Far away from the Zona Sul crowds, this Brazilian hip-hop party is under Madureira's overpass	A dirty corner bar in Lapa where all of the flavors of *cachaça* (sugarcane alcohol) in existence come together.	Upscale, creative cocktail bar, where beautiful and tanned *cariocas* meet and mingle.

Jobi (p92)
BRAZILPHOTOS/ALAMY

BEST BOTECOS

Adega Pérola (p108) Iberian-style tapas in a hole-in-the-wall joint with ice-cold beer.

Jobi (p92) Traditional Portuguese *boteco* from 1956 that's open nearly all night long.

Pavão Azul (p108) Bohemian haunt serving *bolinhos de bacalhau* (deep-fried codfish balls) and beer for more than half a century.

Bar do David (p113) Tucked away behind Leme is some of the best bar food in the city

Bode Cheiroso (p193) If you're going to the Maracanã, Bode Cheiroso is an obligatory pregame stop.

Bar do Momo (p193) This no-frills spot was voted to have the best *boteco* food in the city.

Bar do Serginho (p161) This corner shop in Santa Teresa serving pizza, empanadas and beer is a neighbor-hood gathering point.

or long-standing branded parties (for one example, check out Festa Rara, *@rarafestarara*). Sets can range from house, drum and bass, and electro to hip-hop favorites, along with uniquely Brazilian sounds, like electro-samba or *tropicália*.

For Afro-Brazilian grooves, check out the Baile-Charme at the **Viaduto de Madureira** (p39), playing music that's as close to hip-hop as you'll get, or if you're really down for something new, head to a funk party. Brazilian funk – completely unrelated to American funk music – is a rough, fast-beat favela-born music style with provocative lyrics and dancing that is wildly popular and played at favela-based parties called *bailes*. If you don't feel safe going into a favela for a Baile Funk (it is risky, to say the least), you can check out funk parties at other venues, like in Lapa or at one-off events.

Roda de Samba

One of the most quintessentially *carioca* nightlife offerings in Rio is the *roda de samba*, or samba circle. These live-music performances seat a group of samba musicians around a center table, which becomes the epicenter to a singing, dancing and beer (or *caipirinha*) drinking party.

Some *rodas de samba* are informal and free, in which the musicians play in or in front of a bar, while revelers pour out onto the streets; while others are hosted in closed venues with paid entry and higher-end bar offerings. Groups such as Samba Que Elas Querem (an all-women samba circle: *@sambaqueelasquerem*) and Sambotica (*@sambotica.oficial*) are two frequent attractions. Whichever option you choose, expect a lively, joyful night, where – somehow – everyone around you will seem to know every word to every song.

ONLINE REFERENCES

ONDE TEM SAMBA
(@ondetemsambarj)
If you want to know where to samba, this Instagram account is your daily bible.

MAE BOEMIA
(@maeboemia)
A curation of all the best bars and kid-friendly matinee parties.

AH! SE EU VOU
(@ahseeuvo)
A lineup of the coolest bars, clubs, parties and samba events in Rio.

ABOUT CARNIVAL
(@aboutcarnaval)
The best Instagram lineup of street parties during Carnaval also gives you tips on the best parties in the city all year-long.

T PHOTOGRAPHY/SHUTTERSTOCK

Caiprinhas

Local Spirits

While there are a heap of cool, new bars to check out, for many, nothing beats your neighborhood *boteco.* Although *botecos* are also known for their traditional bar food, many head to the bar for nothing more than an ice-cold beer with friends. You can order a *choppe*: a draft beer, served *com colarinho* or *sem colarinho* (with or without foam); a *longneck* (pronounced longee-neck), which is a simple bottle of beer; or a *seiscentos*: a 600ml beer that comes in a giant insulated holder, meant to be consumed out of small cups and shared among friends – principally so that you're never drinking a warm beer.

While you'll rarely find wine at a *boteco* (or if you do, it might be quite bad), these little bars do serve local spirits like *cachaça*, a sugarcane alcohol that can be quite cheap and burn (as is the case in the most widely found *cachaça* brand, 51) or can be casked and aged, providing a deeper, smokier taste (Salinas is a more easily found upmarket brand). You can also find fruit and spice liqueur-style *cachaças*, in flavors like ginger and honey, mango or clove and cinnamon.

If you've got a nice *cachaça* on your hands, you might opt to drink it from a small shot glass and savor the flavor; however, most imbibe *cachaça* as part of Brazil's national cocktail, the caipirinha. While lime is the traditional flavor, caipirinhas can be made with nearly any fruit – pineapple, tangerine and passion fruit are a few favorites – and can also be served with vodka instead of *cachaça*.

Botecos normally will give you a small piece of paper that serves as your tab, which you'll pay at the end of the night. Some *botecos* are great after-beach or pre-going-out spots; while others, like **Jobi** (p92), in Leblon (which often stays open until sunrise), are the perfect place to end a night on the town.

PABLO FERNANDES/SHUTTERSTOCK

Rock in Rio (p256)

SHOWTIME

The Marvelous City definitely knows how to put on a show, and you certainly won't be at a loss for options.

Rio has a celebrated music scene, with enchanting settings in which to catch live performances, from cutting-edge concert halls to intimate neighborhood spots. Venues range from modern concert halls seating thousands to intimate samba clubs in edgy neighborhoods. Antiquated colonial mansions, parks overlooking the city, old-school bars, crumbling buildings at the edge of town and hypermodern lounges facing the ocean are all part of the mix – there's even a number of large concert halls that attract both Brazilian stars and well-known international bands.

In Lapa, for example, you'll find big-name concerts at both the legendary Circo Voador and its next-door neighbor, the Fundação Progresso, plus plenty of small theaters and samba bars, while the Jockey Club hosts everything from headlining concerts to full-on festivals.

Dance, theater, classical concerts and opera also have their small but loyal local followings, while cinema is an even bigger deal – Rio is one of the leading film centers in Latin America.

Live Music

In addition to samba, Rio is a showcase for rock, rap, hip-hop, jazz, bossa nova, Música Popular Brasileira (MPB), Brazilian funk and fusion styles, which all play at established clubs and venues across the city. Brazil's many regional styles – like *forró* – also appear regularly on the scene. You'll never be at a loss for live music here, and in most cases, you can watch it for free. During the summer months, for example, free music concerts often take place on the beaches of Copacabana, Ipanema and Zona Oeste. In 2024, Madonna headlined a free show on Copacabana Beach that attracted millions.

Dance

Rio has produced a number of successful dance troupes, including the contemporary Companhia de Dança Deborah Colker, which spends much of its time touring abroad.

One homegrown talent you might catch in town is the Cia de Dança Dani Lima, an avant-garde troupe that weaves provocative pieces together through dance and aerial gymnastics.

Also keep an eye out for the Lapa-based Intrépida Trupe, whose talented acrobat-dancers bring surreal works to the stage. There is no space dedicated solely to dance; performances can take place at many venues around the city.

For classical dance, try to see a production by the Ballet do Theatro Municipal, which puts on highly professional performances at Rio's most venerable theater.

Cinema

Rio's many cinemas screen foreign and independent films, documentaries and avant-garde cinema. The latest US blockbusters get ample airtime at movie megaplexes, while cultural centers, museums and old one-screen theaters offer a more diverse repertoire.

Films are shown both dubbed as well as in the original language with Portuguese subtitles.

During Rio's Cinema Week, there are half-price tickets across the city, or check out the Festival do Rio, the city's massive film festival that has screenings all over town.

Teatro Rival (p179)
ZUMA PRESS, INC./ALAMY

LONELY PLANET'S TOP...

Concert Venues

Circo Voador (p169) The most legendary of all of Rio's concert venues still has a full live-music agenda.

Beco das Garrafas (p107) The birthplace of bossa nova still hosts nightly shows, often highlighting the storied music style.

Marina da Glória (p148) On the hill of Rio's main marina is a grassy knoll that regularly hosts concerts and mini-festivals.

Jockey Club (p59) Rio's horse-racing track regularly transforms to host big-name concerts and even full-on music festivals.

Theaters

Teatro Rival (p179) This underground theater also hosts live music and theater, but it's the drag shows it's famous for.

Theatro Municipal (p179) If opera, orchestra or ballet is what you're after, visit this opulent theater in Rio's center.

Clube Manouche (p65) Intimate underground club that hosts small shows and eclectic international acts.

ENTERTAINMENT BY NEIGHBORHOOD

Gávea, Jardim Botânico & Lagoa	Live-music spots and lakeside kiosks.
Ipanema & Leblon	A handful of theaters, cinemas and live-music venues.
Copacabana & Leme	A few storied live-music clubs.
Botafogo, Urca & Humaitá	Good for cinemas and creative venues.
Flamengo, Laranjeiras, Catete & Glória	Large concert venues and small cultural centers.
Santa Teresa & Lapa	A multitude of live-music venues in Lapa.
Centro & Zona Norte	Large selection of concert halls, clubs and theaters.
Zona Oeste	Home to mega-sized concert halls.

Ipanema's Hippie Market (p80)

SHOP

Colorful boutiques, open-air antique markets, lush home goods and folk art mark Rio's shopping scene.

Not all go to Rio to shop, but it's quite unlikely that you'll come to the Marvelous City and leave without buying a single souvenir. There are a few bucket-list items – like a pair of Havaianas or a Brazilian bikini – that nearly everyone ends up with; however, the city is also full of surprising shopping options that are a joy to explore. Imagine small boutiques filled with unique local clothing brands; myriad art and artisan shops; bookstores and vinyl hideaways; and handmade jewelry sold at colorful outdoor markets.

There's a certain joy in wandering in and out of the city's eclectic shopping offerings – especially if you're strolling the medina-like streets of Centro's shopping district Saara; or if you've made it to one of the more sizable *feiras* (lively outdoor markets that take place weekly or monthly), where there's sometimes as much focus on artisan goods, art and clothing as there is on filling your stomach and enjoying a delicious *bebida* (alcoholic drink) en route.

Best Souvenirs

While there are some obvious favorite items for first-time shoppers – your first pair of *sungas* (Brazilian-style Speedo), tanga bikini or homegrown Havaianas, for example – there are plenty of other amazing gift ideas that both you and your loved ones will treasure as holiday memories.

Music

For the musically inclined, consider flipping through the stands selling vinyl at the **Praça XV** market or the **Feira do Lavradio** (p172), where you might just find Brazilian artists like Marcos Valle or Diogo Nogueira looking back at you. If you don't know what you're looking for, opt for a specialty vinyl shop like **Vinil do Mustufá** (p161) in Santa Teresa to steer you in the right direction. Alternatively, a musical instrument might make the perfect gift. If the massive Northeastern Maracatu drums won't fit on your coffee-table, consider a smaller ukulele-like *cavaquinho* (a traditional samba instrument) instead.

Food & Drink

Not all food and drink travels well, however there's nothing wrong with hiding a bottle or two of quality *cachaça* (Brazil's high-proof sugarcane alcohol) in your bag. Other fun favorites include classic sweets such as *paçoca* (sweetened, crumbly peanut-butter-like squares), *goiabada* (a solid guava paste, traditionally eaten with white cheese), or *rapadura* (dried sugarcane juice); hand-made artisan food from the **Junta Local** market (p140); or even some locally produced, forest-restoring chocolate bars by Maré Chocolate.

Artwork & Street Markets

Rio is a very creative city, so there's plenty of art and artisan works on offer. The **Hippie Market** (p80) in Ipanema is a favorite souvenir-shopping stop, as are the small, bohemian galleries and shops in Santa Teresa.Rio also has myriad too-cool street markets that are the perfect places to explore the subcultures beneath the city's surface. There are markets for antique lovers, for up-and-coming or small local brands, for artisanal food and even for art and handmade goods.

Feira da Glória (p148)

JOEL BALSAM/LONELY PLANET

LONELY PLANET'S TOP...

Street Markets

Hippie Market (p80) Sunday market selling art, handmade clothes and artisan wares.

Feira do Rio Antigo (p172) Lapa's very lively, monthly antique street fair.

Feira de Antiguidades (p180) Spend Saturday mornings browsing antiques, used clothes and records.

Feira da Glória (p148) Homegrown brands of all varieties sell their wares every Sunday.

Bookshops & Vinyl

Livraria da Travessa (p123) Locations all around town, including a much-loved Botafogo branch.

Livraria Argumento (p90) Browse books and music and nibble crepes at this Leblon icon.

Vinil do Mustafá (p161) A must-stop in Santa Teresa for fans of vinyl.

SHOPPING BY NEIGHBORHOOD

Gávea, Jardim Botânico & Lagoa	Several small-scale but atmospheric shopping boutiques.
Ipanema & Leblon	High-end boutiques with prices to match.
Copacabana & Leme	Countless stores, although it's mostly markets and tourist fare.
Botafogo, Urca & Humaitá	Small shops as cool as the bar scene, plus bookstores galore.
Flamengo, Laranjeiras, Catete & Glória	Home to some of the best outdoor market shopping.
Santa Teresa & Lapa	Bohemian art and artisan works sold at numerous shops and galleries.
Centro & Zona Norte	Wineshops, bookstores and down-market clothing shops; medina-like browsing in the pedestrian streets of Saara.
Zona Oeste	Beachwear boutiques, sprawling shopping malls and big-box stores.

FROM LEFT: ANDRE LUIZ MOREIRA/SHUTTERSTOCK, MARCIA CHAMBERS/ALAMY

TRIP PLANNER

CARNAVAL

Joy, laughter, music, colors, debauchery, dance, freedom, love. Carnaval in Rio isn't so much a festival as it is an unforgettable, immersive journey through the city, its music, history, culture and people – a creative collective catharsis shared by all. And for many *cariocas*, it's not just an event – Carnaval is a way of life.

Get Ready for the Greatest Party on Earth

While all carnivals can trace their roots back to the Dionysian and bacchanal festivals of ancient Greece and Rome, Rio's Carnaval in particular was brought over by the Portuguese, in the form of a Portuguese carnival tradition known as the *entrudo*. This lively and messy carnival game involves throwing eggs, flour or other food-based goods at each other in the street, and its prevalence in Rio de Janeiro during the early independence period gave space for the Afro-Brazilian community to celebrate more freely in the streets, mingling with Portuguese merchants and forming groups known as Zé Pereiras, which were the predecessors to today's *Blocos*, or street parties.

The wealthy of the era celebrated carnivals in Italian and Parisian style at opulent masked balls. Attendees would later take to the streets, showing off their costumes during lively promenades. These promenades gained a certain independence from the *bailes* (balls) and, over time, formed their own societies, morphing into the first carnival parades.

Competitive parading didn't begin until the 1930s, a decade after the city's *sambistas* began to gain recognition, and samba schools were formed in the city's hillside communities. The first samba school in existence was Deixa Falar (1926), while the second, Mangueira (1928), continues to be a championship samba school to this day. These two, plus a number of other samba schools, paraded against each other informally in Praça Onze

WHEN TO GO

Pre-Carnaval
Carnaval only happens once a year, but if you're a first timer, you might consider joining the warm-up or the cool-down periods as well. The weekend before Carnaval is a less intense, less-messy version of the real thing (and a much cheaper time to travel).

During Carnaval
If you're on a strict budget, look for plane tickets that arrive DURING Carnaval week itself, as they're often much cheaper.

Post-Carnaval
This period can roll on for weeks on end, giving revelers a few more chances to embody the feeling of absolute freedom that everyone is searching for.

during Carnaval, until, in 1932, journalist Pernambucano Mário Filho organized the first official competitive parade, sponsored by *Globo*, Brazil's largest newspaper.

By the 1950s, the parades were such a prominent part of Carnaval that intellectual, artist and middle-class *cariocas* began to join in, and it wasn't long after that the Desfiles de Carnaval became part of the national identity.

BLOCOS DA RUA

At the same time that the samba schools were forming, the former Zé Pereiras were reorganizing themselves into the city's first *Blocos*, starting with Cordão da Bola Preta, which was born in 1918 and continues in existence today. The prevalence of these *blocos da rua* (street parties) grew, often naming themselves with double entendres (although you won't likely understand unless you speak Portuguese), and sometimes adding a theme as well, like Viemos de Egipto (We Come from Egypt).

There are a few *Blocos* known for starting off Carnaval, like Céu na Terra in

Carnaval, Saara (p180)

ESSENTIAL CARNAVAL STRATEGIES

Safety

- Use a belt bag for your things. Carrying a shoulder bag or handbag around during Carnaval won't end well.
- Fill said belt bag with sunscreen, sunglasses, eco-glitter, a phone charger and possibly a toothbrush, in case you don't make it home.
- Use a money belt for your really important things, like keys, cell phone and cash.
- Remove all contactless payment options from your phone and/or credit cards before taking them out.
- Consider switching to an older phone, or travel with a backup in case yours get snatched.
- Use the buddy system. Going solo during Carnaval is cool for locals; but if you're new to town, go with a friend.

Staying Healthy

- It's best not to take drinks or drugs from strangers; even if you're tempted, try to avoid it.
- Hydrate well. Really well. Drink way more water than you think you need. It's hot out there.
- Use sunscreen and keep out of the sun whenever possible. Heatstroke happens.
- Eat a big carb- and protein-filled breakfast before heading out, even if you're leaving at 5am.
- Stop for lunch (or dinner) if you've been going all day. By day four, your body will thank you.

YADID LEVY/ALAMY

Santa Teresa, as well as ones who end it, like Me Enterra na Quarta (Bury me on Wednesday), which parades through the streets on Quarta-feira das Cinzas (Ash Wednesday).

Today, revelers hit the streets in their best, most creative or simply the funniest costume they can imagine (that fits spending the day in 40°C heat), often starting at 5am or 6am and continuing until the sun goes down.

Unlike other cities in Brazil, Rio's street Carnaval remains free of charge – in 2013, the city officially prohibited by law the closure of any public areas or sale of any tickets to street-based Carnaval *Blocos* or events, ensuring that the festival would remain democratic and accessible to all.

THE BEST SHOW IN THE WORLD

The Samba Parade is a different story. Getting in requires buying tickets, but they're very much worth the price. Nicknamed 'the best show on earth', Rio's Carnaval Parade is truly a spectacle of colors, lights, music and dance. Samba schools go head-to-head for the annual title of the city's best, and with all the energy and prowess delivered on the runway, even spectators will feel as if they've levitated into another dimension. The energy in the **Sambódromo** (p188) on parade nights is unimaginable, incomparable and absolutely

Best of the Rest

CÉU NA TERRA
Opens Carnaval at 6am with a parade through the streets of Santa Teresa.

ME ENTERRA NA QUARTA
This *Bloco* performs on Ash Wednesday, at the end of the festivities.

SARGENTO PIMENTA
This Beatles-themed *Bloco* has grown to be one of the city's largest.

Parade, Sambódromo da Marquês de Sapucaí (p188)

unforgettable; and each piece of the parade is a true work of art.

The parades are all-night affairs that start around 10pm and continue until close to sunrise, and if you're not joining in the parade yourself, you can watch from the *arquibancada* (bench seats) or from the *camarotes* (VIP boxes) – just remember to get your tickets well in advance, as they sell out quite quickly.

SAMBA SCHOOLS

Currently, Rio de Janeiro has 12 samba schools in the Grupo Especial (the top group) who, as of 2025, parade over three nights (until 2024, it was only two nights). Portela, Mangueira and Beija-Flor currently hold the most titles of all 12, followed by Imperatriz Leopoldinense and Acadêmicos do Salgueiro (best known for their infamous drum line, the Furiosa.) The parades for the Grupo Especial take place Sunday, Monday and Tuesday of Carnaval, while on the first two days, Friday and Saturday, the schools in the Grupo de Acesso strut their stuff. The following weekend, after the winners are announced, there is a Desfile das Campeãs (parade of champions), where the winning schools take to the av one more time to celebrate their victories.

Tip: If you've missed the parades or couldn't get a ticket, this display is much easier, and cheaper, to attend.

CORDÃO DO BOLA PRETA

One of the largest and most traditional *Blocos* has been on the streets since 1918.

BOI TOLO

This huge, independent *Bloco* traverses half of the city and passes through tunnels during 10 hours of parading.

BANDA DE IPANEMA

This traditional *Bloco* has been cultural patrimony since 2004.

FILHOS DE GANDHI

Bloco celebrating Afro-Brazilian culture and music since the 1950s.

RIO DE JANEIRO

THE GUIDE

Chapters in this section are organised by hubs and their surrounding areas. We see the hub as your base in the destination, where you'll find unique experiences, local insights, insider tips and expert recommendations. It's also your gateway to the surrounding area, where you'll see what and how much you can do from there.

Cristo Redentor (p66)
MARCHELLO74/SHUTTERSTOCK

NEIGHBORHOODS AT A GLANCE

Find the places that tick all your boxes.

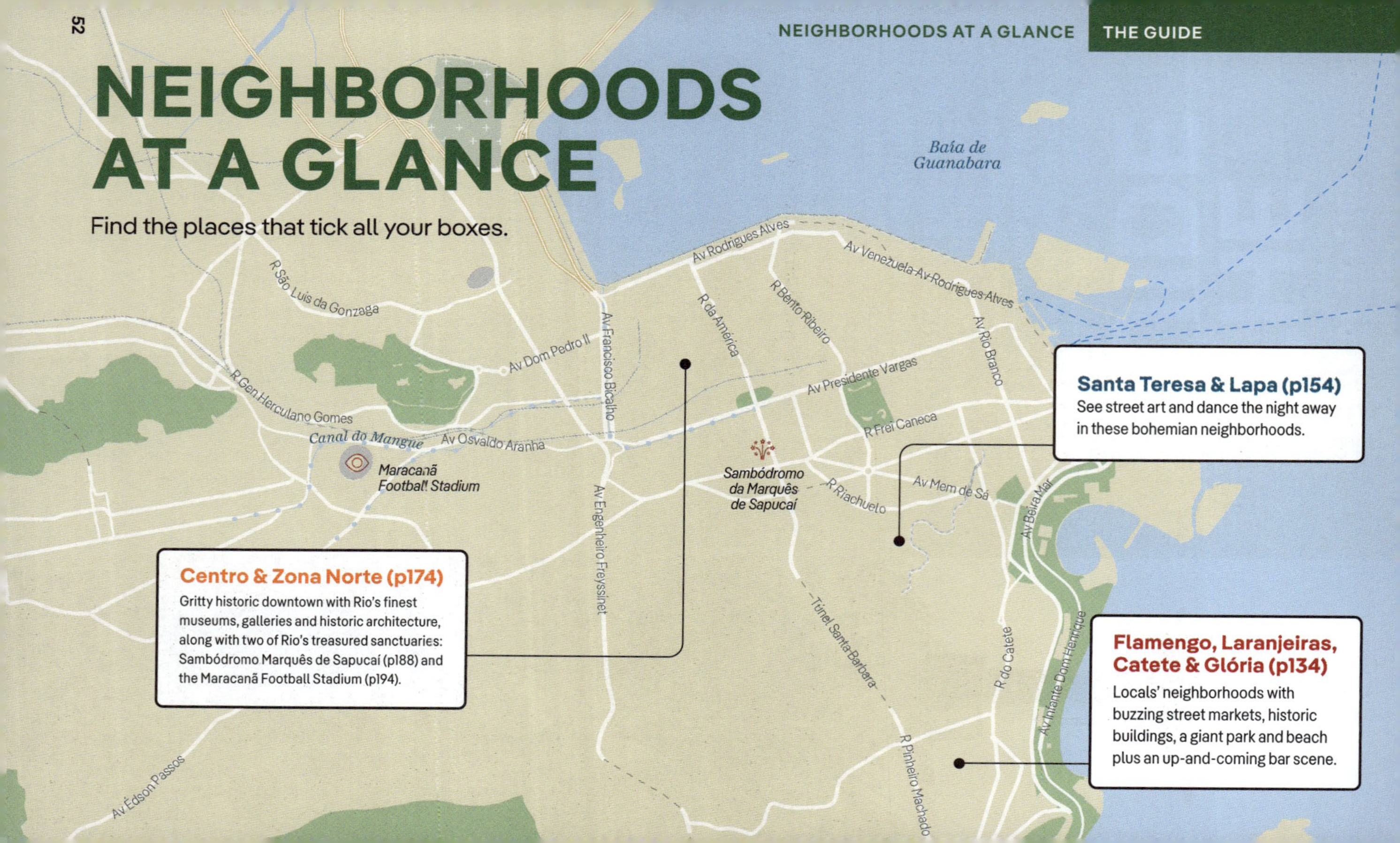

Santa Teresa & Lapa (p154)
See street art and dance the night away in these bohemian neighborhoods.

Centro & Zona Norte (p174)
Gritty historic downtown with Rio's finest museums, galleries and historic architecture, along with two of Rio's treasured sanctuaries: Sambódromo Marquês de Sapucaí (p188) and the Maracanã Football Stadium (p194).

Flamengo, Laranjeiras, Catete & Glória (p134)
Locals' neighborhoods with buzzing street markets, historic buildings, a giant park and beach plus an up-and-coming bar scene.

Gávea, Lagoa & Jardim Botânico (p54)

Rio's world wonder, Cristo Redentor (p66), plus the Parque Lage (p72) mansion, the Jardim Botânico (p68), in upscale neighborhoods surrounding a lake.

Zona Oeste (p198)

Quiet suburbs for surfing and chilling on the beach, visiting an urban island and epic climbs. Visit Sítio Burle Marx (p218) to learn more about Brazil's most famous architect.

Ipanema & Leblon (p78)

Comfortable Zona Sul (South Zone) neighborhoods with spectacular sunsets and Ipanema Beach (p82) to sing songs about.

Copacabana & Leme (p98)

Busy Copacabana Beach (p104) has seen better days, but it's still a must. Nearby Leme has a more local vibe.

Botafogo, Urca & Humaitá (p116)

Hip bars and restaurants, along with peaceful Urca, where you'll be able to climb Pão de Açúcar (p128).

Researched by Marisa Megan Paska

GÁVEA, LAGOA & JARDIM BOTÂNICO

GALLERIES, GARDENS & RAINFORESTS GALORE

While away your days at charming cafes tucked among verdant foliage; or in the botanical gardens, rainforest-filled parks or waterfalls of Rio.

Sitting back-to-back with the Parque Nacional da Tijuca (the largest urban rainforest on the planet), Gávea, Jardim Botânico and Lagoa are alive with lush vegetation, fragrant flora, colorful birds and little monkeys running along the telephone wires.

Wander the green-lined streets or head into the park itself, where you'll quickly find refuge from the crowds and chaos of the beach zones. Whether you're strolling around the Botanical Gardens, cycling around the lake or simply enjoying a coffee in the shade, natural beauty will unfold all around you.

Spend enough time here, and the greenest neighborhoods in Zona Sul will easily enchant you into extending your stay.

INCLUDES

Jardim Botânico (p68)

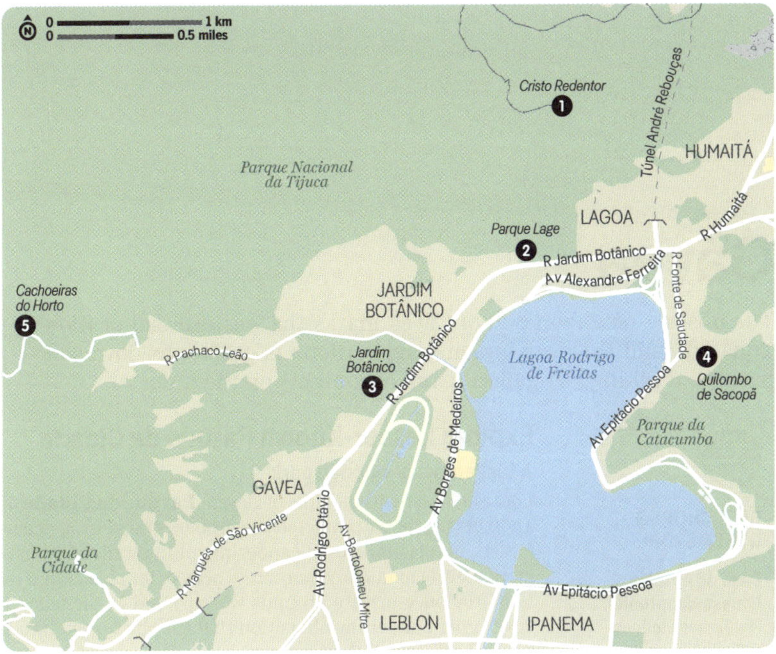
0 1 km
0 0.5 miles
Cristo Redentor
1
Túnel André Rebouças
HUMAITÁ
Parque Nacional da Tijuca
LAGOA
Parque Lage
2
R Humaitá
R Jardim Botânico
Av Alexandre Ferreira
R Fonte de Saudade
Cachoeiras do Horto
5
JARDIM BOTÂNICO
R Pachaco Leão
Jardim Botânico
3
R Jardim Botânico
Lagoa Rodrigo de Freitas
4
Quilombo de Sacopã
Av Epitácio Pessoa
Parque da Catacumba
Av Borges de Medeiros
GÁVEA
R Marquês de São Vicente
Av Rodrigo Otávio
Av Bartolomeu Mitre
Parque da Cidade
Av Epitácio Pessoa
LEBLON
IPANEMA

FROM LEFT: BERNARD BARROSO/SHUTTERSTOCK, BRUNO MARTINS/ALAMY

Highlights

❶ Cristo Redentor
Climb up Corcovado to the city's crowning glory, standing with arms wide open to welcome you to Rio. **p66**

❷ Parque Lage
Wander around a historic, Italian-style palacete with a poolside cafe and art school in the Atlantic rainforest. **p72**

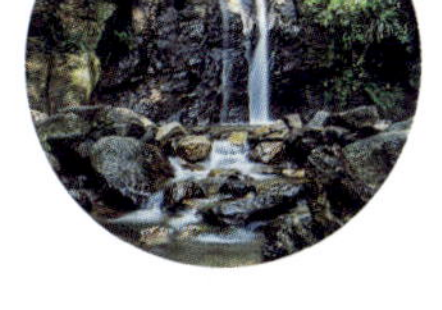

❸ Jardim Botânico
Explore the thematic greenhouses, historic buildings and spot the resident monkeys. **p68**

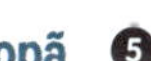

❹ Quilombo de Sacopã
Samba your heart out at the vibrant hillside community overlooking the Lagoa. **p60**

❺ Cachoeiras do Horto
Cool off and escape the crowds at the Horto waterfalls (pictured above), hidden inside Rio's tropical rainforest. **p63**

Getting Around

Bicycle
A lack of public transportation options and an excess of lush greenery make cycling ideal. There are a number of bicycles lanes, although unfortunately, not along all routes, so ride with care.

Buses & Vans
The only public transport options in the area are city buses and minibuses, commonly called vans. There are a large number of lines that run through these zones depending on your destination, so you'll have plenty of buses to choose from – just try to avoid rush hour, as traffic can be intense.

Gávea

The upscale neighborhood of Gávea marks the western end of Rio's Zona Sul, and this leafy-green neighborhood is perfect for lovers of parks and hiking, art galleries and chic nights on the town.

BEST SHOPS & OTHER STOPS

Casa de Antônia (@casa.deantonia): Multibrand clothing shop: the perfect place to delve into the diverse world of *carioca* fashion.

Bauh Móveis (@Bauh Moveis): Bauh's rustic-chic offerings will make furniture lovers swoon.

Feira de Antiguidades da Gávea (@feiradeantiguidadesgavea): Every Sunday morning from 7am onwards in the Praça Santos Dumont you'll find one of the coolest little antique fairs in the city.

Latoog (lattoog.com): A home-design store in a beautiful shop that toes the line between retail space and gallery.

Studio Yoga One (@studioyogaone): Peaceful little oasis in lower Gávea for a blissful Iyengar, Hatha, Vinyasa or Ashtanga yoga class.

Explore Lesser-Known Parque da Cidade

A tucked-away wooded park

Located high up in the hills of Gávea, **Parque da Cidade** is a 470,000 sq meter protected green space comprising dense forests, luxurious lakes, meandering hiking trails and some meticulously manicured gardens – perfect for picnicking. In 1939, the once-private grounds were passed to the federal government under the obligation that they be turned into a public park, which they remain to this day.

The Parque da Cidade also marks the start of a trail through the Tijuca National Forest that connects Gávea to Horto, passing by several of the park's best viewpoints and waterfalls.

Find Fine Art in the Forest

Museu Histórico da Cidade's collection

The Parque da Cidade was once the private residence of Marquês de São Vicente, who built his family home on the land in 1809, at the park's highest point. The house of the Marquês de São Vicente, which still stands, was turned into a museum – the **Museu Histórico da Cidade** – which counts more than 24,000 works of art in its private collection, including pieces by Brazilian artists Eliseu Visconti, Antônio Parreiras and Armando Vianna, and photographer Marc Ferrez. The museum hosts both long- and short-term exhibits, while the patio between the museum's two buildings (one being strictly administrative) is a popular location for concerts, fairs and other outdoor events.

Where the Wild Things Are

A night out in Baixo Gávea

Baixo Gávea (lower Gávea, aka BG) has been a nightlife hot spot since the early 1980s, when a small stretch of the Praça Santos Dumont became a mythological gathering point for Rio's bohemia. **Guimas**, a traditional Portuguese-style

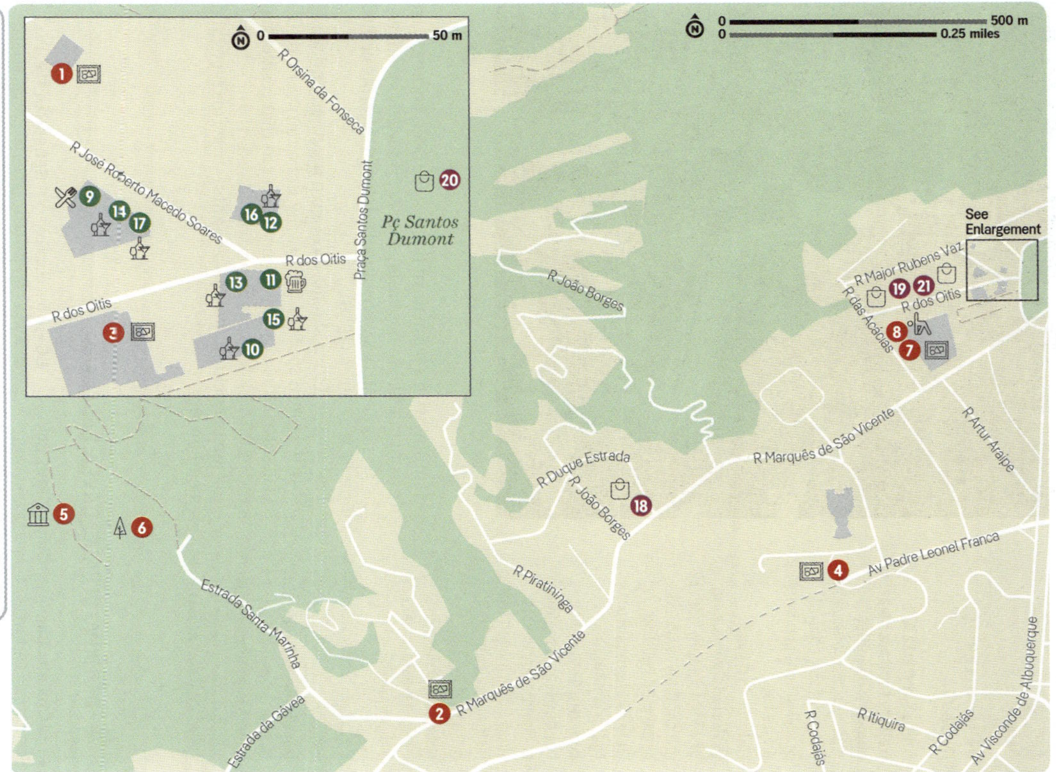

SIGHTS
1 Anita Schwartz Art Gallery
2 Galeria da Gávea
3 Galeria Movimento
4 Galpão de Artes Urbanos
5 Museu Histórico da Cidade
6 Parque da Cidade
7 Silvia Cintra + Box 4

ACTIVITIES
8 Studio Yoga One

EATING
9 Guimas

DRINKING & NIGHTLIFE
10 BG+
11 Braseiro da Gávea
12 Brewteco
13 Ferreirinha
14 Guita Bistro
15 Proa Cozinha Bar
16 Rufi.bar
17 Sebastian

SHOPPING
18 Bauh Moveis
19 Casa de Antônia
20 Feira de Antiguidades da Gávea
21 Latoog

BEST GALLERIES IN GÁVEA

Anita Schwartz Art Gallery (anitaschwartz.com.br): Beautiful gallery space with small but great selection of Brazilian contemporary art pieces.

Galeria da Gávea (galeriadagavea.com.br): Photography gallery in a carefully restored, listed 1888 building.

Galeria Movimento (galeriamovimento.com.br): Gallery that has been representing contemporary artists since 2007, moved to this historic house in 2021.

Galpão de Artes Urbanos: Gallery run by Rio's waste collection program, exhibits art made with recycled materials.

Silvia Cintra + Box 4 (@galeriasilviacintrabox4): Contemporary art gallery in a purpose-built space displaying both known and new artists.

DAVID WALL/ALAMY

Gávea

restaurant with a permanent line out the door, became part of an era marked by *Segundas Sem Lei* (Lawless Mondays). The all-night parties were immortalized in the aptly named film, *Baixo Gávea* (1986).

The area and its residents have aged together, and while it's still a go-to spot for the nearby university crowd, BG has matured (the city government decreed that residential bars had to close at 1am on weekdays), thanks to the addition of cocktail bars, jazz nights, street markets and special events.

DRINKING IN BAIXO GÁVEA: BEST BARS

Proa Cozinha Bar: Seafood culinary haven. Unique drinks and a killer cocktail happy hour 4–8pm weekdays. *noon-midnight Tue-Thu & Sun; to 1am Fri & Sat* $$

Guita Bistro: Chic wine and beer bar, serving excellent healthy-leaning food with some surprising veg options. *9am-1am* $$

BG+: A few classic cocktails, bar food and beers at this age-old hangout. *11:30am-4:30pm Mon; to 1am Tue-Fri, 9am-1am Sat & Sun* $

Sebastian: Creative pub fare, cocktails and beers in a laid-back setting with plenty of sidewalk seating. *noon-1am Tue-Thu & Sun; to 3am Fri & Sat* $$

Ferreirinha: This modern, gastro-pub style *boteco* has cold beers, cocktails and chic snacks on tap. *5pm-1am Tue-Thu, Noon-1am Sat-Sun* $$

Rufi.bar: On Brewteco's rooftop you'll find a cocktail and pizza bar. Live music and DJ sets. *6pm-1am Tue-Fri, 4pm-2am Sat; 4pm-midnight Sun.* $$

Brewteco: Local chain microbrewery. Dozens of craft beers, gastropub fare. *11:30am-1am Sun-Thu, to 2pm Fri & Sat* $$

Braseiro da Gávea: One of BG's oldest establishments. Ice-cold beer and traditional meals till very late. *11am-1am Sun-Thu, 11am-3am Fri & Sat* $$

Lagoa

This high-end neighborhood, backed by lush green hills, wraps around the Rodrigo de Freitas heart-shaped lagoon in Rio's Zona Sul, and is reigned by outdoor living, gastronomy and unique cultural offerings.

A Day at the Races

Horse Racing at the Jockey Club

Between Gávea and the Lagoa Rodrigo de Freitas, the **Jockey Club**, which doubles as a for-rent event space, has been a fully functioning thoroughbred horse-racing track since its inauguration in 1938. It hosts Brazil's premiere horse-racing event, the Grand Prix Brazil (usually held in June), and throughout the rest of year the 640,000-sq-meter track has races on Sunday afternoons at 2pm, as well as Monday and Tuesday evenings at 6pm. Entrance is free and bets can be placed for a little as R$2.

Keep an eye on the city's events calendar (like diariodorio.com) to see what other activities are held here when you're visiting.

Two-Wheeled Exploring

Let's go ride a bike

One of the most quintessential activities in Rio is taking a bike ride along the 7.5km cycling path that encircles **Lagoa Rodrigo de Freitas**. Rent a bike at the Parque dos Patins, or near the restaurants and bars closest to Copacabana. On your route around the lake, you'll pass several wooden docks where you can stop to enjoy the view, lakeside yoga (BYO mat), as well as the Lagoa skate park and skate bowl, and a number of tennis courts, basketball courts and football pitches. You can even follow the red bicycle paths all the way to the Botanical Gardens or down to the beach – just be aware of traffic. Although cycling is widespread, drivers don't typically respect bicycles on the road.

Row, Row, Row Your Boat

Put on your captain's hat

Both the Botafogo and Clube de Regatas do Flamengo (rowing clubs) have boathouses along the lagoon itself. For most, a more accessible way to get on the water is by paddleboat, which can be found on the Copacabana side of the lake near the restaurants and sports fields.

CLUBE REGATAS DO FLAMENGO

In case you're wondering why the city is flooded with red-and-black-striped jerseys, they're from the Flamengo football club: the team with the largest fan base in the country. The **Clube de Regatas do Flamengo**, which has been headquartered along the Lagoa since 1931, also has training programs for a number of Olympic sports, such as rowing, tennis, swimming and gymnastics.

Multi-medal Olympian gymnast Rebeca Andrade and her teammates Jade Barbosa, Flávia Saraiva and Lorrane Oliveira, for example, all proudly sport Flamengo's colors.

The (private) club has a 2023-renovated, on-site (public) museum that tells of the club's history and its most famous players, although it's best for Portuguese speakers.

SIGHTS
1 Casa Museu Eva Klabin
2 Clube de Regatas do Flamengo
3 Lagoa Rodrigo de Freitas
4 Parque da Catacumba
5 Quilombo de Sacopã

ACTIVITIES
6 Lagoa Aventuras

EATING
7 Bar Lagoa
8 Lagoa Sushi Club
9 Quintal do Rio
10 Rancho Português

DRINKING & NIGHTLIFE
11 Badalado Lagoa Club
12 Calçada Bar
13 Clássico Clube Lagoa
14 Kingston Club

ENTERTAINMENT
15 Jockey Club

Get Adventurous at Parque da Catacumba

Picnics, playgrounds and excellent views

This nearly 27-hectare area on the Copacabana side of the Lagoa, which was once an indigenous cemetery, was reforested in the 1970s and turned into a park for the public's enjoyment. Beyond diverse fauna, numerous walking trails and picturesque picnic areas, the **Parque da Catacumba** is also home to **Lagoa Aventuras**, which offers wall climbing, ropes courses and other outdoor adventures for a fee.

The park opens from 8am to 5pm, or until 6pm in the summer, and access is free. Don't miss the hiking trail up to the Mirante da Lagoa lookout point for exceptional views over the lake and out to the sea.

OTHER QUILOMBOS

There are two other *quilombos* in the city of Rio with recognized land titles – **Pedra do Sal** (p186) in Saúde, in the city's center, and the Quilombo do Camorim in the **Parque Estadual da Pedra Branca** (p214) in *Zona Oeste.*

Experience the Unique Quilombo de Sacopã

African history and cultural celebration

In 1929, on an 18,800-sq-meter piece of hillside land next to the Lagoa, Manoel Pinto Júnior established what would become one of Zona Sul's most prominent

EATING IN LAGOA: BEST LAKEFRONT DINING

Rancho Português: Upscale, traditional Portuguese restaurant where plates are served to share. *noon-11pm Mon-Sat, to 8pm Sun* **$$$**

Bar Lagoa: Long-standing restaurant serving German specialties, steaks and creamy draft beers since 1934. *noon-midnight* **$$**

Quintal do Rio: Swanky lakefront restaurant with traditional Brazilian dishes. *6pm-midnight Thu, Noon-1am Fri & Sat, Noon-9pm Sun* **$$**

Lagoa Sushi Club: Japanese sushi bar requiring an invite to get in; inside a members-only club. *6pm-11pm Thu & Fri, noon-11pm Sat, Noon-7pm Sun* **$$**

CAVAN-IMAGES/SHUTTERSTOCK

Harnesses, Parque da Catacumba

quilombos (runaway slave communities), the **Quilombo de Sacopã**. Pinto's descendants have remained on the land since the community's inception, although it wasn't until 2005 that they were recognized as an official *quilombo*; and, in 2014, were given legal rights to their land.

Quilombo de Sacopã, which several dozen Brazilians of African descent still call home, is a place of celebration, promoting music, art, the preservation of Rio's black history and a continuation of cultural traditions.

The site hosts a *feijoada* (bean-and-meat stew) and samba event roughly twice a month that's open to the public and very much worth the visit for a unique look at rural life in the city. Check *@quilombosacopa* for details.

QUILOMBOS

Appearing first during Brazil's colonial period, *quilombos* were self-sufficient communities formed by freed and (more frequently) escaped slaves, who worked together to actively resist slavery.

The most famous *quilombo* in Brazil was called Palmares, located near Recifie. It was founded in 1600, survived for nearly a century (under frequent attack), and had a population that rose to 30,000. Its most famous leader was Zumbi dos Palmares, whose execution date (November 20) is now a national holiday.

In the early 21st century, Brazil began to recognize still-existing *quilombos* across the country and provide land titles for communities still residing on historic property.

Rio de Janeiro state has 53 recognized *quilombos*, although only three have legal rights to their own land.

DRINKING IN LAGOA: BEST NIGHTLIFE

Kingston Club: Reggae-themed restaurant and nightlife spot celebrating flavors and sounds of Jamaican culture. *6pm-1am Fri, 4pm-3am Sat, 4pm-11pm Sun*

Calçada Bar: A busy bar known for its cocktails and festive crowds – beware the slow service. *6pm-1am Thu & Fri, noon-midnight Sat & Sun*

Clássico Clube Lagoa: Simple sophistication, this is the go-to spot for sundowners. *11am-8pm Wed, Thu & Sun, to 10pm Fri & Sat*

Badalado Lagoa Club: Good food, drinks, music and views at this lakefront gastro-bar. *11am-9pm Mon-Wed, to 11pm Thu & Sun, to 1am Fri & Sat*

THE STORY OF A LAKE

The **Lagoa de Rodrigo de Freitas**, was, like most of Brazil, initially indigenous territory. The Tamoios called it home, until they were exterminated by a smallpox epidemic intentionally instituted by the Portuguese to make room for a sugar plantation, called the Engenho d'El-Rey, along the lagoon's edge.

In 1808, the Portuguese royal family claimed the land for their own use, creating a gunpowder factory and the first iteration of the Botanic Gardens.

During the 19th and 20th centuries, the water quality of the lake was already in question, and a canal was created to drain water to the sea. The lake shrunk in size and improved slightly, although the problem of water quality, unfortunately, remains to this day.

NATURE'S CHARM/SHUTTERSTOCK

Lagoa de Rodrigo de Freitas

Enjoy the Well-Preserved Casa Museu Eva Klabin

One widow's ancient-art collection

Eva Klabin (1903–91) was one of the most prolific classic-art collectors of her era, and when the 88-year-old widow passed on, her home turned into a museum and her collection of over 2000 pieces, spanning ancient Egypt to the impressionist period, was put on permanent exhibition.

The **Casa Museu Eva Klabin** is open for free to the public from 2pm to 6pm every Wednesday to Sunday, where you'll find paintings, sculptures, furniture and other decorative objects on display. The space has also become a de facto cultural center, hosting lectures, concerts, courses, films, temporary exhibitions and more. There is no parking on-site, so arrive on foot (the Cantagalo metro station is quite close) or by rideshare *(evaklabin.org.br)*.

Jardim Botânico

This affluent neighborhood's namesake – the Botanic Gardens – may be the central attraction, however it's also a gastronomic powerhouse, home to chic shops and galleries, and the gateway to the Tijuca National Park.

World of Waterfalls

A freshwater escape

Jardim Botânico is a world of water, and its numerous waterfalls are the perfect place to escape summer heat.

The **Cachoeiras do Horto**, **da Gruta** and **dos Primatas** (waterfalls) are three of the most popular in the area, and relatively easy to reach. Do Horto's trailhead starts inside of the Tijuca Park and has a slightly more difficult trek to the bathing pool, while da Gruta (aka da Imperatriz) is reachable by an easy 30-minute trail from behind the Solar da Imperatriz. The trail to Cachoeira das Primatas, which starts in a residential part of the neighborhood, is a 40-minute, not-too-taxing hike that's a favorite for families.

Rare Colonial Architecture

Semirural Solar de Imperatriz

Just up the road from the Jardim Botânico in the Horto neighborhood you'll find one of the last standing examples of 19th-century semirural architecture in Rio: the **Solar da Imperatriz**. The charming bright-yellow building – part of the old Fazenda do Macaco – was declared cultural patrimony in 1973 and is now part of the Jardim Botânico's research arm.

Entry to the grounds is free – the gardens were designed by the office of renowned landscape artist Burle Marx – although visits to the inside of the building are limited to special events. To the building's left, you'll also find the trailhead for some great waterfall hiking.

Cycling to Cristo

Two wheels uphill

Climbing the hills in the Parque Nacional da Tijuca is a popular pastime for road cyclists in Rio. A seemingly

INDUSTRIAL ROOTS

Jardim Botânico and Horto were originally industrial zones, thanks to an abundance of water that could support machinery of large factories. One of the first was the Companhia de Tecidos Carioca (Carioca Fabric Factory), founded in 1884 on the street just behind Jardim Botânico (modern-day Pacheco Leão street). The factory, which built housing for its workers, was responsible for the development of the neighborhood, and when it closed shop in 1962, the former factory workers organized a resistance to ensure they wouldn't be thrown out of their homes. Their plea worked, and the entire neighborhood was listed as a historic villa, with the requirement that the workers and their families be allowed to stay in their houses.

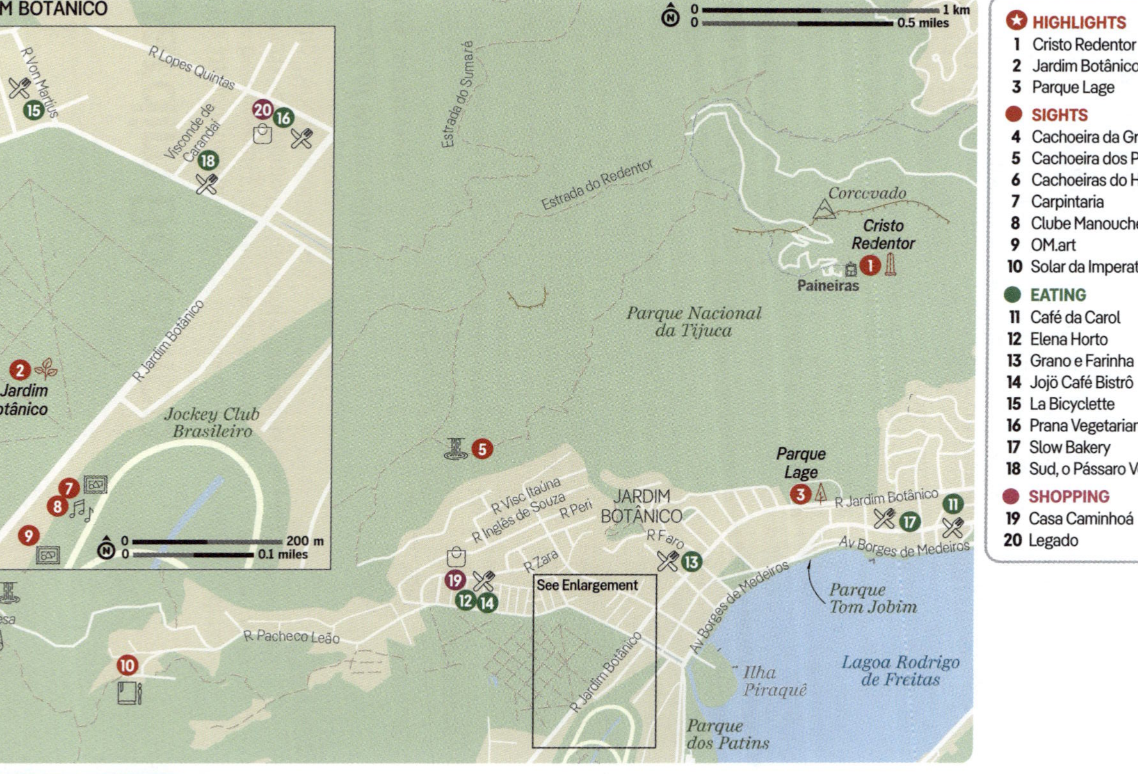

HIGHLIGHTS
1 Cristo Redentor
2 Jardim Botânico
3 Parque Lage

SIGHTS
4 Cachoeira da Gruta
5 Cachoeira dos Primatas
6 Cachoeiras do Horto
7 Carpintaria
8 Clube Manouche
9 OM.art
10 Solar da Imperatriz

EATING
11 Café da Carol
12 Elena Horto
13 Grano e Farinha
14 Jojö Café Bistrô
15 La Bicyclette
16 Prana Vegetariano
17 Slow Bakery
18 Sud, o Pássaro Verde

SHOPPING
19 Casa Caminhoá
20 Legado

KAROL KOZLOWSKI PREMIUM RM COLLECTION/ALAMY

Vista Chinesa

constant stream of bicycles wheel by on weekend mornings, with several bars and shops catering to this specific clientele.

One of the most popular end points is Cristo Redentor, a roughly 2½-hour uphill cycle (if you're quite fit) that takes you past some of the Serra da Carioca's most famous sites, such as **Vista Chinesa**, a Chinese-style pagoda with exceptional views, and the Mesa do Imperador, where Dom Pedro II famously lunched in the forest with his court. If you're up for the challenge, Nattrip *(nattrip.com.br)* has cycling tours to Cristo.

BEST CULTURAL STOPS

Carpintaria Art Gallery (fdag.com.br): Rio's outpost of Fortes D'Aloia & Gabriel Gallery represents more than 40 artists, and holds 15+ exhibitions year-round.

OM.art (om.art.br): Art gallery by designer and visual artist Oskar Metsavaht, the man behind Brazilian fashion house Osklen.

Legado (@legado arte): This chic little home-goods store turned gallery holds many treasures.

Clube Manouche (clubemanouche.com.br): This small bar and basement club hosts concerts, theater performances and special events.

Casa Caminhoá (@casacaminhoa): A beautiful house on a bucolic street that holds pop-up shops, expositions and special events.

EATING NEAR JARDIM BOTÂNICO

La Bicyclette: Very popular French-style cafe in front of Globo TV Studios. Ideal stop for bread lovers. *8am-9pm* $$

Grano e Farinha: Old-school bakery for traditional breakfasts, juices, sandwiches, along with plenty of pastries and coffee. *7am-8pm* $$

Café da Carol: Breads, sweets and brunches served in a charming, corner red brick building. *7:30am-6pm Tue-Fri, 8am-6pm Sat & Sun* $$

Slow Bakery: One of several outlets in the city, serves artisanal breads, pastries and locally sourced, delicious meals. *8am-8pm Tue-Sat* $$

Elena Horto: Creative contemporary restaurant where live music and spectacular cocktails set the scene. *7pm-1am Tue-Thu, to 2am Sat & Sun* $$$

Prana Vegetariano: Mouthwatering vegetarian fare favoring local producers, artisanal products and the slow-food movement. *noon-4pm* $$

Jojö Café Bistrô: Charming bistro with mostly outdoor seating. Champagne-and-oyster Thursdays. *6pm-midnight Tue-Fri, 1pm-1am Sat, 1-7pm Sun* $$

Sud, o Pássaro Verde: Renowned chef Roberta Sudbrack serves innovative dishes. *6-10pm Tue-Thu, noon-4pm & 6-10pm Fri & Sat; noon-5pm Sun* $$$

SHAWN EASTMAN PHOTOGRAPHY/SHUTTERSTOCK

TOP EXPERIENCE

Cristo Redentor

Perched atop Corcovado Hill with arms open wide is Rio's most emblematic site: Cristo Redentor (Christ the Redeemer). At more than 700m above sea level, the iconic art deco statue – elected one of the Seven Wonders of the Modern World – is visible from across the city, welcoming residents and visitors alike to Rio's sandy shores.

DON'T MISS

- Cristo Redentor
- Corcovado Train
- Parque Lage–Corcovado Trail
- The Heart of Christ
- The Chapel
- Sunset from the top

Corcovado

Corcovado (which means 'hunchback' in Portuguese) is the 710m (2330ft) granite peak in the center of the Tijuca National Forest from where Cristo reigns – and it was a tourist attraction long before Christ's arrival. The Corcovado railway, inaugurated in 1884, was Brazil's first tourist train, taking visitors up to enjoy the incredible views for nearly half a century prior to the statue's inauguration.

Cristo Redentor

The Cristo Redentor statue, which clocks in at 38m tall (the equivalent of a 13-story building), is the largest art deco statue in the world. Its creation was a collaborative effort that began in

PRACTICALITIES

Scan this QR code for prices and opening hours.

1922 with a project by Brazilian architect and engineer Heitor da Silva Costa and Italian-Brazilian artist Carlos Oswald. But the actual sculpting took place in France, where artists Paul Landowski (Polish-French) and Albert Caquot (French) took the helm, along with Romanian Gheorghe Leonida, who was responsible for creating the face. Upon the statue's arrival in Brazil, local engineer Heitor Levy, who would become known as the statue's master-builder, was charged with the monumental task of dismantling the 1100-ton statue and managing a crew of nearly a thousand people as they transported Christ to the top of Corcovado (primarily by train), and remounted him at the peak's summit. The statue was inaugurated after five long years of work on October 12, 1931.

Inside the monument are 12 plateaus connected by stairs that create a very precarious walkway up to the openings in the arms and head of the statue. While travelers can't enter, here's a fun fact: there is an Argentinian religious restoration artisan named Pablo Cardoso who lives inside the statue; in a small apartment under Christ's left arm.

The Heart of Christ

It may surprise you to know that Cristo Redentor has an actual heart. The 1.3m-tall hollow soapstone heart is visible from both inside and outside the statue (although you'll need to be at the height of his chest, 9 stories up, to see it). What's more, inside the heart is a bottle that contains the family tree of head engineer Heitor Levy.

The Chapel

Cristo Redentor is also a religious sanctuary – there is a small Catholic chapel around the backside of the statue that you're welcome to visit, with 22 seats and standing room for another 10–15 people. Via the chapel's website *(santuariocristoredentor.com.br)*, you can request to take part in Mass, join a pilgrimage group or even schedule a baptism or wedding (depending on availability).

Visiting

There are three ways to arrive at the top of Corcovado: by train, by van, or on foot.

The distinctive red train leaves from its station in Cosme Velho on a 20-minute journey to the top – buy tickets in person or online *(tremdocorcovado.rio)*. Official vans, which leave from Largo do Machado, Copacabana, Barra da Tijuca or the Paineiras Visitors Center, can be prebooked online *(paineirascorcovado.com.br)* or in person at a departure point.

If you're feeling particularly fit, there is a hiking trail from Parque Lage to Corcovado (it's a two-hour, entirely uphill hike); or you can cycle through the Tijuca National Forest from Horto (also entirely uphill). Either way, purchase your entrance ticket to the site upon arrival at the Paineiras Visitors Center.

STORM RISKS

While the gigantic statue was engineered to withstand winds up to 250km/h (as strong as a Category 5 hurricane), Cristo Redentor has a lightning problem. According to the National Institute of Spatial Studies, the statue is hit on average by six lightning bolts per year, so to minimize damage, the statue sports a metal crown of thorns that functions as a lightning rod.

TOP TIPS

- Cristo Redentor is open from 8am to 7pm, with periodic extensions until 8pm during summer.
- While you'll have to arrive late if you're keen to catch the sunset from the top, to avoid crowds, it's recommended to arrive as early as you can, and avoid weekends and holidays.
- The first vans leave from Paineiras Visitors Center at 7:20am, or you can leave from Largo do Machado or Copacabana at 8am.
- Rideshares, taxis and private vehicles are not allowed past the Paineiras Visitors Center – from there, you'll have to get out (beware, there is no parking) and buy a ticket for the official van, or continue on foot.

IAN G DAGNALL/ALAMY

Orchid House

TOP EXPERIENCE

Jardim Botânico

Officially known as the Instituto de Pesquisas Jardim Botânico do Rio de Janeiro (Institute of Studies of the Botanical Garden of Rio de Janeiro), the Botanical Garden is one of the most important research centers for botany and botanical conservation in the world – and this peaceful 54-hectare space is a must-visit during your stay in Rio.

DON'T MISS

- Arboreto
- Imperial Palm Walk
- Orchid House
- Japanese Garden
- Medicinal Plant Garden
- Jardim Botânico Museum
- Jardim Sensorial

History

The Botanical Gardens were founded by Dom João VI in 1808 as a place to acclimatize plants collected from around the world. After Brazil proclaimed its independence from Portugal in 1882, the garden opened to the public. In 1937, Rio's Botanical Gardens were declared Brazilian historic and artistic patrimony, and in 1991 became a UNESCO biosphere reserve.

PRACTICALITIES

Scan this QR code for prices and opening hours.

Arboreto

The arboretum, which begins at the park's entrance and encompasses the majority of the grounds, is composed of nearly 9000 different plant species from ecosystems across Brazil and around the world. Hidden among the trees are four lakes, six thematic gardens and four greenhouses, each dedicated to a different type of plant. There is even a stretch of the garden designed to evoke the dense vegetation of the Amazon region, complete with cacao, rubber and pau-mul trees. Keep an eye out for the friendly monkeys found around the park – they're up for photo ops, but please don't feed or approach them.

Imperial Palm Walk

Many visitors beeline for the Aleia Barbosa Rodrigues – a walking path named in homage to Brazilian naturalist João Barbosa Rodrigues, director of the Jardim Botânico Institute from 1890 to 1909. This charming dirt lane is symmetrically lined with towering Imperial Palm trees, and it's easily one of the garden's most picture-perfect sites.

Greenhouses

Orchid House

One of the most popular places on the grounds is the Orchid House, as much for its constructon as for its collection. This greenhouse, which has more than 700 species of orchids as residents, sits inside a beautiful octagonal structure that was first built in wood in the 1800s, then remodeled in 1930 in iron and glass in the style of the European greenhouses of the era.

Bromeliad House

Another one of the garden's amazing greenhouses brings together nearly 1600 species of bromeliads from Central and South America, including those from the Amazon and the local Atlantic rainforest. These ornamental, adaptable plants are located inside the Roberto Burle Marx Greenhouse, named in honor of Brazil's famous landscape artist and botanist.

Carnivorous Plants

For those coming with kids, the carnivorous plant house is a must. The small but centrally located greenhouse is home to a horde of carnivorous plants – the type that feed on unsuspecting insects – and although they're mostly quite small-scale specimens, it's still a very cool visit.

Jardim Sensorial

The Botanical Gardens has a special greenhouse designed specifically for visitors with sensory challenges. The Jardim Sensorial, or Sensory Garden, houses a collection of particularly aromatic plants, as well as fauna with unique and diverse textures to allow for a different sort of botanic experience. Information and labeling is provided in braille for those with severe visual impairments.

A RESEARCH INSTITUTE

Beyond being a pretty oasis in the center of the city, the gardens are a research institute, responsible for keeping records of all of the species of flora in the country and evaluating their risks of extinction. There are nearly 6500 live specimens on site along with more than 600,000 dried samples, with nearly 20,000 new samples added annually.

TOP TIPS

- Purchase tickets in advance online (by card) or upon arrival at the visitors center (cash only), just outside the park's main gate.
- The gardens can be wandered freely, or you can opt for a guided tour (also bookable online or on-site, pending availability) or for golf-cart transport for less-mobile visitors.
- There are also night tours available several times throughout the month.
- At the visitors center you'll find information and maps available in a variety of languages.
- You can also book your guided tour on-site (subject to availability), and peruse the art in the visitors center's exhibition area.

JON ARNOLD IMAGES LTD/ALAMY

PLAYTIME

Built on the grounds of the Royal Gunpowder Factory (1808–31), the Jardim Botânico's playground is still surrounded by some of the factory's original stone and brick walls. The 2022-renovated kids' park is a perfect stop if you're roaming the gardens with little ones – there's even a small snack bar with drinks, coffees and to-go snacks.

Gardens

Cacti & Succulents

Just to the left of the main entrance is one of the largest collections of cactus and succulents in Brazil. The 2023-revamped cactus collection includes nearly 150 different species of cacti and succulents located in a mostly outdoor area with observation and lookout points, as well as 'micro-world' collections, which give visitors a look at different micro-landscapes where cactus and succulents might live in the wild.

Japanese Garden

In 1935, the Japanese economic mission donated 65 typical Japanese plant species to the Botanical Gardens, the catalyst for the creation of a unique Japanese Garden inside of the institute's grounds. The space was inaugurated in 1995, and includes a traditional stone garden, bonsais, bamboos, cherry trees, weeping willows and two ponds with lotus flowers and Koi Carp.

Medicinal Plant Garden

The Botanic Garden's collection of medicinal plants began in 1976, and currently counts more than 185 species of both native and exotic plants used in healing and rituals by cultures across the world.

Fountain of the Muses, the Imperial Palm Walk (p69)

Rose Garden
Roses – a non-native plant – were introduced to Brazil by the Jesuits during the colonial period, with records of them at the Botanical Gardens since 1873. The institute's Rose Garden was built in 1914, and its collection has changed over time to favor varieties that best adapt to the city's hot and humid climate.

Casa dos Pilões

Between the main entrance and the orchid house is an adorable colonial structure that used to be a part of the area's old gunpowder factory. The Casa dos Pilões has since been turned into a very small archaeological museum where you can see remnants of life on the site and learn a bit about the water mill that once ran the factory.

Museum

The **Jardim Botânico Museum**, inaugurated in March 2024, is a beautifully renovated exposition space with immersive installations, cultural exhibitions and educational offerings for all ages. While art and fauna facts are on display, the main themes are the environment and sustainability. The museum sits on the Garden's grounds but outside the official entrance, so you don't need to pay to visit; however, you will need to book a free ticket online prior to arrival.

CATARINA BELOVA/SHUTTERSTOCK

The Palacete

TOP EXPERIENCE

Parque Lage

Parque Lage is a 52-hectare park located just a few streets off the Lagoa and a short walk from Jardim Botânico. Sitting at the feet of Cristo Redentor, melting into the Mata Atlantica, it is a favorite for family outings and picnics, as well as a magnet for the artists and art-lovers of the city.

DON'T MISS

- The Palacete
- Plage Café
- Artificial Caves
- Parque Lage-Corcovado Trail
- Aquarium
- Children's Playground
- EAV Art School

The Palacete

Parque Lage was the former residence of married couple Henrique Lage and Italian opera singer Gabriela Besanzoni. In 1920, Lage remodeled the mansion that had been built by his father with the help of Italian architect Mario Vodret, who designed an eclectic *palazzo romano* to please Besanzoni. The couple quickly became known for their magnificent parties – all the rage on the *carioca* social scene – and Besanzoni even founded a theater society that met on the grounds. But it would all end in the 1950s when Lage found himself in financial trouble and had to trade the land to pay off his debts.

PRACTICALITIES

Scan this QR code for prices and opening hours.

Luckily, Parque Lage was declared cultural patrimony in 1957, and after part of the grounds were sold to build the Globo TV Studios in 1960, the remaining area was opened to the public. In 1966, the Institute of Fine Arts was installed in the park's mansion, although it was dismantled during the dictatorship and reopened as the Escola de Artes Visuais (EAV; School of Visual Art) in 1975, which it remains to this day.

EAV: An Intellectual Encounter

From the second half of the 1970s, the EAV became the place where artists and intellectuals met. It was known to be one of the most liberal and intellectually free spaces in the city, where the strict censorship imposed by the regime was frequently challenged. It was at EAV where Francisco Bittencourt founded the city's first and most important LGBTIQ+ magazine, *Lampião*, in 1978; and where vanguard psychoanalysts of the era founded the first Escola Freudiana do Brasil (Freudian School of Brazil).

These days, the EAV is still very much a part of the city's artistic heartbeat. Beyond hosting regular theater performances, concerts, lectures and events, the school also offers rotating exhibitions and cultural immersions, and of course, a full calendar of classes. If you have some local language skills, you can join one of the continuing art courses – simply pay the monthly fee and arrive with your materials in hand.

Grounds & Gardens

The gardens were originally projected by English landscape artist John Tyndale in 1840, and although the area is significantly smaller than the original 52-hectare estate, the grounds retain their whimsical quality, featuring ponds and pathways, artificial caves, castle-like towers, a children's playground and even a small aquarium, all encased in the Mata Atlantica.

Visiting

You can visit the park for free daily from 8am to 6pm, while the mansion itself is open from 9am to 5pm; but be aware of long lines if you're hoping to take the iconic poolside photo. Inside the mansion you can brunch at **Plage Café** by the pool – the lovely setting is more of an attraction than the food; however, if you don't mind the wait (tables are first come, first served), it is a special place to have a coffee.

A TRAIL TO CORCOVADO

The park also hides the trailhead for the trek to Corcovado, a two-hour uphill hike through the forest that takes you to Cristo Redentor. Departure is permitted from 8am to 3pm daily, however it's important to note that the Panieras Visitors Center ticket office at the top (where you can buy your entrance to the statue itself) only functions until 5pm.

TOP TIPS

- There are often long lines to take a poolside photo inside of the mansion, so if you're a really keen Instagrammer (or really keen on having brunch), make sure to arrive very early.
- In summer, the building often runs over capacity, and the Park's management will sometimes require that you reserve a free entry pass online to be allowed in, so check the website *(eavparquelage.rj.gov.br)* before heading out.
- Note that the mansion is often closed on weekends for events and weddings, and will be undergoing renovations starting in 2025, so part or all of the building may be closed during your visit.

Parque Nacional da Tijuca

The Tijuca National Park is home to the largest urban rainforest in the world, and it's got enough sites, trails, waterfalls and breathtaking viewpoints to keep you busy for days on end.

REWILDING

The Tijuca National Forest is home to more than 350 different animals and 1600 species of plants, 48% of which exist nowhere else on Earth. However, many species were lost during the early development of the city, and many relocated when the forest was cleared in the 16th and 17th centuries and never returned.

Without these animals spreading seeds and fertilizing young growth, the forest can't thrive, so rewilding organization **Refauna** *(refauna.org.br)* is working to introduce displaced animals back into different sectors of the forest.

Due to safety concerns for both animals and visitors, the project mostly works with smaller species, although the aim is to move up the food chain as time goes on.

A Mesmerising Museum Location

Sublime setting for art encounters

The **Museu do Açude** *(museuscastromaya.com.br/museu-do-acude)*, which sits in four reformed colonial buildings among well-manicured gardens, is the only museum inside the Tijuca National Forest. Its buildings, which were reformed in the early 1920s by Raymundo Ottoni de Castro Maya, became a museum in 1964 in order to display Castro Maya's private collection of oriental art, furniture, ceramic panels, lithography, historical photographs of the city and personal effects, as well as to provide gallery space for contemporary and performance artists to exhibit their works. The site and its buildings are breathtaking on their own, however they become especially magical if you manage to catch a special event, music performance, theater or cultural brunch.

The gardens are open from 9am to 5pm; while the interior opens at 11am, although both close Tuesday. There's free entry on Thursdays, otherwise tickets are R$8 or R$4 for students and 60+; while those under five and over 80 are free.

MUSEUS CASTRO MAYA

The Museu do Açude is one of two Museus Castro Maya. The other, **Museu da Chácara do Céu** (p162), resides in Santa Teresa.

Trails & Peaks

The summit series

With over 200km of trails, the park also has some of the best urban hiking in the world, with exceptional viewpoints around every corner. The 19km-long **Circuito dos Picos** (peak circuit) is a challenging trek that takes you to 10 of the sector Floreta's main mountaintops, including the popular **Pico da Tijuca**, as well as the **Bico do Papagaio** (p77), the second-highest peak in the park. If you're keen to hike the whole circuit, plan for two or three days so you'll have ample time to enjoy, or opt for individual summits. Both the Pico da Tijuca and Bico do Papagaio hikes, for example, start along the same trail, leaving from the Largo de Bom Retiro. When you hit the fork, head left for Bico de Papagaio, and right for Tijuca. Pico da Tijuca takes about 1½ hours up and back and has stairs carved into the rock, while the just over 5km of the Bico do Papagaio trail involves a bit more rugged trekking.

A FAMILY-FRIENDLY PARK CIRCUIT

Hiking the Parque Nacional da Tijuca doesn't have to be hardcore – there are plenty of cool sites just steps away from the park's main entrance.

START	END	LENGTH
Praça Afonso Viseu	Bar da Praçinha	8.8km, 2hrs, 15 min

Start off at the 1 **Praça Afonso Viseu**, the central square in the Alto da Boa Vista. Head through the park's main gate and 450m up the road, where you'll find the 2 **Cascatinha Taunay**, a 35m-high waterfall – the tallest in the park. Opt for a swim in the chilly waters, or continue to the charming 3 **Capela Mayrink**, a pastel-pink chapel built in 1855 (open 2pm to 4pm daily).

Next you'll pass the 4 **Recanto dos Pintores**, a leisure area with lakes, picnic tables and playgrounds, followed by the 5 **Jardim dos Manacás**, where Empress D Leopoldina used to hold tea with her ladies of court. Just ahead sits the 6 **Restaurante Os Esquilos**, currently the only sit-down venue in the forest, located in the former home of the Baron d´Escragnolle, who led the area's reforestation efforts in the late 1800s (reservations recommended).

You could take a five-minute detour from the parking lot to Cascata Gabriela for an after-lunch dip. Continue on foot to the 7 **Cascata da Baronesa** waterfall, then the 8 **Vista do Almirante** for some exceptional views of the surrounding mountains.

As you loop back around, enjoy the enchanted atmosphere at the 9 **Lago das Fadas** (fairy lake), before heading back down the road to whence you came, where the 10 **Bar da Praçinha** awaits to reward you with some ice-cold beers.

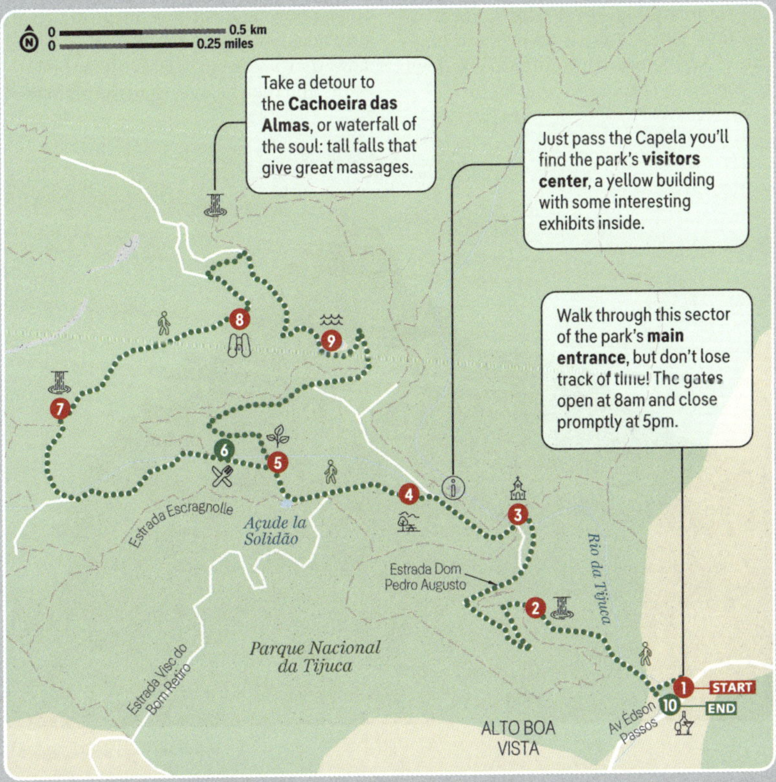

0 0.5 km
0 0.25 miles

Take a detour to the **Cachoeira das Almas**, or waterfall of the soul: tall falls that give great massages.

Just pass the Capela you'll find the park's **visitors center**, a yellow building with some interesting exhibits inside.

Walk through this sector of the park's **main entrance**, but don't lose track of time! The gates open at 8am and close promptly at 5pm.

Estrada Escragnolle
Açude la Solidão
Estrada Dom Pedro Augusto
Rio da Tijuca
Parque Nacional da Tijuca
Estrada Visc do Bom Retiro
ALTO BOA VISTA
Av Edson Passos
1 START
10 END

HIKING TRAIL

A Trek on the Transcarioca

Spearheaded by environmentalist Pedro Menezes, the Transcarioca Trail is the longest urban hiking trail in the country. Its 180km connects all of the city's six major conservation zones – starting from Barra de Guaratiba in the far west reaches of the city, and ending at the Morro da Urca in Zona Sul – and is divided into 25 sections. This hike of over 6.6km covers section 12 of the Transcarioca.

1 Morro do Archer

Starting at the Largo do Bom Retiro, follow the trail markers – yellow boot prints on a black background – toward Bico do Papagaio and Cova da Onça, and soon after you'll see a left trail branch off that leads you to your first stop, **Morro do Archer**, a hilltop named in honor of the man responsible for the reforestation of the Tijuca Forest in the late 1800s. Take a moment to enjoy the views before continuing back down to the main trail.

The hike: Back on the main trail, you'll walk another kilometer before seeing the Circuito das Grutas on your left.

2 Circuito das Grutas

Take a detour through the **Circuito das Grutas** – the cave circuit – where you can hike through the aptly named Gruta de Navio (ship cave), reminiscent of an ocean liner's bow, and the awe-inspiring Gruta do Papagaio. The entire circuit is 9.5km, however you can opt to just visit the first two caves and then head back to the main trail.

VITORMARIGO/SHUTTERSTOCK

View from Bico do Papagaio

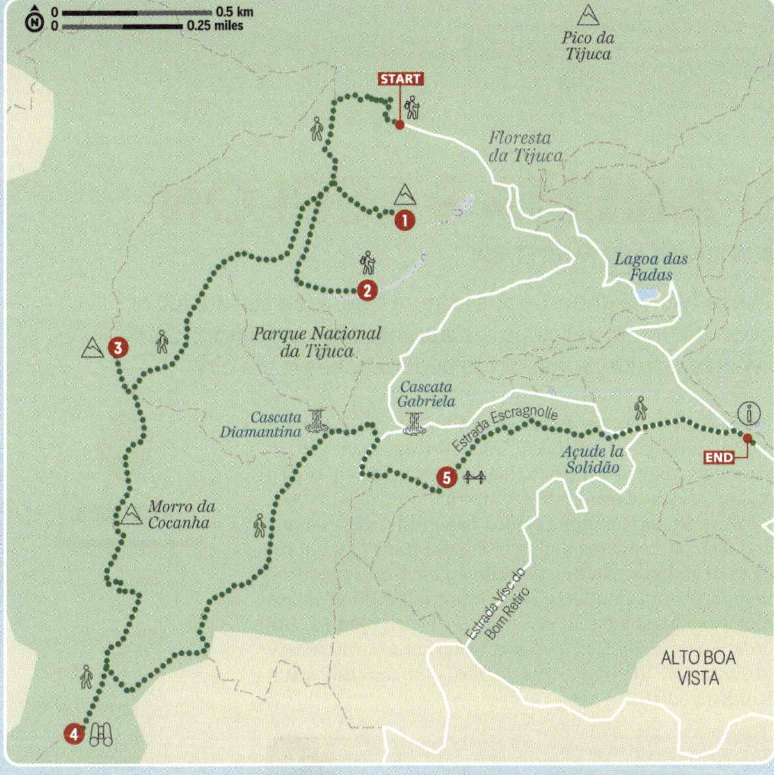

The hike: Continuing along the main path, it's another 300m walk until you come to a fork in the trail.

3 Bico do Papagaio

While the Morro da Cocanha is on your left, the trailhead to the **Bico do Papagaio**, one of the park's most famous peaks, sits on your right. If you're not afraid of a bit of a climb, opt for the right fork and hike the roughly 300m, steeply uphill trail to the top of the Bico do Papagaio, where exceptional views await you.

The hike: When you're back down, walk past a rock outcropping with some beautiful views before heading downhill, past a plateau overlook, to where the trail branches to the right.

4 Morro e Castelos da Taquara

Here you'll find the entrance to the **Morro e Castelos da Taquara** (hill and castle of Taquara), a 600m trek that rewards you with another set of exceptional views over the city's west zone. There's also a unique cactus at the top, which makes for some pretty cool photography options.

The hike: There's quite a bit of hiking past forks in the trail, streams and small rivers. Simply follow the trail for approximately 2.5km to your next stop.

5 Ponte Pênsil

Next on your list is the **Ponte Pênsil**. The 27m-long hanging bridge was reconstructed in March 2024 to meet both safety and conservation standards, however do note that its still recommended to not have more than four people on the bridge at a time.

The hike: All that's left is another 1.4km trek to the park's visitors center, where your hiking adventure ends.

Researched by Marisa Megan Pasaka

IPANEMA & LEBLON

SUN KISSED AND FANCY FREE

These twin neighborhoods feature tree-lined streets full of open-air cafes, delicious restaurants, high-end shops and lively bars; plus, some of the best beaches in the city.

When Antônio Carlos (Tom) Jobim and Vinícius de Moraes wrote 'Garota de Ipanema' ('The Girl from Ipanema') in the 1960s, they had no idea their song would help turn a 3.5km stretch of sand into an international destination.

The headquarters for *carioca* beach life, gastronomy and fashion, Ipanema and Leblon hold some of the most coveted addresses in Rio. Walk down the roads where the famous Garota sauntered, step into high-fashion shops, rent a chair and an umbrella from the beach vendors, and order an *água de coco* (coconut water) or a *caipirinha* – in short, live life like a true *carioca, sungas* (tiny swim trunks) and all.

INCLUDES

Ipanema Beach (p82)

See p223 for places to stay in Ipanema and Leblon.

FROM LEFT: CATARINA BELOVA/SHUTTERSTOCK, M.SOBREIRA/ALAMY

Highlights

1 Ipanema Beach
Visit the beach immortalized in the song 'Garota de Ipanema.' It isn't just breathtakingly beautiful – it's a whole lifestyle. **p82**

2 Pedra do Arpoador
Catch sunset from the Arpoador's rocky outcropping that sits jutting out over the sea. **p88**

3 Hippie Market
Shop till you drop at General Osório's outdoor art and artisan market that's been on the Ipanema circuit since the 1970s. **p80**

4 Dias Ferreira
Wander down a road full of bars, restaurants and shops in Leblon; the perfect spot to meet up or make new friends. **p90**

5 Casa de Cultura Laura Alvim
Delve into *carioca* culture at an oceanfront house turned cultural center (pictured above). **p80**

Getting Around

Metro
The metro runs all along Ipanema, ending at the praça and station Antero de Quental in Leblon. Most places in these neighborhoods are less than a 10-minute walk to the nearest station.

Bicycle
There's a bike path running along the entire beachfront (possibly one of the most beautiful cycling lanes in the world), along with several branches connecting to the Lagoa – ideal for cycling.

Walking
Walking around Ipanema and Leblon is a joy – the whole area is completely flat, full of shops, restaurants, bars and enticing views, and only a 45-minute walk from end to end.

Ipanema

Although the Tupinambá indigenous called 'Ypanema' the place of 'bad waters', this breathtaking beachfront zone was destined to develop into the place to be for the *carioca* elite.

VINÍCIUS DE MORAES

One of Ipanema's most famous residents was the Brazilian poet, composer, musician and diplomat best known as one of the founders of bossa-nova music, and coauthor of the song 'Garota de Ipanema.'

Vinicius de Moraes (1913–80) wasn't just one of his era's great creative minds – he was a fixture of Rio's bohemia. Moraes was a bon vivant who made easy friends, loved cooking and was known to write poems in his bathtub.

He married nine times in his life – three of these partnerships resulted in children – and had countless lovers, although ironically, one of his most famous poems, written to his first wife in 1939, was entitled *Soneto de Fidelidade* (the sonnet of fidelity).

Bohemian Art & Artisan Market

General Osório Hippie Market

Every Sunday, General Osório Square in Ipanema hosts the **Hippie Market**, an unpretentious gathering of artisans and artists from across the city selling their work and wares. It was once a *carioca*-only event, but the arrival of backpackers in the late 1960s transformed this weekly market into the bohemian open-air art gallery that it is today.

The Hippie Market is the best place to buy handcrafted gifts, clothing, paintings or home decor, as well as sample the street-fair delicacies from across the country. Head towards the white-clad women serving street food from Salvador for some exceptionally delicious treats.

A Beachfront Home for the Arts

Casa de Cultura

The Ipanema beachfront is home to one of the most important cultural centers in the city – the **Casa de Cultura Laura Alvim**. Laura Alvim dreamed of being an actress, but her family wouldn't allow it, so instead she spent her life as a dedicated supporter of the arts. Alvim built a stage in the back of her Ipanema home and provided space for friends and other artists to meet and rehearse. Six months before her death in 1983, Alvim willed her house to the Government of Rio to continue to be used for this purpose, and in 1986 the Casa de Cultura Laura Alvim opened its doors.

The space has a theater, a cinema, an auditorium and three rooms where artistic and cultural courses are offered, along with an art gallery used for exhibitions as well as book- and album-launch parties. The house is open from Tuesday to Sunday, and nearly all events and performances are open to the public.

HIGHLIGHTS
1 Ipanema Beach

SIGHTS
2 Casa de Cultura Laura Alvim

ACTIVITIES
3 Bodhi Float Center
4 Museum of Yoga
5 Samba Fit
6 Spa Maria Bonita

SLEEPING
7 L'Homme de Rio
8 Mango Tree

EATING
9 ASA Açaí
10 Aussie Coffee
11 Barraca do Uruguai
12 Casa Mohamed
13 Copanema Mix
14 Didier
15 Ferro e Farinha
16 Le Pulê
17 Maria Açaí
18 Nôa Ipanema
19 Oakberry
20 Rudä Restaurante
see 6 Spazziano
21 Tapí Ipanema
22 Teva
23 Zazá Bistrô

SHOPPING
24 Blue Man
25 FARM Rio
26 Hippie Market
27 Osklen
28 Redley
29 Salinas

LAZYLLAMA/SHUTTERSTOCK

Bikini seller

TOP EXPERIENCE

Ipanema Beach

Heading to Ipanema Beach is a daily ritual for residents of this coastal enclave, and an entire industry runs in turn. Beach vendors, *quiosque* (kiosk) owners and equipment renters all make a living from the sun worshippers, while rigorously trained lifeguards keep watch over the scene, often enacting multiple rescues per day. It's a place where you'll find every social class and walk of life.

DON'T MISS

- Posto 9
- Biscoito Globo
- Posto 7
- Posto 8
- Barraca do Uruguay
- Vendedores ambulantes
- The Lifeguards

A Quick Breakdown

Rio's beaches are a world unto themselves, and knowing where to go will help you find your tribe. Ipanema's beach runs from Posto 7 in Arpoador to Posto 12 in Leblon, lined with *barracas* (stands) – where you rent beach chairs, umbrellas and buy ice-cold drinks – conveniently numbered so you can more easily find your friends among the crowds.

Finding the Best Spot for You

Each zone attracts a different type of beachgoer – here's a quick breakdown:

Posto 9

The best-known spot in Ipanema is Posto 9 – the place to go to see and be seen. Here, you're likely to find young celebrities and their entourages stretched out on the sand next to models and influencers having informal photo shoots on blue beach chairs. The scene is young, the vibe is carnal, and there are great drinks and even some decent food to be found to keep you going – try the sausage sandwich from the **Barraca do Uruguai** (Anthony Bourdain ate here).

Posto 7

Arpoador's Posto 7 has two claims to fame: 1) It's the heart and soul of the *carioca* surf scene, where everything from surf lessons to local surf competitions take place; and 2) it's the place where crowds gather at the end of the afternoon to get ready for another spectacular sunset. Besides having these two popularity claims, it's also frequently a cradle of funk culture, thanks to its location close to the metro and the nearby Cantagalo and Pavão e Pavonzinho favelas. The late afternoons in the summer can get rowdy, crowded and quite loud (watch your belongings).

Posto 8

Posto 8 is typically a tourist spot, due to its location in front of the Fasano hotel, and if you continue up a bit toward Farme de Amoedo street, you'll quickly enter into rainbow-flag territory.

Posto 10 & **Posto 11**

On both sides of the canal that separates Ipanema from Leblon you'll find some of the quietest areas of sand on the strip. Posts 10 and 11 are marked by beach tennis and beach volleyball courts, sand dunes and book lovers. These zones are also favorite spots for families or those looking for some peace and quiet away from the crowds.

Vendedores Ambulantes

The beach isn't just a beach – it's a lively, moving street market, where *vendedores ambulantes* (itinerant salespeople) are hawking anything you might need to make your day more comfortable. You can purchase *cangas* (used instead of towels), bikinis, hats, sunglasses, sunscreen, tanning oil, beach toys, and all manner of food and drink. Local favorites include Mate Leão, the *carioca* equivalent of ice tea that's mixed with lemonade or passion-fruit juice; and Biscoito Globo, a tapioca-based cracker that's a Rio de Janeiro icon.

Bombeiros

The numbered Postos are actually lifeguard towers, and they are where to go if you need a (paid) bathroom or free first aid. The *bombeiros* (lifeguards) are also the emergency responders on the sand, whether you have lost a child or have a health emergency. Rio's lifeguards pass through extremely intensive training, and are considered to be some of the best in the world.

BEACH ETIQUETTE

You'll likely be elbow to elbow with your closest neighbor, especially on weekends in the summer, so be careful of your belongings. Don't hesitate to ask a friendly face to watch your bag so you can pop in the water for a *mergulho* (a dip) to help beat the heat. It's common courtesy to do the same for your neighbors – a task that takes more vigilance as the crowds roll in.

TOP TIPS

- For peace and quiet, arrive early. In the morning, Ipanema is a haven for fitness lovers, bookworms, dog owners and families, and in contrast to late afternoon vibes, the morning beach is both quiet and safe (although you can still get a caipirinha at 9am, if that's your thing).
- As the day goes on, the crowds begin to roll in and the ambience shifts, sometimes quite drastically. The *vendedores ambulantes* (with their persistent sales pitches) appear, as do the larger groups of beachgoers with their portable speakers.
- By late afternoon on the weekend, Ipanema turns into a veritable party on the sand.

BEST CARIOCA CLOTHING BRANDS

Osklen: Perhaps Brazil's most internationally famous brand, Osklen walks the line between laid-back beach style and upscale chic.

Haight Clothing: High-quality, swim- and beachwear that's as good on the sand as it is for a night out.

Salinas: For the perfect bikini, or a go-to beach look inspired by the *carioca* sands, head to this upscale (mostly) women's brand. Its first store in Ipanema opened in 1988.

Redley: What started as a shoe brand inspired by California surf culture has gone on to become one of the country's coolest menswear brands.

Blue Man: These Brazilian bikinis – an Ipanema staple for decades – have also graced catwalks in Paris, London and Milan.

IAN TROWER/ALAMY

Beach, Life & Style

Your Rio de Janeiro wardrobe

A far cry from the sleek runways of São Paulo, fashion in the 'Marvelous City' fits the lifestyle it portrays. *Carioca* style is colorful, laid-back and ready for everything. You need to be chic enough to hit the sand and still head straight for a night out while looking fabulous. High heels are rarely seen, while tropical-inspired patterns are everywhere – one of the city's favorite brands, **FARM Rio**, is known for them. When the temperatures begin to drop, the satirical side of *carioca* style comes out of the closet – picture jackets and beanies matched with board shorts and *havaianas* on a 'cold' winter's day.

Get Involved in Wellness Activities

Yoga, spas, Pilates and more

Ipanema and Leblon are all about living well, so it's no surprise these neighborhoods are overflowing with yoga and Pilates studios, salons, spas and sports teams. **Spa Maria Bonita** is the go-to for excellent massages that won't break the bank, while at the **Bodhi Float Center**, you can hop in a sensory deprivation tank to give your overstimulated brain a break.

EATING AÇAÍ IN IPANEMA: OUR PICKS

ASA Açaí: If you're a purist, this is the best *açaí* in town: all organic and sustainably sourced ingredients from the Amazon. *9am-10pm* $$

Maria Açaí: This is the spot for those who love their *açaí* to resemble ice cream: full of sugar, toppings and happiness. *10am-10pm* $

Oakberry: The *açaí* chain that's hit the global market; in between healthy and gluttonous – depending on how you order. *10am-9pm* $$

Tapí Ipanema: This organic *açaí* from the Amazon comes pre-mixed with banana and honey. Choose your own toppings. *8am-8pm Mon-Sat* $

Yoga session

Yogis can check out the **Museum of Yoga** *(Museu do Yoga)*, where you'll find a full schedule of all types of yoga classes and plenty of bilingual teachers.

Or opt for a free outdoor yoga or fitness classes with **Mude** *(page.mude.fit/app)*: an organization leading a movement across the city, occupying outdoor spaces with free wellness activities. Simply download the Mude App on your phone to see its full calendar of classes, then register yourself on the app to join in.

Get Samba Fit

Shake it out

It's hard to hang out in the land of Carnaval if you don't know how to samba. But if you weren't born and raised on Rio's golden sands, it can be a tricky step to learn. Luckily, in Ipanema, there's a dance studio devoted to teaching foreigners the art of samba during a fun, fitness-style dance class that's been attracting visitors from all over the world for more than 25 years.

Owner of the **Samba Fit** studio, Carla Campos, a veteran of the samba parade circuit, offers both open and private classes for anyone – regardless of age, level or language spoken.

BISCOITO GLOBO

In 1953, *carioca* brothers Milton, Jaime and João Ponce were sent to live with their cousin in Ipiranga, São Paulo, where they learned to make tapioca biscuits.

They took the recipe back to Rio, where the biscuits were so well received that the brothers were hired by a bakery – named 'Globo' – to sell their product. Demand grew, and the Ponce brothers partnered with Portuguese bread aficionado Francisco Nunes Torrão in 1963 to make and sell **Biscoito Globo**.

Still found all around Rio (but especially on the beach), Biscoito Gobo has never marketed its product, never changed its label and never opened any franchises, yet it may just be the most popular snack in the city.

EATING IN IPANEMA: LAID-BACK DINING

Spazziano: Vegan spot inside Spa Maria Bonita. One of the least expensive and most delicious buffets for lovers of healthy food. *noon-4pm* $

Alva Bakery: Artisan micro-bakery; its sweet, flaky pastries and bread have developed their own cult following. *8am-6pm Tue-Sat* $

Aussie Coffee: Specialty coffee to a small gallery in Ipanema. One of the best flat whites in the city. *8am-5pm Mon-Fri, to 4pm Sat, to 2:30pm Sun* $$

Copanema Mix: This corner snack bar serves everything from *açaís* and sandwiches to traditional lunch and dinner dishes. *24hr* $

WHY I LOVE IPANEMA

Marisa Megan Paska, Lonely Planet writer

To me, Ipanema isn't just a place – it's an entire lifestyle. It's waking up early and walking to the beach with just a bikini, towel and flip-flops for an early morning swim; it's your daily *açaí* and coffee at the corner cafe. It's a small town inside of a city, where you actually get to know your neighbors and you're constantly late because you're constantly running into people you know on the street.

It's stopping work to watch the sunset; cycling to get your groceries and meeting friends at the bar in the afternoon because really, what's better than some beers while the samba musicians set up their gear behind you. Get ready, it's almost time to dance the night away.

Partake in Carioca Sports

Patrimony of the sands

Ipanema is full of fitness fanatics, and when in Rio, you'll want to join in. Beach volleyball, beach tennis, ocean swimming, Hawaiian canoeing and stand-up paddleboarding are just some of the sports you'll see every morning – just ask any friendly athlete where you can rent equipment or take a lesson.

Three of the most popular beach sports in Brazil were born on Rio's sands: *altinha* (a group game of juggling with soccer touches, played in the sand), *frescobol* (aka paddleball by the sea) or *futevôlei* (exactly like volleyball but with, you guessed it, soccer touches). These sports all evolved on Rio beaches in the 1950s, 1960s and 1970s, and are a veritable part of *carioca* heritage. Both *frescobol* and *futevôlei* now have organized leagues, tournaments and championship circuits, while *altinha*, the most informal of the three, went on to be declared Cultural Patrimony in 2020.

Enjoy an Amazonian Superfood

How to order açaí

Açaí is a purple superfood from the Amazon, and although you may have an exported version in your hometown, you haven't had a true experience till you've been in Brazil. Typically, the purple berry is frozen and blended into a thick smoothie and eaten with a spoon; and in Rio, *açai* is a bit like coffee in that everyone has their order. *Açaí* in Rio generally comes mixed with guaraná syrup – very sugary and caffeine-like – although you can opt for *pouco xarpoe* (a little bit of syrup) or *sem xarope* (no syrup), then pick your favorite fruits to blend together – banana, *graviola* (custard apple), passion fruit – you name it. Finally, choose your toppings, which could be anything from condensed milk and M&Ms to granola, cut fruit and honey. Your favorite *açaí* spot says a lot about your style; while some shops cater to the healthy crowd, others can be just downright gluttonous.

EATING IN IPANEMA: UPSCALE OPTIONS

Nôa Ipanema: Serving coastal Mediterranean cuisine in a 1930s historical house, noted on Michelin's 2024 Guide. *noon-11pm* $$$

Teva: Vegan, sustainable, organic and very chic. Perfect for dates, with yourself or otherwise. *noon-midnight Mon-Sat; to 10pm Sun* $$

Zazá Bistrô: Brazilian fare with an Asian twist in brightly colored corner mansion. *6:30pm-12:30am Mon, noon-12:30am Tue-Sat, noon-11:30pm Sun* $$

Le Pulê: In General Osório square you'll find this chic, French-style bistro with a solid wine selection and a stylish crowd. *noon-1am* $$$

Rudã Restaurante: Brazilian classics from north and southeast served in a charming historic 1930s house. *noon-midnight Tue-Sat, to 8pm Sun* $$

Casa Mohamed: Middle Eastern restaurant's old family-style recipes and wood-fired bread make for a winning combination. *11:30am-11pm Tue-Sun* $$

Ferro e Farinha: Only pizzeria in the city named in the top 100 in the world. Great cocktails and ambience. *6pm-midnight Sun-Thu, to 1am Fri & Sat* $$

Didier: French restaurant with a Michelin Bib Gourmand serves traditional French cuisine/French takes on Brazilian classics. *11:30am-11pm* $$$

HISTORICAL BUILDINGS & UNIQUE ARCHITECTURE OF IPANEMA

Walk along Ipanema's leafy streets and learn about the history of the neighborhood via its historical houses and buildings.

START	END	LENGTH
Praça General Osório	Edifício Marajoara	2.8km; 40min

Start at the Praça General Osorio's 1 **Chafariz dos Saracuras**, a granite fountain first built in 1795 for the internal courtyard of the Convento da Ajuda, Rio's first all-female convent. Ajuda was demolished in 1911 and the fountain reinstalled in Ipanema.

Head to the beachfront to walk past 2 **Edifício Vieira Souto** (1938), the only oceanfront art-deco building in Ipanema and former home to Vinícius de Moraes, before continuing to the 3 **Edifício Garota de Ipanema**. It was in this 1961 construction that Heloísa Pinheiro, the famed Girl from Ipanema, lived. She would pass in front of the old Bar Veloso (now the bar 4 **Garota de Ipanema**), where Tom Jobim and Vinícius de Moraes sat watching – from where, in 1962, they composed their famous song.

Next, walk up to 5 **Rua Nascimento Silva 107**, the residence of Jobim and his wife Thereza, immortalized in the bossa-nova song 'Carta Ao Tom 74', then head to the 6 **Casa de Pedra**, a 250-sq-meter house constructed in 1930 that's been lovingly preserved (and is now a multi-brand shop). On the same road, you'll walk past the 7 **Gabinete de Leitura Guilherme Araújo** (former house of Guilherme Araújo; one of the co-founders of Tropicalia), which has been turned into a cultural center, before heading through the Praça Nossa Senhora da Paz to end at the 8 **Edifício Marajoara**, Ipanema's first skyscraper.

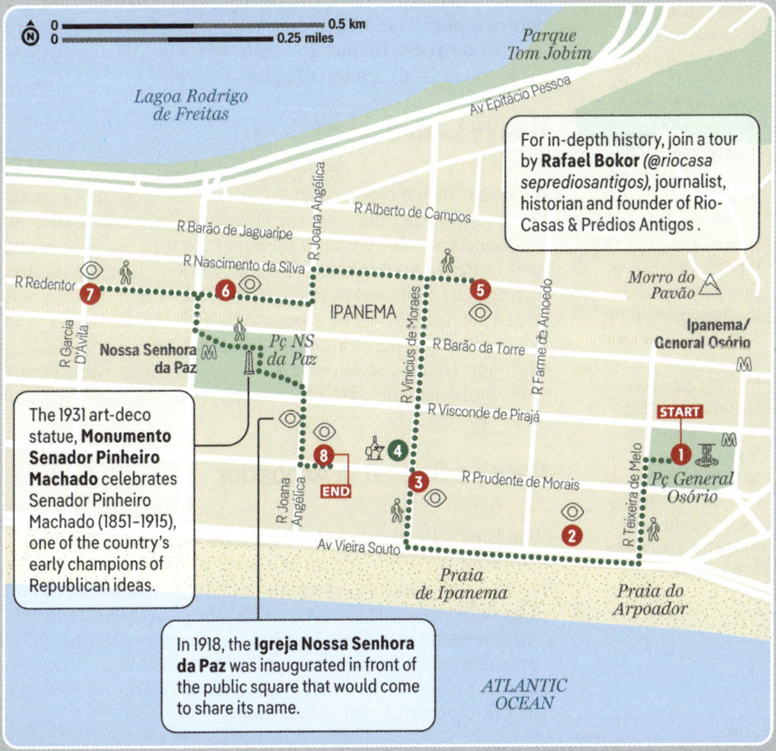

For in-depth history, join a tour by **Rafael Bokor** *(@riocasasprediosantigos)*, journalist, historian and founder of Rio-Casas & Prédios Antigos.

The 1931 art-deco statue, **Monumento Senador Pinheiro Machado** celebrates Senador Pinheiro Machado (1851–1915), one of the country's early champions of Republican ideas.

In 1918, the **Igreja Nossa Senhora da Paz** was inaugurated in front of the public square that would come to share its name.

Arpoador

Arpoador – Arpex to its friends – sits at the far end of Ipanema Beach, separated from Copacabana by a rocky outcrop and the sea. This unique corner of the city is where surf, fitness and breathtaking sunsets set the scene.

WHAT'S IN A NAME?

Arpoador is as much a beach as it is a rock formation. The rock sits in between Praia do Diablo and the sands of Ipanema, and is a *carioca's* favorite sunset spot; while the stretch of sand in question runs about 500m along Ipanema Beach.

Both got their name from a fishing practice that both the native Brazilians and later the Portuguese took part in in the 16th and 17th centuries: whale hunting. Arpoador loosely translates in Tupi-Guarani to 'harpoon thrower,' due to the fact that it was the main spot where locals would go to throw their harpoons to hunt whales.

Get Into Surf Culture

Learners, legends and legendary lefts

Surfers, aspiring or otherwise, will find their tribe at Arpoador Beach, which has been the heart and soul of *carioca* surfing since the sport first took hold of Brazil in the 1950s and 1960s.

While the West Zone has the best waves in the city, there are plenty of surf schools inside of the South Zone at Posto 7 (p83), where you can rent gear, take a lesson or find a photographer to shoot your mad skills. **Surf Glória** *(@surf_gloria)* and **Team Bispo** *(@teambispo)* are two reliable options for learners of all levels and ages.

Heavy Lifting

Arpoador Beach's workout culture

Arpoador Beach is a magnet for fitness fanatics – not just for the sports taking place on the strand or the sand, but for its outdoor **Arpoador Gym**. At the very far end of the boardwalk, next to **Praia do Diablo,** you'll find workout lovers pumping iron on the bright-yellow painted concrete weight benches and matching dumbbell sets. The space is used day and night, and it remains well maintained by the local fitness community. The vibe is generally friendly and welcoming, even during early mornings and late afternoons, when the space is at its most crowded.

Catch a Sunset in Arpoador

Yes, there is clapping

Watching sunset from the **Pedra do Arpoador** is a quintessential *carioca* experience. After a beautiful day on the beach, crowds gather on a giant rock in Arpoador at the end of Ipanema to watch the sun go down over the Atlantic Ocean, with the distinctive **Dois Irmãos** *(Two Brothers Mountain)* in the background. Caipirinhas are imbibed. Clapping ensues. On the most perfect day, you'll even get to turn around to watch the full moon rise over Copacabana.

SIGHTS
1 Parque Garota de Ipanema
2 Pedra do Arpoador
3 Posto 7
4 Praia do Diablo

ACTIVITIES
5 Arpoador Gym

SLEEPING
6 Hotel Arpoador

EATING
7 ARP Bar
8 Balcão
9 Parada Voadora
10 Tapí Arpoador

The Revival of Parque Garota de Ipanema

Outdoor leisure and events

Set just behind Arpoador Beach, **Parque Garota de Ipanema**, once abandoned and dangerous, now has full-time security patrols so locals can use the revived spaces: children's playground, dog park, outdoor gym, games tables, as well as an amphitheater space that hosts outdoor markets and concerts in the summer. It's still recommended to visit the two skate bowls with a group.

CIRCO VOADOR

The Parque Garota de Ipanema was the site of the original **Circo Voador** (p169), where the performance space had its initial three-month run in 1982 before moving to Lapa later in the year.

Embrace Rooftop Yoga

Zen with a view

At **Hotel Arpoador** (the only hotel that's actually located ON the sand, and not across the street from it) you'll find the wellness crowd making the best of the mornings – and of the views – with an open-air yoga class, offered Monday to Friday at 8am on the rooftop. Make a reservation at the reception or online *(cityandsea.shop/collections/experiencias/products/yoga-no-terraco)*.

EATING IN ARPOADOR: OUR PICKS

Tapí Arpoador: Tapioca is a Brazilian tradition, and this is the place for gourmet tapioca, with a side of organic *açaí* and coffee. *8am-10pm* $

Parada Voadora: This food truck that opened in 2024 inside Parque Garota de Ipanema serves post-beach snacks. *11am-8pm Tue-Sun* $

Balcão: Corner kitchen serving mouthwatering international street food to customers sitting on barstools. *11am-10pm Wed-Sat to 9pm Sun & Tue* $

ARP Bar: Chic hotel restaurant-bar has the best breakfast (and breakfast view) in the area. Lunch and cocktails also shine. *7am-11pm* $$$

Leblon

This upscale neighborhood – the second-most expensive in Brazil – is the beachfront playground for the beautiful, tanned and carefree *cariocas* of the upper echelons. Expect high-end shops and gastronomy, open-air cafes and bars.

BAIXO LEBLON

Between Av Ataulfo de Paiva, Dias Ferreira and Aristides Espínola streets is a section of Leblon that in the 1970s and 1980s became the meeting point for intellectuals, artists and bohemia of the neighborhood. They called it 'Baixo', meaning 'lower' in Portuguese, in reference to Timóteo da Costa street just up the road, which climbed a steep hill and thus became known as 'Alto Leblon'.

But the term *baixo* came to take on another meaning, and was coined by *cariocas* to informally define an area with a high concentration of bars where one goes for nights out. Although other areas, like Baixo Gávea, would soon follow the trend, Baixo Leblon was the first spot in the city to use the term.

Experience the Famed Dias Ferreira

More than just a street

Dias Ferreira isn't just any road. This 700m street lined with bars, restaurants, shops and galleries has turned into an entire lifestyle. It's as much of a place to run into friends, converse across parked cars and meet for lunch, as it is to put on your best frock for a night out.

Originally called Rua do Sapé, this upscale stretch of Leblon –only a 10-minute walk from end to end – gained fame when it was featured in *telenovelas* (TV soap operas) by Manoel Carlos in the late 1990s and early 2000s. Recently, author Fernanda Gentil even published a book about it. *Uma rua chamada Dias Ferreira (A Road Named Dias Ferreira)* is an 118-page ode to the street itself, written in English and Portuguese, and recounting its history and the culture that's since developed here.

For those more interested in parties, events and openings, follow all the happenings on this little stretch of asphalt on Instagram *(@diasferreira.rio)* – and keep an eye out for the website and app, set to launch in 2026.

Absorb Leblon's Artistic Culture

Intellectual hot spots

While Leblon is best known for its high fashion and gastronomy, it's also a place where polished artistic culture quietly thrives. The best known epicenter for the neighborhood's intellectual crowd is the **Livraria Argumento**, a small bookstore which, when it opened in 1978 in the middle of Brazil's dictatorship, quickly attracted students, professors, journalists and the like, thanks to its wide selection of otherwise difficult-to-find titles.

These days, it's still a cultural meeting point, where book launches, author signings and live-music events are frequent happenings.

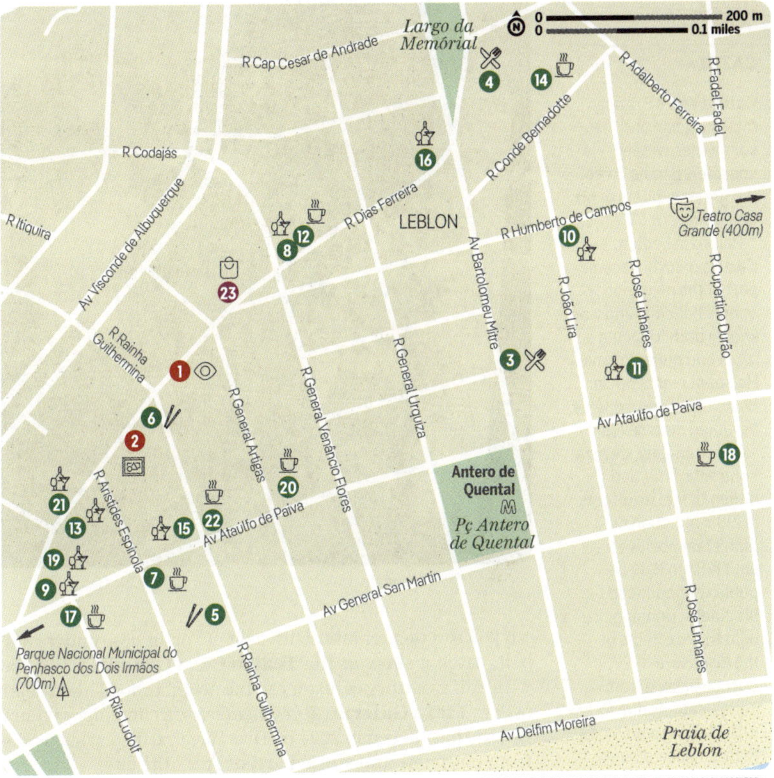

SIGHTS
1 Dias Ferreira
2 Flexa Galeria

EATING
3 Giuseppe Grill
4 Mesa do Lado
5 Nam Thai
6 Sushi Leblon

DRINKING & NIGHTLIFE
7 BB Lanches
8 Belmonte
9 Boteco Boa Praça
10 Boteco Princesa
11 Bracarense
12 Café Severino
13 Esch Café
14 Grâu Artesanal
15 Jobi
16 Liz Cocktail & Co
17 Nusa Leblon
18 Okanossa
19 Stuzzi
20 Talho Capixaba
21 Venga!
22 Verso Café Cultural

SHOPPING
23 Livraria Argumento

EATING IN LEBLON: OUR PICKS

Sushi Leblon: Rio's first ever Japanese restaurant (opened 1986) always attracts a crowd. *noon-12:30pm Mon-Wed, to 1:30am Thu-Sat, 1pm-midnight Sun* $$$

Giuseppe Grill: Upscale surf and turf served grilled or barbecued in a rustic dining room. *noon-midnight Mon-Fri, to 1am Sat, to 11pm Sun* $$$

Nam Thai: Modern, sophisticated Thai food. Over two decades on the *carioca* scene. *6-10pm Mon; noon-10pm Tue, Wed & Sun; noon-11pm Thu-Sat* $$$

Mesa do Lado: Tiny 12-seater dining room with a unique gastronomic experience aimed to awaken all five senses. *8-10.30pm Wed-Sat* $$$

CAZUZA

Cazuza was a Brazilian rock musician and songwriter, widely considered to be one of the greatest poets of his generation.

Raised in Leblon, Cazuza quickly became part of the neighborhood's bohemia and was known both for being a rebel and quite polemic. He spent nights out in Baixo Leblon and openly assumed his bisexuality.

Unfortunately, Cazuza contracted HIV and began to feel its effects in 1985, although he didn't test positive until 1987. In 1989 he publicly announced his illness, bringing light to the effects of the disease. In 1990, Cazuza passed from complications due to AIDS, having sold more than 5 million albums, recorded 126 songs and made 11 number-one singles during his only nine-year-long career.

FOTO ARENA LTDA/ALAMY

If you're a theater lover with a bit of Portuguese under your belt, catch a show at the **Teatro Casa Grande**, a theater with half a century of history in the neighborhood, then head over to **Flexa Galeria** *(@flexa.galeria)*, a contemporary art gallery that opened in 2024 on Dias Ferreira, displaying works from both new and storied artists from the city.

Extraordinary Views from a Tiny Park

A window to the sky

At the far end of Leblon, right at the start of Av Niemeyer you'll find the entrance to a small, often overlooked park with some excellent trails and even better views.

DRINKING IN LEBLON: OUR PICKS

Liz Cocktail & Co: Stylish cocktail bar offers delectable dishes and thematic drinks for events (eg cocktails inspired by your Tarot card selection).

Belmonte: This chain of bars are Rio icons, and this Leblon address is one of the most popular. Go for afterwork drinks or to find your next date.

Stuzzi: Upscale Italian tapas bar featuring what's been called the best cocktail menu in the city.

Venga!: Cozy tapas bar with an excellent wine list, typical Spanish food and an animated crowd.

Jobi: One of the oldest and most traditional pubs in Leblon, this classic Portuguese bar is a magnet at the end of any night out.

Boteco Princesa: This traditional corner pub is perfect for lunch, dinner or afternoon beers.

Boteco Boa Praça: Go-to spot for after-beach beer, to meet with friends or to make some new ones.

Bracarense: Serving delicious bar snacks and ice-cold beer, this *boteco*-style pub attracts crowds at all hours.

Parque Nacional Municipal do Penhasco dos Dois Irmãos

The **Parque Nacional Municipal do Penhasco dos Dois Irmãos** – more frequently called the Parque dos Dois Irmãos or simply Parque do Penhasco – sits on the lower end of the Two Brothers mountain, offering picnic areas, playgrounds, beautiful gardens and six different lookout points with views stretching across Leblon, Ipanema and Lagoa.

The best sits at the very top, at the end of an approximately 1.5km trail called Janela do Céu (Window to the Sky), which leads you up the slope of the smaller of the two brothers.

MANOEL CARLOS' LEBLON

Brazilian *telenovelas* are a global phenomenon. In Latino countries across the world, these overdramatic television series are broadcast to obsessive viewers, bringing bits of life in Brazil to living rooms in Mexico, Portugal, Spain and beyond.

Some of Rede Globo's (Brazil's main TV station) most popular *novelas* were written by *Paulista* Manoel Carlos and set on the streets of Leblon: *Viver a Vida*, *Mulheres Apaixonadas* and *Por Amor* were just a few that became national phenomena.

Fun fact: nine of the *novelas* written by Carlos featured a protagonist named Helena, a reference the writer made to Helen of Troy (*Helena de Troia*, in Portuguese), whom he considered to be 'the perfect woman.'

CAFES & JUICE BARS: OUR PICKS

Talho Capixaba: Deli and bakery serving artisanal breads, pastries, breakfast spreads and stuffed sandwiches since 1958. *7am-10pm* **$$**

BB Lanches: Named in honor of Bridget Bardot. Some of the best *açaí*, fresh juices and savory pastries in the city. *8am-1am Sun-Wed, to 3am Thu-Sun* **$**

Verso Café Cultural: Downstairs is a chic cafe-bar; while upstairs you'll find book launches, lectures, concerts and more. *8am-8pm Mon-Sat* **$$**

Café Severino: Literary-inspired cafe serving coffees, drinks and snacks inside the Argumento bookshop. *10am-10pm Mon-Sat, 9am-9pm Sun* **$$**

Grâu Artesanal: Hidden away in a gallery in Leblon, this little artisanal bakery has your daily bread. *9am-7pm Tue-Fri; 8am-7pm Sat; 8am-1pm Sun* **$$**

Esch Café: Cuban cigars, cocktails and delicious plates and bar snacks at this slightly off-beat cafe-bar. *12:30pm-1am Tue-Sat; 1-9pm Sun* **$$$**

Nusa Leblon: One of the best spots in the neighborhood for a healthy breakfast or brunch; as delicious as it is photogenic. *8am-6.30pm* **$$**

Okanossa: Tiny colorful cafe serving healthy, vegetarian and vegan breakfasts along with specialty coffee. *10am-5:30pm Tue-Fri, 9am-5pm Sat & Sun* **$$**

Vidigal

Spilling down the hillside of Dois Irmãos mountain, you'll find the favelas Vidigal and Chácara do Céu. These communities are some of the most frequented in the city, with restaurants and guesthouses geared towards tourists.

BEST NIGHTLIFE SPOTS

Faro Beach Club (farobeachclub.com.br): With an oceanfront pool and daytime views, this event space on Av Niemeyer hosts public events and parties.

Bar da Laje (@bardalaje): Swinging samba, *pagode* and *sertanejo* music with breathtaking views. The go-to spot for sunset parties Friday to Monday.

Alto Vidigal (@altovidigalbrasil): One of Vidigal's original party spots got a makeover as a beer garden and live-music venue.

Mirante do Arvrão (mirantedoarvrao.com.br): Vidigal's only high-end hotel, hosts samba, funk and MPB (Música Popular Brasileira) events on its terrace bar with spectacular views.

Trek to the Top

Where sunrise views reign

Dois Irmãos is better known as the backdrop for Ipanema's sunset, however the hike to the top via **Trilha Dois Irmãos** is just as exciting.

The approximately 1.5km, 40-minute (each way), relatively easy trail starts where the favela ends, which means to get to the trailhead you'll have to take a Kombi or mototaxi up to the favela's highest point. The tourist rate in either mode of transport to the Campo de Vidigal, where the trail begins, is R$10, and there's a R$10 (cash only) fee to enter the trail, paid to the community.

When you're on the trail, there's nothing to do but enjoy the views – São Conrado and Rocinha feature, while at the top you'll find the entire Zona Sul at your feet, with the heart-shaped Lagoa looking back at you.

Rio's First Public Food Garden

From trash to treasure

The 8500-sq-meter **Parque Instituto Sitiê**, once a giant trash heap, was transformed by volunteers into the city's first public park with a food-producing garden.

Besides incredible (free) ocean views, educational opportunities for local schoolchildren, and nearly two tons of fresh fruit and vegetables annually for local residents, approximately 75% of the park is Mata Atlantica, where more than 50 new plant species have been successfully reintroduced by the park's volunteers.

Yoga on High

Well-being classes

Started in the Pavão Pavãozinho community behind Copacabana, **Ame Viva** *(ameviva.org; @favelayogi)* is a locally

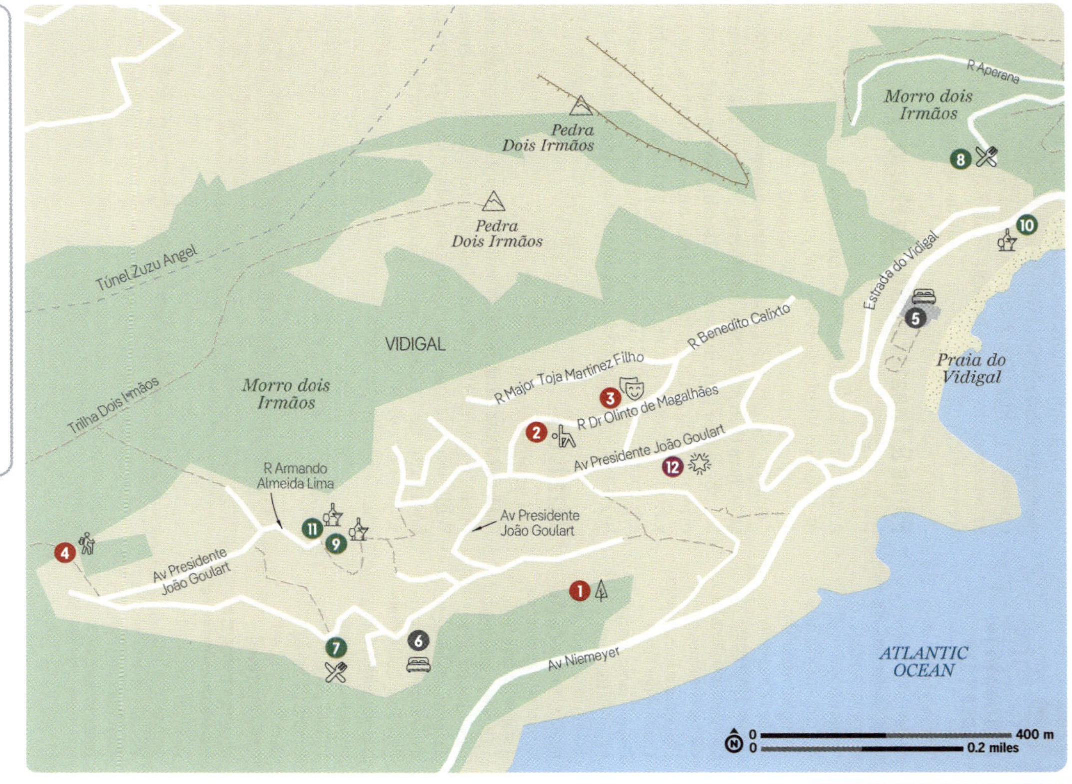

SIGHTS
1 Parque Instituto Sitiê

ACTIVITIES
2 Ame Viva
3 Nós do Morro
4 Trilha Dois Irmãos

SLEEPING
5 Sheraton
6 Varandas do Vidigal

EATING
7 Café e Mar
8 Flor do Céu

DRINKING & NIGHTLIFE
9 Alto Vidigal
see 9 Bar da Laje
10 Faro Beach Club
11 Mirante do Arvrão

ENTERTAINMENT
12 OJ&OS Jazz Club

HISTORY TO THE MODERN DAY

The area known as Vidigal was once inhabited by the Carijós indigenous group, however the arrival of European invaders changed everything. By the 19th century, the land had been usurped, and the area carried the name of Portuguese Royal Guard commander Major Miguel Nunes Vidigal. In the 1940s, when fishing families began to inhabit the hillside, the community as we know it started to take form.

Decades later, the hillside haunt, with exceptional views and a privileged location in Rio's Zona Sul became popular with artists, musicians and even famous people from around the world. David Beckham, Vincent Cassel and even Madonna were just a few who invested in real estate in the hillside community, helping Vidigal turn into the 21st most valorized property zones in the city.

run nonprofit organization offering local children, teens and adults opportunities to learn about healthy eating, meditation and physical well-being. The main center, which opened in Vidigal in 2020, has weekly yoga and martial-arts classes, as well as baskets of all-natural food items for free to local children (powered by donations).

Films & Theater at Nós do Morro

Hill of the artists

A number of Brazilian actors and musicians were born, raised or lived in Vidigal, giving the community the nickname *Morro dos Artistas* (hill of the artists).

One of the city's longest-running nonprofits (since 1986) gave them their start: **Nós do Morro** *(gruponosdomorro.com.br)* offers free activities and courses in theater and cinema, providing job training for future actors, stagehands, scriptwriters, directors, camerapeople and producers. All teachers are volunteers and all classes are free; visitors are welcome to join in for film screenings and theater productions.

Jazz it Up

Get your Swing on

OJ&OS Jazz Club is an offbeat little spot where owner and talented pianist Hugo Braule belts out jazz, blues and samba. While officially open from 8pm to 1am Thursday to Saturday, hours can be sporadic, so call ahead for reservations *(+55 21-97548-2186: Whatsapp)*.

EATING IN VIDIGAL: OUR PICKS

Flor do Céu: Exceptional Italian-fusion restaurant in Chácara do Céu with ocean views. Reservation only. *noon-6pm Wed, Thu, Sun; to 8pm Sat* $$

Café e Mar: Brunch café with Mykonos-inspired decor serves US-style breakfast specialties with a Brazilian twist. Reservation only. *8:30am-5pm Thu-Sun* $$

Bar da Laje (p94): Vidigal's most famous bar/restaurant is known for views, *feijoada*, laid-back vibes and weekend samba. *noon-8pm Mon-Fri, to 10pm Sat & Sun* $$

Alto Vidigal (p94): Better known for its dance parties, Alto Vidigal daylights as a gastro-bar with a view. *noon-8pm Sun-Thu, to midnight Fri* $$

SOPA IMAGES LIMITED/ALAMY

Script-writing workshop, Nós do Morro

Researched by Joel Balsam

COPACABANA & LEME

STILL THE PLACE TO BE

Copacabana put Rio de Janeiro on the world travel map, and it's still a classic. Go to lesser-known Leme to eat and chill with locals.

It's been just over a century since a striking French-style hotel transformed a stretch of beach in southern Rio into a hub for the glitziest global stars and visitors from everywhere. For the rest of the 20th century, Copacabana cradled the invention of bossa-nova music and countless films. While the hype has died down, and Copacabana has become extremely busy, it's still a must. Walk the vivacious white-and-black-tile boardwalk with a coconut, catch a bossa-nova show, and lounge on the 4km beach. Then head to Leme, north of Av Princesa Isabel, a quieter beachfront neighborhood with a calmer, more inclusive vibe and some stellar restaurants.

INCLUDES

Copacabana Palace (p101)

See p223 for places to stay in Copacabana and Leme

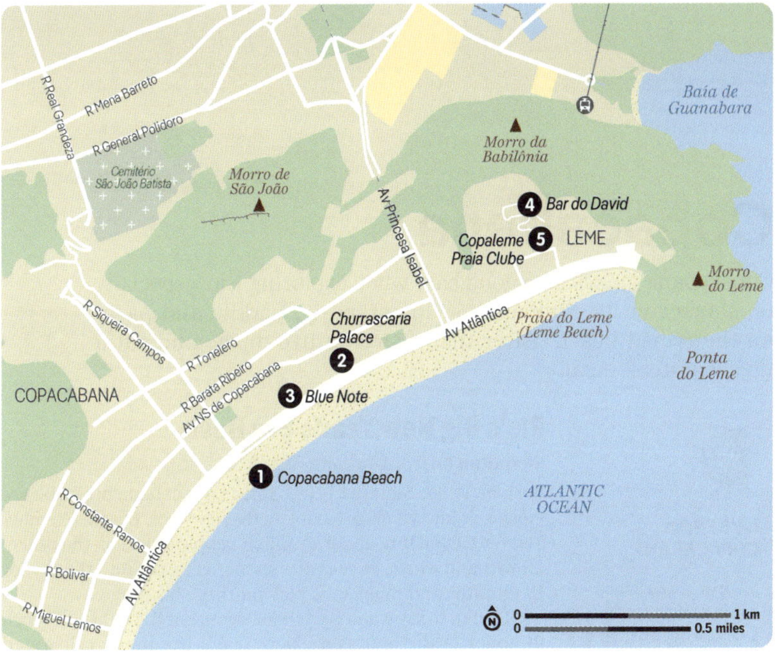

R Real Grandeza
R Mena Barreto
R General Polidoro
Cemitério São João Batista
Morro de São João
Av Princesa Isabel
Morro da Babilônia
Baía de Guanabara
4 Bar do David
Copaleme Praia Clube 5
LEME
Morro do Leme
Praia do Leme (Leme Beach)
Ponta do Leme
R Siqueira Campos
R Tonelero
R Barata Ribeiro
Av NS de Copacabana
Churrascaria Palace 2
Av Atlântica
COPACABANA
3 Blue Note
1 Copacabana Beach
ATLANTIC OCEAN
R Constante Ramos
R Bolivar
R Miguel Lemos
Av Atlântica
N
0 1 km
0 0.5 miles

Highlights

1 Copacabana Beach
Sunbathe on the beach that put Rio on the travel map a century ago. **p104**

2 Churrascaria Palace
Prepare for an all-you-can-eat steak extravaganza at this local institution. **p100**

3 Blue Note
See live bossa nova in the neighborhood that birthed the genre, as well as jazz (pictured above right). **p108**

4 Bar do David
Award-winning bar snacks inside one of Leme's favelas. **p113**

5 Capoeira at Copaleme Praia Clube
Learn to play capoeira and find out where the pros are playing next. **p114**

Getting Around

Walking
Walk Copacabana's famous boardwalk; though be warned, the beach is exhaustingly long.

Metro
Copacabana lays claim to three metro stops: Cardeal Arcoverde, Siqueira Campos and Cantagalo. Leme doesn't have any.

Bicycle
The dedicated bike path along the beach is a common, highly enjoyable route to get from Leme to Ipanema. Rent an Itaú bike via its app or directly through Uber's.

Copacabana

Copacabana makes for a good base when exploring Rio, especially on shorter visits. Sunbathe, swim, stand-up paddle and party on the famed beach. After that, listen to live music and eat a gigantic steak meal.

LIVE FROM COPACABANA

If Copacabana Beach can host New Year's Eve, why not a gigantic concert? That was the thinking of Rod Stewart, or perhaps his marketing team, when the British pop singer decided to play at Réveillon in 1994. Piggybacking off the existing crowd, Stewart played in front of more than three million people – the biggest rock concert ever.

Copacabana Beach has held more giant shows since, including the Rolling Stones in 2006 and Live Earth in 2007. In May 2024, Madonna played in front of 1.6 million screaming fans. For Réveillon 2024, Copa was headlined by Brazilian legends Caetano Veloso, Maria Bethânia, Anitta and Ivete Sangalo.

Rio's Big New Year's Eve Bash

Révellion on Copacabana Beach

Besides Times Square in New York, Copacabana might be the most well-known place to ring in the new year. Every December 31st for **Réveillon**, about 2 million people crowd on the beach, all wearing white, as sea rafts shoot fireworks into the sky for 15 minutes and musicians play on three big stages.

It's tough to say when Réveillon began, but the name is French in honor of the high-class New Year's Eve meals celebrated in France. Rio could have borrowed this name as part of its attempts to be seen as the Paris of the South at the turn of the century.

The reason people wear white is attributed to the Afro-Brazilian religions Candomblé and Umbanda. Followers of these religions, among others, throw flowers, fruit and messages in a bottle into the sea as an offering to sea *orixá* (spirit) Iemanjá. They'll also jump in the water and get splashed by seven waves to honor seven deities. Another Réveillon tradition is to wear colored underwear, depending on your desires for the upcoming year: white is for peace, blue brings harmony, yellow wealth, orange creativity, red passion and wear pink to find love.

Festivities kick off at 7pm and are free if you're on the sand. If you want to go all-out, book a hotel room in one of Copacabana's beach-facing hotels and pop Champagne from the balcony.

All You Can Meat

Gorge on steak at Churrascaria Palace

Try a Brazilian *churrascaria* (steakhouse) *rodízio* for an all-you-can-eat extravaganza. Going strong since 1951, **Churrascaria Palace** has waiters coming to your table with juicy cuts of meat on a spit, where they'll slice it directly onto your plate – catch the cuts before they fall with the provided tongs. Mouthwatering meats include *picanha*, Brazil's most celebrated beef cut – known for its thick layer of fat; and *chorizo*, Argentina's beloved sirloin. Servers also bring other

ALEXANDRE ROTENBERG/SHUTTERSTOCK

New Year celebrations, Copacabana Beach (p100)

meat, including *pirarucu* (a giant Amazon fish) and chicken hearts, and there's a hot-and-cold buffet with sushi, salads, cheeses, Brazilian classics like *feijoada* (bean-and-meat stew) and a lineup of sauces. You may also request sides such as grilled banana. Drinks and desserts are extra.

STOP & GO

At many *rodízios* (Churrascaria Palace being a rare exception), you'll find a card on your table that has two colored sides. Green is to indicate to the server to bring on the meat, while red is the equivalent of a white flag – for heaven's sake, stop! Note that Brazilians usually spend four or five hours at a *rodízio*, so slow down and take it easy on the carbs if you want to get your money's worth.

While *rodízios* usually serve *churrasco* (grilled meat), you can also find all-you-can-eat pizza, sushi or *petiscos* (snacks).

The Hotel that Changed Rio

Famous Copacabana Palace

Copacabana Palace *(belmond.com/hotels/south-america/brazil/rio-de-janeiro/belmond-copacabana-palace)* isn't just the most famous hotel in Rio, it's the most iconic accommodation in Latin America. Built in 1923 and now owned by international luxury brand Belmond, the glamorous white hotel remains a postcard of Rio and is a big reason the neighborhood became so famous.

The hotel's impetus was in 1919 when Brazil's 11th president, Epitácio Pessoa, wanted to welcome distinguished guests to Rio (then the capital) for the country's centennial. Rich businessperson Octávio Guinle answered the call and hired French designer Joseph Gire to build a hotel and casino on Copacabana Beach.

continued on p107

WHERE TO STAY

Copacabana Palace out of your budget? Whether you're looking for a hostel or a boutique hotel on a mountainside, find more options to stay across Rio de Janeiro in our 'Where to Stay' section on p223.

DRINKING IN COPACABANA: CAFES

Revigorante: Cafe on quiet street good for some peaceful moments, as it's also a coworking space. *11am-8pm Mon-Sat* $

Cultura: Tasty cakes, breakfasts and lattes, including iced coffees and matchas – rarities in Rio. *9am-7pm Mon-Sat, to 6pm Sun* $

Tiny Cat: Lattes in cat-shaped mugs, *pão de queijo* and a good place to work. A favorite with local digital nomads. *9am-7pm Mon-Sat* $

Mini Joe: Pastries, breakfast casseroles, sandwiches and coffees, including ginger-flavored latte. Quite chilly. *8am-7pm Mon-Sat, 9am-3:30pm Sun* $

HIGHLIGHTS
1 Copacabana Beach

SIGHTS
2 Forte de Copacabana

ACTIVITIES
3 BikeZRio
4 Eco Clube SUP

SLEEPING
5 Copacabana Palace
6 Pura Vida
7 Selina

EATING
8 Adega Pérola
9 Amir
10 Bar do Adão
11 Bardana Cozinha Natural
12 Bibi Sucos
13 Cantón
14 Cervantes
15 Churrascaria Palace
see 5 Cipriani
16 Confeiteria Colombo
17 Crums
18 Farro
19 Galeto Sat's
20 Haru
see 5 Mee
21 Momo
22 O Caranguejo

23 Os Imortais
24 Panamá
25 Pavão Azul
see 5 Pérgula
26 Sova Natural
27 Teva Deli

DRINKING & NIGHTLIFE
28 Barraca Ponto G
29 Black Cat
30 Cafe 18 do Forte
31 Cultura
see 34 Mini Joe
32 Pink Flamingo
33 Revigorante
34 Tiny Cat

ENTERTAINMENT
35 Beco das Garrafas
36 Bip Bip
37 Blue Note
38 Réveillon

SHOPPING
39 Alternativa Carioca
40 Av Atlântica Fair
41 Fluminense Store
42 Gilson Martins
43 Havaianas
44 Oficina Muda

CELSO PUPO/SHUTTERSTOCK

TOP EXPERIENCE

Copacabana Beach

Praia de Copacabana (Copacabana Beach) contends with Ipanema as the most iconic slice of sand and waves in the world. While not as pretty as Ipanema, Copacabana is a place for everyone, from visitors to Brazilians of all social classes, all sipping *água de coco* (coconut water) under hundreds of umbrellas along the wide 4km strip of perfectly curved beach.

DON'T MISS

- Sunbathing
- Cruising the boardwalk
- Coconut water
- Caipirinhas
- SUP surfing
- Futevôlei
- Cycling
- Live samba

History & Setting

There are no signs of indigenous people living on what was originally named Sacopenapã ('the way of the *socós* bird') by the indigenous Tupi people. The beach was renamed Copacabana after the patron saint of Bolivia – a statue of the saint used to be in a now-destroyed church on the rocks where Forte de Copacabana is currently.

Copacabana was a humble fishing village for most of the 19th century, but that changed in 1892 when an underground tunnel made the beach accessible from Centro. The 1923 arrival of Copacabana Palace lit the fire to make the neighborhood a hot

PRACTICALITIES

Download the Brazilian Mude app for daily free workouts like yoga and HIIT in Rio.

destination for foreigners as well as Brazilian elites. Lower-income Brazilians wanting a taste of beach life came too, and every single family home was destroyed in favor of apartments. To protect the population from wave surges, Rio extended the beach by 50m using landfill from tunnel projects, and hired world-famous landscape designer Roberto Burle Marx to make the gorgeous waterfront boardwalk we see today.

The Beach

Copacabana Beach is laid out from Av Princesa Isabel, near Posto 2, to the military fort (Forte de Copacabana) after Posto 6. The water is calmer the further south you go.

Park yourself and your *canga* (beach towel) anywhere on the beach – all beaches are public in Brazil. Umbrellas and chairs are governed by numbered *barracas* (tents). Small umbrellas are between R$15 to $R20, while larger cost between R$20 and $R30. Chairs are R$5 to $R10 each, and tables are often free.

Cruise the Boardwalk

Copacabana's boardwalk and Av Atlântica are almost as famous – and certainly as fun – as the beach itself. Wavy white-and-black tiles, just like the ones used in Lisbon's Rossio Square, provide a dance floor for one of the liveliest places to walk in Zona Sul. Here, you'll face vendors coaxing you into a tour or to eat at their restaurant *quiosques* (kiosk restaurants), street carts slinging churros, and vendors selling yellow-and-green Brazilian soccer jerseys. When nightfall hits, the Copacabana boardwalk becomes a big party, with boardwalk *quiosques* hosting live samba and blasting pop hits.

Cycling & Scooters

If strolling isn't your speed, hop on an Itaú bike and cruise along the dedicated path, which was added in the 1990s. Anyone can rent one via Uber or Itaú's dedicated app. Or whizz on a new Whoosh scooter.

If you want your own wheels, order a bike or seated electric scooter at least a day in advance from **BikeZRio** *(021-8732-63040, bikes R$20/hr or R$70/day, 9am–9pm; card payments are extra).*

You'll have even more room to spread out on Sundays and holidays, as Av Atlântica shuts to car traffic from 7am to 6pm.

SUP Sunrise

One of the best ways to experience Copacabana Beach is from out on the water atop a stand-up paddleboard (SUP). The view is even more spectacular for sunrise, when the sky lights up in incandescent colors over this Cidade Maravilhoso (Marvellous City).

Rent a board from **Eco Clube SUP** *(@ecoclubesup, 30min/1hr/2hr sunrise R$50/70/150)* at Posto 6 on the southern end of Copacabana Beach. The water is less wavy at this end. The experienced operator has been around since 2011 and can

BEACH DRINKS

Água de coco (coconut water) directly from the coconut is a must and has much-needed electrolytes.

For something boozy, try a caipirinha (sugarcane *cachaça* cocktail), made with fresh fruit like lime, passionfruit, mango and watermelon, and plenty of sugar. Beer is always served ice cold and usually in large bottles: *seiscentos* (600ml).

TOP TIPS

- Most *barracas* take card payment.
- Keep your possessions in front of you, never out of sight.
- Ask a friendly face to hold onto your stuff when you go for a dip.
- Don't walk on the beach late at night, nor sleep there after dark.
- Don't swim if you see a red flag on the sand.
- Always apply sunscreen.
- Volleyball and *futevôlei* groups usually offer free trials.
- You may be charged for taking photos of elaborate sandcastles.
- Head to **Pedra do Arpoador** (p88) for sunset.

PÉ NA AREIA

All you need to know about what to do at the beach is covered in the instant-classic 2016 samba track by Diogo Nogueira called *Pé na Areia*. The lyrics go: *Pé na areia* (feet in the sand), a *caipirinha* (cocktail), *água de coco* (coconut water), a *cervejinha* (little beer), *beira do mar* (dip in the sea).

teach you the basics: how to row on the board, how to stand up etc. If all goes well, you'll row out past Forte de Copacabana, to paddle on calmer water. It's a lot more exhausting to get out if it's windy.

Sunrise paddles are worth the price if you can manage to wake up before 4am (sunrise times vary by season). Once you're settled in calmer water, instructors can come out and take photos of you on a GoPro (included). You can also take photos on your phone with the free waterproof pouch provided. Reserve and pay ahead on WhatsApp *(021-9801-16062)*.

Beach Food

You'll be bombarded with offers of drinks and snacks by vendors when on the beach. The most quintessential Rio beach snack is Biscoito Globo (round donut-shaped tapioca-based cracker) swished down with a sip of cold *maté* (iced tea). Vendors will ask if you want your *maté* sweetened or not and flavored with or without *maracujá* (passion fruit).

Another common beach snack is the Levantine *esfiha* (savory pastry filled with meat, cheese or spinach). *Açaí* (frozen Amazon berry mixed with sugar and usually banana) comes in a small cup and is topped with fresh fruit, granola and the option of *cobertura* (topping), including *leite condensada* (condensed milk) or a chocolate or fruit syrup. *Queijo coalho* is a thick, salty cheese similar to Halloumi, grilled to order on tiny coal barbecues. *Milho* is corn freshly cut off the cob and put in a bowl with butter. *Sacolé* are frozen-fruit treats, sometimes mixed with booze. Lastly, you'll see vendors selling *camarão* (shrimp) on a stick, which we don't recommend unless you want to risk getting sick.

FOCUS PIX/SHUTTERSTOCK

Drinks vendor

continued from p101

Gire's designs were inspired by the beaux-arts Le Negresco in Nice and the neoclassical Carlton in Cannes.

The resulting splendor that is Copacabana Palace opened in 1923 and soon caught the eye of the world's glitzy and glamorous. A who's who of US, Brazilian and French stars stayed here, many of whom played in the hotel's Golden Room concert hall, which hosted its first performance in 1938. Famous faces, such as Brazilian soccer legend Pelé, Madonna and King Charles III, all have a picture in Copacabana Palace's hall of fame.

The casino was removed in 1946. Renovations in 2014 added colorful tiles to the windows, spotlights on the facade and a renewed interior, which refreshed the hotel to modern standards. Other updates have included a pool (open only to guests), a spa and a tower with more spacious rooms (originally designed as longer-term apartments for seafaring visitors).

Nonguests may visit by attending a show at the renovated performance theater (most shows are in Portuguese) or by eating at its three restaurants: **Pérgula** (*6am-4pm & 6-10pm $$$*) for casual poolside Brazilian food; **Mee** (*7pm-late Tue-Sun $$$*) serves pan-Asian cuisine and proudly holds a Michelin star; and **Cipriani** (*7pm-late Mon-Sat $$$*) does contemporary Italian tasting menus.

See Live Music

Bossa nova, jazz and samba

The early half of the 20th century saw the development of two groundbreaking rhythms in two special pockets of the African diaspora: samba in Rio de Janeiro and jazz in New Orleans. By the 1950s, both samba and jazz were everywhere in Rio, so it was only natural for them to fuse together. Officially, that happened in 1958 when poet Vinícius de Moraes and composer Antônio Carlos 'Tom' Jobim recorded the song 'Chega de Saudade' on Elizeth Cardoso's album *Canção do Amor Demais*. The special sauce was added by Bahian guitarist João Gilberto, who ingeniously slowed down samba rhythms.

As legend has it, it was at Copacabana's **Beco das Garrafas** (*becodasgarrafas.com.br, R$60*), a small Copacabana club in a tiny alley, where Jobim, Gilberto and Moraes first unveiled 'Garota de Ipanema,' later translated to 'The Girl from Ipanema,' in 1962. After being shuttered for years, Beco das Garrafas reopened in 2014 and hosts bossa-nova and jazz shows nightly at its two enchanting venues, Little Club and Bottle's Bar.

CPF

While Brazil feels laissez-faire when you look at it from the beach, it's actually quite bureaucratic.

One big example is the **Cadastro de Pessoas Físicas** (CPF; p238). This 11-digit number given to Brazilians at birth is used for pretty much everything in Brazil. You'll be asked for one when going to the gym, buying groceries and buying items online. Some things, like booking local flights, purchasing concert or soccer-match tickets, or getting a local SIM card, may be impossible without a CPF.

You can get a CPF as a foreigner, but it takes a couple of weeks and only makes sense if you're staying a while in Brazil. If you're desperate, ask a Brazilian friend to borrow their CPF.

EATING IN COPACABANA: HEALTHY FOOD

Teva Deli: Vegans, rejoice! This deli has extraordinary plant-based meals, pastries and dips to eat in and take away. *7am-10pm* **$$**

Bardana Cozinha Natural: Yes, you can still try Brazilian classics if you're vegan. Just fill your plate, weigh and pay. *11am-6pm* **$$**

Farro: Bakery and pay-by-kilo restaurant, with plenty of healthy options, including salads, lean meats and quality pastries. *7am-8pm* **$$**

Bibi Sucos: Reliable chain great for *açai* (Amazon berry smoothie), fresh juices and a snack. Good option for kids. *8:30am-midnight* **$$**

BEST SONGS ABOUT RIO DE JANEIRO

Go beyond 'Garota de Ipanema' and listen to more songs about Rio.

'Samba do Avião': Tom Jobim sang about the beauty of seeing the city from an airplane, prompting the international airport to be named after him.

'Meu Lugar': Arlindo Cruz' song about 'his place': the Zona Norte neighborhood of Madureira. Always gets everyone singing along.

'Do Leme ao Pontal': Psychedelic MPB singer Tim Maia's song about Rio's neighborhoods – 'there's nothing like it'.

'As Caravanas': Chico Buarque sings about the beauty of Copacabana when it's painted by the sun.

'Aquele Abraço': Bahia-born *tropicália* legend Gilberto Gil smooth-talking the city, and everyone in it.

LMASCARETTI/SHUTTERSTOCK

Newer, yet no less atmospheric, **Blue Note** (*bluenoterio.com.br*), actually originated in New York City and hosts nightly (except Monday) bossa-nova and jazz shows. On Saturdays, Blue Note has live samba and *feijoada* from 1pm to 5pm, and music in the piano bar any night of the week.

Last but certainly not least, **Bip Bip** (*@rodadobip*) – cutely pronounced 'bipee bipee' in Portuguese – is another legendary Copacabana venue with bossa nova on Wednesdays, samba on Sundays and Thursdays, as well as *choro* (instrumental samba-adjacent genre) on Tuesdays. Note that it's closed on Fridays, Saturdays and Mondays. The tiny storefront can't fit much more than the musicians, forcing a crowd of spectators to bulge out on the street – but it's an unparalleled vibe. Bip Bip is cash only. Tell the guy seated at a table what drink you want to order, go get it yourself, then pay at the end.

Go Shopping

Where to find the best stuff

Whether you want a bikini in Brazil's unmissable national soccer team colors (lemon-yellow and lime-green) souvenirs or stylish locally made clothing, Copacabana has you covered.

EATING IN COPACABANA: SNACK BARS

Adega Pérola: Choose from a mouthwatering lineup of Portuguese-style tapas from the glass bar counter. *11am-1am Mon-Sat* $$

Pavão Azul: Corner bar with bountiful *bolinhos* (fried balls) stuffed with codfish, *feijoada* and more. *noon-midnight* $

Os Imortais: Large selection of Brazilian snacks, sandwiches and meals like *feijoada* on weekends. *noon-1am Fri-Wed, from 6pm Thu* $

Bar do Adão: Local chain known for its fried stuffed *pasteís* and *croquetas* along with ice-cold beer. *11am-midnight* $

Confeitaria Colombo

ORIGIN OF THE BRAZIL JERSEY

Brazil's bright-lemon yellow and lime-green Seleção (national football team) jersey might be the most memorable uniform in pro sports, but the team didn't always wear these colors. Brazil used to compete in white shirts with blue collars, but a devastating 1950 World Cup loss at the hands of rival Uruguay prompted a change.

Newspaper *Correio da Manha* published a callout for a new design, and Aldyr Garcia Schlee, a newspaper illustrator from a small town near the Uruguay border, answered with a jersey design colored like the Brazilian flag. Out of 401 options, the iconic *canarinho* (canary) jersey stuck and has been used in various forms ever since.

Lined with top Brazilian brands, Rua Santa Clara is the go-to shopping street in Copacabana. A great one to check out is **Oficina Muda** *(@oficinamuda)*, which restores defect clothing from Brazilian brands like Farm and Maria Filó and resells them at a discount. Just off Rua Santa Clara, local designer **Gilson Martins** (*@gilsonmartinsbrasil*) sells cute bags, faux fur, jewelry and wallets in the shape of Rio symbols like Cristo Redentor and Dois Irmãos. Items are all made without animal products.

Pop-up **Av Atlântica Fair** around beach marker Posto 5 is where you'll find your souvenir shirts, sundresses and beach gear like volleyballs, hats and *cangas* (beach blankets that also work as skirts). You'll also find these on the boardwalk and from vendors as you lie on the beach.

If it's Carnaval season and you're looking to dress up, or if you simply want something unusual, horseshoe-shaped **Alternativa Carioca**

THE CHEAPEST MARKET

If you're looking for Brazil jerseys, cheap clothing, souvenirs and knockoff shoes, you'll find the best deals around the **Saara metro** (p180) in Centro.

EATING IN COPACABANA: SWEETS

Confeitaria Colombo: Branch of the historic Centro cafe, known for its pastries. Has picturesque views from the fort. *10am-7pm Tue-Sun* $$

Crums: Enticing menu of cakes, pastries and breakfasts along with friendly service. Has fast wi-fi if you have some work to do. $

Momo: It's a struggle to decide which of the many tasty gelato flavors to pick at this shop in front of Copacabana Palace. *noon-10pm* $

Sova Natural: Sourdough bakery with fluffy oven-baked pizzas and crumbly pastries. *8am-10pm* $$

Serves chocolate pizza – a Brazil favorite.

'T' IN TROUBLE

While Rio de Janeiro's Zona Sul might feel like an LGBTIQ+ paradise, elsewhere in Brazil, trans people are under attack. In 2023, Brazil saw the most trans murders of any country in the world with 145 – an average of one every three days, according to the Associação Nacional de Travestis e Transexuais (Antra). In 2022, Brazil was also the world's worst for trans murders, with 131.

Recently, there have also been at least 77 anti-trans laws passed in 18 states. They prevent gender-neutral language, prohibit shared bathrooms, and block transgender children and adolescents from accessing certain health services.

Learn more at antrabrasil.org, or Associação Brasileira de Lésbicas, Gays, Bissexuais, Travestis, Transexuais e Intersexos (ABGLT; *abglt.org*).

(*@alternativacarioca*) is a lot of fun, with plenty of sparkly outfits. And visit one of the four **Havaianas** (*havaianas.com.br*) shops in Copacabana to grace your feet with a pair of the world's most famous flip-flops. Other stores will sell cheaper Havaianas knockoffs, but the official stores have the real deal, along with the best styles and colors.

Latin America's Top LGBTIQ+ Destination

Bars, clubs and festivals

Rio de Janeiro is one of the most gay-friendly cities in the world, with an abundance of beach hangouts, bars, clubs and festivals catering to its thriving LGBTIQ+ community. Copacabana Beach (p104) is exceptionally gay-friendly. However, the more in-vogue beach spots are **Barraca Ponto G** (*8am-6pm*) in Leme and around Posto 9 on Ipanema Beach (p82).

Black Cat (*11pm-6am Fri-Mon, to midnight Thu*) is a two-story nightclub with a dark room in Copacabana that caters to the erotic. **Pink Flamingo** *(opening times vary)* features wild club nights with drag queens spinning in the DJ booth, as well as drag brunches.

Aside from Réveillon (p100) on December 31st, and Carnaval (both top events for LGBTIQ+ travelers), there's **Rio Pride**, which takes place every November during Rio's spring. Join more than a million people on the Copacabana beachfront at the official parade to celebrate diversity and acceptance.

Every July, Rio hosts its **LGBTIQ+ International Film Festival** (*riolgbtqia.com.br*) at venues across the city. The festival started in 2011 and has grown to feature nearly 100 films.

Military Fort & Views

Impressive Forte de Copacabana

Brazilians love to talk about how few wars their country has fought in. There was the war with Paraguay in the 19th century, and Brazil only made brief appearances in the two World Wars. The country didn't even have a war for independence with Portugal – it simply declared a republic. Yet Brazil has a strong military, and it's on full display at the active **Forte de Copacabana** (*@fortedecopacabana, adult/child & senior R$10/5*).

An Anthony Bourdain favorite!

EATING IN COPACABANA: OUR PICKS

Amir: Heaping platters of Levantine favorites like hummus, falafel, *kibe*, *kafta* and shawarma plates. *noon-11pm* $$

Cantón: Peruvian-Chinese *chaufas* (fried rice) and noodle dishes with stylish photogenic decor. *noon-4pm & 6-11pm* $$

Haru: Fresh sushi specials for lunch, as well as ramen, in a classy atmosphere. *12-4pm, 6-11:30pm Tue-Sun* $$

Galeto Sat's: Non-pretentious Copacabana classic since 1962 known for its *galeto* (spring chicken) and *picanha* (steak). *noon-4am* $$

CESAR LIMA/SHUTTERSTOCK

Forte de Copacabana

Built in 1914, directly into the rock on Copacabana Beach's southernmost point before Pedra do Arpoador (p88), the Copacabana Fort has impressive 12m-thick walls and a couple of armored cupola domes holding Krupp canons. The fort also has a patriotic museum, showcasing memorabilia from 1889 (when the military exiled Princess Isabel after she abolished slavery) to the end of WWII in 1945. The museum is nothing special and information is only in Portuguese, but it's worth checking out, if only for the air-conditioning on a hot day.

The biggest attraction here are the two cafes outside, which while pricey, offer sublime views of the beach. Confeiteria Colombo (p109) is a branch of the 1894 confectionary located in Centro and known for its *bolos* (cakes) and classic Brazilian dishes. A little further along, **Cafe 18 do Forte** (*10am-7pm Tue-Sun $$$*) serves more contemporary dishes.

DIGITAL NOMAD RIO

Thinking about staying a while in Rio de Janeiro to study or work as a digital nomad? Learn more about Brazilian visas and how to get that pesky CPF on p238.

SOUTH AMERICA'S BLOODIEST WAR

The Triple Alliance War (1865–70) between Paraguay and a trio of allies – Brazil, Argentina and Uruguay – was the largest and last major war on the continent. Its effects are still felt today, both as a lynchpin of Brazilian national identity and in the struggling economy of the war's loser, Paraguay.

The war began when Paraguayan President Francisco Solano López launched an attack against Brazil after a Brazil-supported coup in Uruguay. Landlocked Paraguay also wanted access to the coast. The gamble backfired, as the Triple Alliance overpowered Paraguay, killing López in 1870 and wiping out more than half the country's population.

EATING IN COPACABANA: OUR PICKS

Cervantes: Its trademark filet mignon and pineapple sandwich is truly one of the world's great sandwiches. *10-5am* $$

Panamá: A locals' *boteco* (bar) with R$20 lunch specials that have no business being so tasty for that price. *8am-midnight* $

O Caranguejo: Seafood (especially crab) served in various fried and stewed forms. Try its *moqueca* (seafood stew). *8am-midnight* $$

Churrascaria Palace (p100): Famous *rodízio* (all-you-can-eat steakhouse). Served to your table in a cavernous setting since 1951. *noon-midnight* $$$

Leme

More relaxed and less touristy than Copacabana, Leme, located north of Av Princesa Isabel, has fabulous restaurants, vistas, accommodations and an inclusive beach vibe with refreshingly fewer vendors.

FAVELA ORGÂNICA

When Regina Tchelly moved to Rio at 19 years old from Paraíba, she noticed how much food waste there was while so many were going hungry, including in the favela she lived in: Babilônia.

In 2011, Tchelly launched Favela Orgânica *(@favela_organica)*, a program to teach favela residents how to avoid food waste by cooking with discarded produce and ingredients from their backyard, such as jackfruit.

She also wanted to teach people how to compost and grow urban gardens. In the first week of crowdfunding, Tchelly earned just R$140, but Favela Orgânica has since taken off to become a thriving nonprofit, teaching at schools in Brazil and abroad in France and Uruguay.

Chill, Inclusive Beach

Join locals on Praia do Leme

Despite being steps away from Copacabana Beach, **Praia do Leme** (Leme Beach) has a totally different vibe. It's more laid-back and remarkably less touristy, and generally more inclusive than the rest of Rio's southern beaches. This is especially the case at **Rasta Beach** (*9am-6pm Mon-Wed, to 8pm Thu-Sun*): *barraca* (tent) number 20, owned by two brothers who live in the Babilônia favela above Leme. Underneath Rastafarian flags to the beat of chill music, you'll find *cariocas* from favelas alongside anyone else. Nearby, Barrca Ponto G (p110), *barraca* 26, represents a different kind of inclusivity, as it has become one of the LGBTIQ+ beach spots du jour.

Leme Beach also sees fewer vendors selling *cangas* (beach towels) – if you need one or some cool clothing, there's a little market in Praça Almirante Júlio de Noronha. Don't worry, you'll still be asked by vendors if you want *maté* (iced tea) and other beach snacks.

If you walk to the end of Leme Beach, you'll find the **Mureta do Leme** – a rock wall with restaurant kiosks and fishers. This is an awesome spot for photos that include mountains Dois Irmãos, Pedra do Gávea, Corcovado and Copacabana all in one snap. The path continues for a few minutes – you'll really be able to get a feel for the power of the ocean when the waves crash into the rocks below.

Hunt for Rio's Best Snacks

Comida di Buteco

To Brazilians, *botecos* (classic local bars) are beloved places where young and old come to watch a game, sip light local beer and eat *petiscos*. To honor and support these local institutions, more than 1000 *botecos* across 25 Brazilian cities, including Rio de Janeiro, compete in the annual **Comida di Buteco** (*comidadibuteco.com.br*). The 'u' is for how the word is pronounced in Minas Gerais, where the competition originated in 2000.

Every April, *botecos* dream up the most scrumptious *petiscos* – such as fried *croquetas* filled with strange and sensational

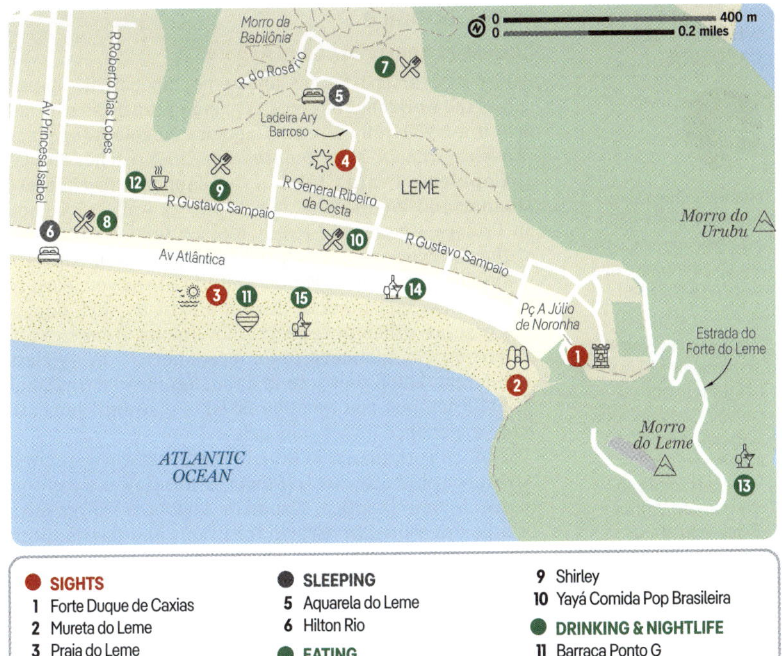

SIGHTS
1 Forte Duque de Caxias
2 Mureta do Leme
3 Praia do Leme

ACTIVITIES
4 Copaleme Praia Clube

SLEEPING
5 Aquarela do Leme
6 Hilton Rio

EATING
7 Bar do David
see 8 Joaquina
8 S-Bistrô
9 Shirley
10 Yayá Comida Pop Brasileira

DRINKING & NIGHTLIFE
11 Barraca Ponto G
12 Frédéric Epicerie
13 Quiosque Espetto Carioca
14 Quiosque Ginga
15 Rasta Beach

ingredients – and invite everyone to taste them. Diners are given a form to rank each snack, and winning *botecos* are determined half by the public, half by judges – the bottom 20% is eliminated for the following year, just like soccer leagues and samba schools. Comida di Buteco is a great way to explore different bars and neighborhoods in Rio, and of course to eat.

In Leme, **Bar do David** is a proud Comida di Buteco participant and multi-award winner. Its owner, former fisher David Bispo of the Chapéu Mangueira favela, has become a local legend, famously participating in the Rio 2016 Olympics torch relay and hosting former New York City Mayor Michael Bloomberg.

At David's bar, taste winning *petiscos* like 2017's Ressurgência, a heaping bowl of seafood, white beans and vegetables in a purple cabbage bowl; or 2022's Referência, pumpkin, shredded coconut, *oro-pro-nobis* (cactus) and shrimp *bolinhos* (fried balls) served in a transparent shell. Bar do David, which has locations in the favela above Leme and in Copacabana, also serves great cocktails like Pé Na Favela, a riff on the classic samba track *Pé Na Areia* by Diogo Nogueira. The drink is made with pineapple juice, cinnamon *cachaça*, almond liqueur and topped with a burnt cinnamon stick.

WHERE TO SEE CAPOEIRA

Mestra Juliana Lima *(@julianalima_angola)* recommends where to see capoeira *rodas* and more Afro-Brazilian culture.

Every second Friday of the month, there's a **Ngoma** *(@ngoma_capoeira_angola) roda* at Praça da Babilônia in Leme at 7pm.

Every second Saturday there's a **Unificar** *(@gucangola) roda* at **Centro do Teatro do Oprimido** *(@centrodeteatrodooprimido)* in Lapa at 5pm.

Every last Thursday, there's a **Mocambo de Aruanda** *(@grupomocambodearuanda) roda* at **Instituto Pesquisa da Cultura Negra** *(@ipcnbrasil)* in Lapa at 7pm followed by Northeastern dances *jongo* and *coco* under Arcos da Lapa.

Every first Saturday, there's an **Aluandê** *(@institutoaluande) roda* on Rua do Lavradio at 10am. In the evening, there's *baile charme* (coordinated dance to pop music).

Play Capoeira

Classes at Ngoma Capoeira Angola

Part martial art, part dance and game, capoeira has spread across the world, but its roots are here in Brazil, so why not give it a try? Group Ngoma Capoeira Angola (*@ngoma_capoeira_angola, trial/month R$40/200*) teaches classes at **Copaleme Praia Clube** in the Babilônia favela every Monday and Wednesday at 6:30pm, as well as in Lapa on Fridays. Classes are led by Mestra Juliana Lima, one of the few women to reach the highest level of capoeira training and teaching. Follow and imitate as you learn to play drums, smash sticks during *maculelê* (stick dance) and practice different capoeira movements, from kicks to *bananeira* (handstands) to *aú* (cartwheels) – every class is different. You'll then join in a *roda* (game in a ring), but don't be nervous, you won't be asked to play until you have more experience under your belt.

Capoeira's origins are in Brazil's northeast when enslaved Africans would disguise self-defense training as a game or dance. Ngoma practices Capoeira Angola, a slower form of capoeira rooted in African traditions and resistance to systems of oppression. Capoeira Regional, a more common form, is not only faster, but also involves more *acrobacia* (acrobatics like flips). When you go to a class, wear long pants, a T-shirt and flat sneakers – and be prepared to sweat!

Hike the Leme Fort

Forte Duque de Caxias

Stretch your legs and soak in spectacular views at the far end of Leme at **Forte Duque de Caxias** (*cep.eb.mil.br/apresentacao, adult/child & senior R$10/5*), better known as Leme Fort. Built in 1776, the fort was an important point of defense for Rio de Janeiro against foreign attacks at the mouth of Baía Guanabara, and is still staffed by active military. It's also a beautiful, short 20-minute hike up 800m through lush reclaimed Atlantic Forest.

The fort is open 9:30am to 4pm, Tuesdays to Sundays. Find the entrance on the road just north of Praça Almirante Júlio de Noronha and pay the entrance fee. Bikinis and see-through clothing are prohibited. It's also a good idea to wear sneakers, as it's a steep hike.

EATING IN LEME: OUR PICKS

Joaquina: Tasty and reliable Brazilian food beyond beans and rice with an ambience-filled beach-facing patio. *noon-midnight* $$

Shirley: Succulent Spanish seafood dishes, such as paella, amid classic decor in the heart of Leme since 1954. *11am-midnight* $$$

S-Bistrô: Romantic beach-facing restaurant with a funky vibe and French cuisine. *noon-1am Wed-Sun, from 6pm Mon & Tue* $$

Yayá Comida Pop Brasileira Chef Andressa Cabral honors her Afro-Brazilian heritage with flavorful dishes. *12-11pm Mon-Sat, to 8pm Sun* $$

Does seafood or vegan cashew cream moqueca.

BERNARD BARROSO/SHUTTERSTOCK

Forte Duque de Caxias

The path is along a cobblestone road and climbs almost directly up. Keep an eye out for tiny wild monkeys, but don't feed them or put your hand out. The path is decorated by beautiful round sculptures depicting bible scenes. At the top, you'll be treated to panoramic views over Leme Beach and Rio's dream team of mountains: Corcovado, Dois Irmãos, Pedra da Gávea and Pão de Açúcar. You'll also have a good viewpoint of Leme's favelas and Urca's Praia Vermelha below.

Inside the fort, on the right, is a tiny museum with signs explaining a few important battles for the base, as well as its involvement in restoring the Atlantic Forest. At the top, take a rest among several armored canons before hiking back down.

FOREST COMEBACK

Before Europeans arrived, lush Atlantic Forest stretched the entirety of Brazil's coastline, including in Rio. Centuries of development and reckless agriculture means just 15% of that forest remains today.

In recent years, different pockets of the city have aimed to bring the forest back, including Leme Fort, which had been taken over by Guinea grass and military installments.

In 1987, the army, along with civil society and volunteers, removed the grass and replanted trees. Thanks to Rio's glorious tropical climate, the Fort became the flora- and fauna-rich forest we can hike today.

Leme Favelas

Carioca life on a hilltop

Above Leme, find two sister hilltop *comunidades*, or favelas: Babilônia and Chapéu Mangueira. Filled with graffiti murals and lush Atlantic Forest at the top of the hill, these neighborhoods represent vibrant *carioca* life and community interconnectedness. However, as with other favelas, they still pose risks to travelers and we don't recommend wandering around on your own, especially at night.

That said, you should be fine if you stick close to the entrances at Ladeira Ary Barroso. Around there you'll encounter some cool murals, beloved *botecos* (bars), a *capoeira* school and popular guesthouses.

DRINKING IN LEME: OUR PICKS

Frédéric Epicerie: Belgian-owned cafe with espresso drinks, delicious pastries and pizzas, and a relaxing atmosphere. *8am-7pm Tue-Sun*

Bar do David (p113): A former fisher serves award-winning snacks and cocktails from the Chapéu Mangueira favela where he grew up. *Noon-10pm Tue-Sun*

Quiosque Ginga: Expats love this Leme beach kiosk's cocktails and live music, with tables in the sand. *24hrs*

Quiosque Espetto Carioca: Soak in the sights from the Leme wall with drinks, decent snacks and occasional live music. *9am-midnight*

Researched by Joel Balsam

BOTAFOGO, URCA & HUMAITÁ

NIGHTLIFE, GASTRONOMY & MOUNTAIN VIEWS

Check out Botafogo and Humaitá's food scene and meander around peaceful Urca after seeing its world-renowned peaks.

Peel yourself off the beach to some of Rio de Janeiro's oldest neighborhoods. Botafogo has a lineup of restaurants that puts the rest of Zona Sul to shame. Stay through the night to party with the young ones on the street and in impossibly-hip cocktail bars. No visit to Rio is complete without mounting Urca's Pão de Açúcar (Sugarloaf Mountain). Urca is also a treat to walk around, with pretty shaded streets and a couple of quiet beaches capped off by sunsets on the Mureta da Urca (bay wall). If there's time, schedule a visit to Humaitá's indoor market and street block party.

INCLUDES

Street cafes

See p223-4 for places to stay in Botafogo, Urca and Humaitá.

Highlights

❶ Pão de Açúcar
Climb or ride the cable car up to Sugarloaf Mountain for epic views. **p128**

❷ Treme Treme
Party with the cool crowd on the street with some of Rio's coolest bars and tastiest restaurants. **p118**

❸ Cemitério de São João Batista
Pay your respects to Brazil's biggest stars and leaders who are buried in this astounding cemetery. **p120**

❹ Mureta da Urca
Sip beer and munch on fried snacks while taking in the sunset. **p125**

❺ Cobal do Humaitá
Procure a picnic from this market in the heart of Humaitá (pictured above). **p131**

Getting Around

Subway
A lone metro stop is the main way in/out of Botafogo. Urca and Humaitá aren't connected to metro lines.

Walking
Urca is safe to walk around, thanks to active military bases. Botafogo and Humaitá aren't too bad, but be careful.

Bus or Taxi
There are few dedicated bike lanes in these neighborhoods, so either take a city bus or taxi/Uber to get from point A to B.

Botafogo

One of the first residential neighborhoods in Rio, Botafogo is a strange mix of (polluted) beach, modern apartment buildings, car mechanics and historical mansions along with some of the trendiest restaurants and bars in Rio.

WHAT'S GOING ON TONIGHT?

It can be tough to find out about the cool stuff going on in any new city as a visitor, and Rio de Janeiro is no different. Most bars and events are posted on the organizer's Instagram accounts, so you have to be already following them to know what's happening on any given night.

Follow aggregator accounts like @ondetemsambarj, which posts lists of all the sambas happening on any given weekend. The same trick is used for Carnaval *blocos* (drumming and dancing processions): @blocosrj.oficial.

For DJs and club events, see what's going on with the Shotgun app. Sympla is another vendor to look for ticketed events, especially larger concerts.

Go Out in Botafogo

So many bars and restaurants

From *à la mode* cocktail bars to live jazz to some of the best Italian, pizza and vegan food in Rio, Botafogo is an abundance of riches when it comes to going out.

The heart of the action on any given night is at the intersection of Rua Arnaldo Quintela and Rua Fernandes Guimarães, where a student-age crowd hang out in front of the *boteco* (no-frills bar) **Treme Treme** (*6pm-late Tue-Sun*). Thursdays are particularly popping on this strip, thanks to the live jazz show that plays upstairs at **Macuna** (*7pm-2am Wed-Sat, 5pm-midnight Tue*) – be prepared to sweat. Thursdays are also Mundo Lingo (*mundolingo.org*) nights at **Bar Bukowski** (*7pm-late Thu-Sat*), the oldest rock-and-roll club in the city located inside a huge historic house with a spacious back patio. While Mundo Lingo is intended as a place for foreigners and locals to practice languages, it usually ends up being one big hookup fest.

Zona Sul is LGBTIQ+ friendly in general, but Botafogo is a focal point. There are several fun queer bars to pick from, including chill pink-lit bar **Calma** (*6pm-late Tue-Sun*) and the dance bar **Mãe Joana** (*noon-2:30am Tue-Sat, from 5pm Sun*). Botafogo doesn't really have dance clubs, but if you're looking to shake it, your best bet is **Vuvu** (*6pm-1am Tue-Sun*), which has live music and DJs throughout the week.

Stunning Vista & Holocaust Memorial

Somber historic point

Sweeping views of Enseada de Botafogo, Pão de Açúcar and Corcovado await visitors who make the journey up Pasmado. It's best reached in early morning or late afternoon, when the light is at its optimum for capturing the postcard panorama. Since 2023, the viewpoint is also Rio's Holocaust memorial, **Monumento Memorial às Vítimas do Holocausto** (*memorialdoholocaustorio.org.br, free*). The monument in

SIGHTS
1 Casa Firjan
2 Cemitério de São João Batista
3 Monumento Memorial às Vítimas do Holocausto
4 Museu Casa de Rui Barbosa
5 Museu Nacional dos Povos Indígenas

ACTIVITIES
6 Evolução Escalada Indoor

SLEEPING
7 Farfalla
8 Injoy

EATING
9 Da Roberta
10 Dainer
11 Elias
12 Empório Jardim
13 Ferro e Farinha
14 Fogo de Chão
15 Galeto Sat's Botafogo
16 Hoba
17 Magna Cozinha
18 Marchezinho
19 Slow Bakery
20 Sult
21 Vegan Ti Burger
22 Vegan Vegan

DRINKING & NIGHTLIFE
23 Bambina
24 Bar Bukowski
25 Bar Tero
26 Belisco
27 Botica
28 Calma
29 Chanchada
30 Embrazza
31 Hocus Pocus
32 Livraria da Travessa
33 Macuna
34 Mãe Joana
35 Maz
36 Quartinho
37 Treme Treme
38 Vuvu

SHOPPING
39 Botafogo Praia Shopping
40 Rio Sul Shopping

MICHAEL JACKSON'S VISIT

In 1996, US singer Michael Jackson came to Brazil to film the video for 'They Don't Care About Us'. The locations for filming were Pelourinho in the heart of Salvador in the state of Bahia, and the Santa Marta favela over Botafogo.

In 2010, the city erected a statue of MJ in the favela, partly to celebrate the singer, partly to declare that it's safe to visit after the government's Unidade de Polícia Pacificadora (UPP) 'pacification' project of policing favelas.

Today, UPP's effectiveness is subject to debate, as inequality in Rio remains as rampant as ever and theft is a persistent problem. Unfortunately, it's just too risky for us to recommend you visit.

SERGIO SHUMOFF/SHUTTERSTOCK

Cemitério de São João Batista

remembrance of the victims of the Nazi genocide features a 20m pillar with the inscribed words: *Não Matarás* (Thou Shalt Not Kill). Below the monument, enter a circular museum remembering the Holocaust with photos, video and audio.

Wander the 'Cemetery of the Stars'

Cemitério de São João Batista

Surprisingly off the map for many visitors, **Cemitério de São João Batista** (*concessionariariopax.com.br/project/cemiterio-sao-joao-batista, free*) is one of the most impressive cemeteries you'll find anywhere in the world. Built in 1851 following yellow-fever outbreaks, the 225,000-sq-meter necropolis has marvelous mausoleums, above-ground tombs and stacks of columbariums (drawers filled with ash remains) – each a work of art unto themselves. Buried here are a who's who of Brazilian elites and celebrities, including nine presidents, writers, poets, singers

EATING IN BOTAFOGO: OUR PICKS

Ferro e Farinha: Perfect thin-crust pizza, cheesy garlic bread and a cool setting in the heart of the action. *6pm-midnight* $$

Sult: Delicate pasta, Wagyu beef risotto and 'tiramisult' (housemade tiramisu) for a blissful date night. *12-11pm Tue-Sat, to 5pm Sun* $$$

Da Roberta: Roberta Sudbrack tributes international street food from this casual restaurant in a renovated garage. *noon-10pm Tue-Sun* $$

Dainer: Gussied-up US diner with comfort food (mac & cheese, chicken nuggets, milkshakes). *9am-10pm Wed-Sat & Mon, to 7pm Sun* $$

and artists. Among them are 'Queen of Samba' Clara Nunes; author Joaquim Machado de Assis; the fathers of bossa nova, Tom Jobim and Vinícius de Moraes; as well as Jorge Selarón, the man behind **Escadaria Selarón** (p166), fittingly buried beneath a staircase of colorful tile steps. Tombs of notable figures have QR codes.

Tour Historic Mansions

Linger amid the legacies

Take a refreshing break from the buzz of Botafogo at the gorgeous former mansion of Rui Barbosa, a journalist and diplomat who played a pivotal role in shaping Brazil's socio-economic development in the early 20th century. Cotton candy-colored **Museu Casa de Rui Barbosa** (*gov.br/casaruibarbosa/pt-br, free*) was built in 1849 and was Barbosa's home from 1895 to 1923. Behind the house are lovely gardens for quiet contemplation. Inside features guided tours (Portuguese only) that display much of Barbosa's original furniture. You'll see Barbosa's collection of 37,000 books in six languages (all of which he spoke fluently) and impressive gifts from abroad, including urns from Japan, China and Switzerland. Barbosa's legacy includes advocating for Brazil to join the Allies in WWI and introducing more than 1000 amendments to the Brazilian Civil Code. Controversially, as Minister of Finance, Barbosa ordered that all records of slaves be burned. While this prevented owners from seeking compensation after slavery was abolished, it also stopped former enslaved from seeking reparations and made it impossible to trace their lineage back to Africa.

Shift from learning about the past to being excited about the future at **Casa Firjan**, an innovation school in Botafogo. There are a few small exhibits showing students' work (like photography and 3D printing), but the biggest attraction is the carefully restored palace formerly owned by the Guinle family. While the striking white building looks like a French palace from the 17th century, it was built in the early 20th century as a wedding present to Celina Guile and Linneo de Paula Machado. Wander around the building and up its majestic marble staircase indoors. There's a delicious plein-air breakfast and lunch spot, Empório Jardim (p123), in the garden.

STARS OF THE CEMETERY

Historian **Milton Teixeira** *(02 19886 00480)* shares some of the stars buried in the cemetery.

Santos Dumont
Inventor of the airplane who considered himself responsible for all the victims of aviation and killed himself.

Carmen Miranda
Recorded 14 Hollywood films and made so much money that, in 1943, she was the largest individual taxpayer in the US.

Tom Jobim
One of the fathers of bossa nova who partnered with Vinícius de Moraes (also buried here), composing many songs, including 'Garota de Ipanema' (Girl from Ipanema).

Luís Carlos Prestes
Brazil's greatest communist leader is buried next to Hélio Beltrão, minister of the military dictatorship he fought against.

Don Pedro II
Brazil's emperor for almost 50 years is buried in the São João Batista chapel.

EATING IN BOTAFOGO: OUR PICKS

Marchezinho: Creative French-style small plates with market-fresh ingredients for lunch/dinner. Natural wines. *11:30am-midnight Mon-Sat* $$

Galeto Sat's Botafogo: Airier version of the Copacabana classic, legendary for spring chicken, *picanha* (steak) and chicken hearts. *11:30-5am* $$

Elias: Middle Eastern weigh-and-pay-by-kilo buffet with a wide array of fresh salads and lean meats. *11:15am-3:15pm* $$

Fogo de Chão: *Churrascaria* from Rio Grande do Sul that sent Brazilian steakhouses global, with 52 locations worldwide. *11:30am-10pm* $$$

'TROPICAL SILICON VALLEY'

Eduardo Paes, Rio mayor from 2009 to 2017 and again from 2021, is hoping to position the city as a hub for tech and innovation. One way he plans to do that is by hosting events; after all, Paes was the mayor when Rio hosted the 2014 World Cup and 2016 Summer Olympics.

Tech events in Rio include April's Web Summit Rio *(rio.websummit.com)*, which gathers more than 30,000 tech innovators from around the globe, and Rio Innovation Week *(rioinnovationweek.com.br/en)* in August, the largest technology and innovation event in Latin America.

Rio is also aiming to become a South American hub for digital nomads, thanks in part to the remote-work visa the country introduced in 2022.

SPP SPORT PRESS PHOTO./ALAMY

Indigenous History of Rio

Learn about Rio's indigenous people

Much is said about the influence of Portugal and African descendants on Brazil, but woefully less about the country's indigenous peoples. Yet names we're familiar with like Ipanema, Maracanã and the term for residents of the city, *carioca*, all have origins in indigenous languages.

Learn about Brazil's indigenous peoples at **Museu Nacional dos Povos Indígenas** (*gov.br/museudoindio/pt-br*), operated by Funai (the National Foundation of Indigenous Peoples). The museum, situated in an impressive Botafogo mansion, has an archive of tens of thousands of objects, photographs and sound recordings. Along with a permanent exhibition in the building, it hosts handicraft fairs, films, celebrations and storytelling.

EATING IN BOTAFOGO: VEGAN FOOD

Magna Cozinha: Vegan lunch buffet paid per kilo inside a cute and colorful historic Botafogo house. *noon-4pm* **$$**

Vegan Ti Burger: Tasty burgers, mostly made with tofu, and quality *maté* (a sweet tea-like drink) made in-house. *noon-3pm Mon-Thu, 6pm-11pm Thu-Sun* **$$**

Hoba: Cool off with creamy, 100% vegan ice cream. There are plenty of enticing flavors, including cookie with *brigadeiro* chocolate. *11am-9pm* **$**

Vegan Vegan: Art-filled enchanted garden restaurant on quiet street near Humaitá. *noon-4pm Tue & Wed, to 10:30pm Thu-Sat, 9am-8pm Sun* **$$**

Estádio Olímpico Nilton Santos

Cheer on Botafogo

Botafogo plays at Nilton Santos

Black-and-white striped Botafogo is one of of Rio de Janeiro's four club football teams, and the 2024 champion of South America's largest club competition: CONMEBOL Libertadores Cup.

Like a few of Rio's other clubs, Botafogo started out as a rowing club in the late 19th century and quickly embraced football after the game's popularization in the early 1900s. During the 1950s and 1960s, some of Brazil's greatest footballers played for Botafogo, such as Garrincha, who overcame limb length discrepancy to become one of the best dribblers of all time. Another legendary player was Nilton Santos, a defender so revered that the club decided to rename their home stadium after him in 2015.

EUROPEAN'S DIDN'T 'DISCOVER' RIO

When Europeans arrived in Rio de Janeiro in the early 1500s, an estimated 120,000 Guarani and Tupinambá (better known as the Tupi) indigenous people lived here in 30 or 40 villages.

Though little is known specifically of the original inhabitants, we know that they were seminomadic and had a varied diet from hunting, fishing, gathering and farming, with cassava being the most important crop.

Within the first century of contact, most of Rio's indigenous people were killed by diseases or armed conflict. The rest were enslaved – Arcos de Lapa, for instance, was built by enslaved indigenous hands. Today, there are about 7000 people who identify as indigenous in Rio and 1.7 million across Brazil.

EATING & DRINKING IN BOTAFOGO: CAFES & BAKERIES

Livraria da Travessa: Beautiful bookstore (some English options). Read them while sipping coffee upstairs. *9am-10pm* $$

Empório Jardim: Attractive cafe, breakfast and lunch spot, famous for its *pão de queijo* with Gruyère cheese. *9am-6:30pm* $$$

Slow Bakery: Super sourdough baked on-site, delicious pastries and an exciting breakfast and lunch menu. *8am-8pm Tue-Sat, to 4pm Sun* $$

Maz: Stylish cafe, brunch and enticing plates, as well as a good place to get some work done. *8am-7pm Tue-Sat, to 4pm Sun* $$

PRICEY SHOPPING

Botafogo is one of the best places to shop for top international brands, as it has a couple of huge malls: **Rio Sul Shopping** and **Botafogo Praia Shopping**. But don't expect products to be cheap.

Federal taxes on imported goods range from 10% to 35%, and items delivered by mail from abroad can get slapped with 60% postal import duties. For instance, Apple iPhones sold in Brazil are the second most expensive in the world after Türkiye.

Take this as a good opportunity to shop for local brands and save the rest for when you're home.

PRADEEP SUBRAMANIAN/ALAMY

Botafogo Praia Shopping

Botafogo plays its home games at **Estádio Olímpico Nilton Santos** (also known as Engenhão) in Zona Norte. The stadium can seat 60,000 people and hosted track and field events in the 2016 Summer Olympics. During big matches, Botafogo plays at the larger-capacity Maracanã Stadium (p194). Foreigners can get tickets without a CPF online at ingresse.com two or three days before game time. You'll need to use your smartphone to scan your face and share a photo of your passport. You may also buy tickets on game day at the stadium.

Indoor Climbing Gym

Evolution Indoor Climbing

Rio de Janeiro has some awesome mountains for climbing, especially Pao de Açúcar and Morro de Babilônia, as well as some terrific spots outside of the city. Train for those or just have some fun at **Evolução Escalada Indoor** *(Evolution Indoor Climbing; evolucaoindoor.com.br, R$40)*.

Rio's largest indoor climbing gym is located in a spacious warehouse in a gated area, a short walk up a steep staircase from the Botafogo metro station. Evolution has two large bouldering walls – one 3m tall, one 5m – plus an extensive wall for rope climbing and a resistance-training room. Courses change every six weeks, and there are plenty of classes for kids aged 6 to 16.

DRINKING IN BOTAFOGO: OUR PICKS

Try the maté cocktail.

Bambina: Sing your heart out at this karaoke dive bar with plenty of pool tables. *7pm-late*

Embrazza: Burger bar over three art-filled stories, including a rooftop often with hip-hop music. *6pm-midnight Tue-Sat, 2-10pm Sun*

Quartinho: This cocktail bar is always packed inside and out with the coolest of the cool. *6pm-1am Tue-Sat*

Belisco: If you like wine, this chill bar has an extensive list of international vintages plus tapas. *6pm-midnight Mon-Sat*

Hocus Pocus: Rio de Janeiro's most recognizable craft beer brand's brewery. Serves food. *noon-midnight Mon-Thu, to 2am Fri & Sat*

Bar Tero: Vintage decor, vermouth cocktails and lunch specials, with occasional live *chorinho* and samba. *noon-midnight Tue-Sun*

Botica: Cocktails and Mediterranean small plates. Bookish atmosphere. *6pm-2am Tue-Fri, from 1pm Sat & Sun*

Chanchada: Tiny bar that stretches almost a full block, with tables on the sidewalk. Its small plates are so good. *noon-midnight*

Urca

Idyllic neighborhood offset from the action, with shaded streets lined by stunning architecture, several calm beaches and one of Rio's must-do sights in both meanings of the word. Plan to come for sunset.

Quiet Beaches with Calm Waves

Quiet beaches for swimming

The waves at Copacabana and Ipanema are often dangerous – make your own splashes by swimming at 200m-long **Praia Vermelha** *(Red Beach)*, a pretty beach squashed between Morro da Urca and Morro da Babilônia where the water is almost always calm. Vendors at Praia Vermelha sell coconuts and snacks, and there are often *blocks* (street parades) here during Carnival season.

If you want to stretch your legs, Pista Cláudio Coutinho (p129) to the left of the beach is a paved 1.2km trail that winds along the southern contour of Morro da Urca. About 300m into the trail is Trilha do Morro da Urca (p129) up to Urca Hill.

On the other side of the mountains, **Praia da Urca** is a non-busy beach popular with families. No need for a picnic, as there are several bars and restaurants surrounding the beach.

Beers, Bolinhos & Beautiful Views

Sunsets on the Mureta

Every day before sunset, the short stone **Mureta da Urca** (bay wall) that lines the coast of Urca becomes one of the most romantic spots to end the day. Since 1938, **Bar Urca** *(8am-11pm)* has fueled the fun with ice-cold beers and *bolinhos de bacalhau* (deep-fried codfish balls) and *pastel de siri* (fried pastry stuffed with crab).

Closer to the entrance of Urca, **Urca Grill** *(6am-11pm)* also fuels the sunset spectators with beers and snacks. The crowd tends to be younger, with local Casanovas bringing along their saxophones for impromptu shows.

Another option for sunset is to take a wooden ferry *(R$10)* a few minutes over to **Flutante** *(noon-10pm Tue-Fri, from 8am Sat & Sun)*, a floating restaurant just off the coast of Urca. While we don't love the food at this price, the drinks and vibes on this floating bar are worth the trip.

BEER, BEM GELADA

Beer only arrived in Brazil in 1822 – before that, the Portuguese only permitted their wine. Afterward, Brazil became beer-obsessed, and drinking it on plastic tables and chairs is a national pastime.

Brazilian beer is served *estupidamente geladinha* (stupidly cold) in 600ml bottles kept cool in a *camisinha* (insulated beverage holder that hilariously has the same name as a condom in Portuguese) and poured into small cups. Popular local brands – Antarctica, Brahma, Bohemia and Skol – are made by US-Belgian-Brazilian brewing company InBev/AmBev.

Flavor is sparse in these lagers and pilsners, but they're very refreshing. If we were to pick a favorite, it'd be Original from Antarctica. *Cheers* (cheers)!

URCA

HIGHLIGHTS
1 Pão de Açúcar

SIGHTS
2 Fortaleza de São João
3 Morro da Urca
4 Mureta da Urca
5 Praia da Urca
6 Praia Vermelha

ACTIVITIES
7 Pista Cláudio Coutinho
8 Trilha do Morro da Urca

SLEEPING
9 Hotelinho Urca
10 Urca Hotel

EATING
11 Árabe Urca
12 Casa Que Doce
13 Clássico Sunset Club
14 Gal

DRINKING & NIGHTLIFE
15 Bar Urca
16 Flutante
17 Garota da Urca
18 Terra Brasilis
19 Urca Grill

TRANSPORT
20 Parque Bondinho Pão de Açúcar

EATING IN URCA: OUR PICKS

Casa Que Doce: Cute cafe in a splendid structure, with a bevy of enticing sweets, bagels and eggs. *10am-7pm* $

Arabic Urca: Grab a meal or snack of Levantine delights (like *esfiha* and *kibe*) before heading up the mountains. *6am-10pm* $

Gal: A pretty former residential building with hearty Brazilian dishes, such as seafood *feijoada* and *moqueca* (fish stew). *noon-11pm* $$

Bar Urca: Classic restaurant and bar since 1939, serving seafood upstairs and snacks from the bar counter below. *8am-11pm* $$

ROBERT WALLWORK/ALAMY

Fortaleza de São João

Military Base Where Rio Began

Tour Fortaleza de São João

Armed forces have been in Urca since 1565 when the Portuguese fought the French, as well as natives, from their base known as Forte de São José, located on the northeastern tip of Urca. After kicking out the French, the Portuguese expanded the fort in 1618 to become **Fortaleza de São João** (*funceb.org.br/copia-cas-historica-de-deodoro*), an active military base and physical-education school that offers free guided tours – email sitiohistorico.fsj@gmail.com to book.

The tours take you through the private military compound to a museum filled with medals, signed jerseys and other paraphernalia from athletes tied to Brazil's military, including soccer GOAT, Pelé, who did military service a year after winning his country the 1958 World Cup.

You'll then visit the grounds to see an art-deco gymnasium and replica canons before hiking over the hill to see windswept Forte de São José. The huge granite blocks and canons are the tour's highlight, and there's a small museum recounting Brazil's military history.

MILITARY SERVICE

Technically, military service in Brazil is mandatory for men – they must register in the first six months of their 18th year and serve for 10 to 12 months. However, in practice, only a fraction of men serve; if they really don't want to go, they won't be forced.

As of 2025, women may also join the army at 18 as volunteers. Previously, they were only admitted after undergoing training courses and served in administrative roles. In June 2024, the first women were trained for combat roles in the Brazilian Marines.

DRINKING IN URCA: OUR PICKS

Bar Urca (p125): The original Urca sunset spot. Grab a beer and *petiscos* (snacks) to enjoy on the *mureta* (bay wall). *8am-11pm*

Garota da Urca: The girl from...Urca. A classic bar facing the beach for pints, snacks and hearty meals. *11am-midnight*

Urca Grill (p125): Grab an ice-cold beer, fried *torresmo* (fried pork rinds) and take it to the *mureta* for sunset with a young crowd. *6am-11pm*

Terra Brasilis: The food is pricey and not great, but the live music, drinks and views are worth waiting in line for. *noon-11pm*

JOAO PAULO TINOCO/ALAMY

The Bondinho

TOP EXPERIENCE

Pão de Açúcar

If you even have just one day in Rio de Janeiro, make sure you make time to hike, climb or cable-car up to Urca's mountains: Pão de Açúcar (Sugarloaf Mountain) and Morro da Urca (Urca Hill). The views from here prove why Rio is called the Cidade Maravilhosa (Marvelous City). Stay for sunset to see live samba and DJs.

DON'T MISS

- The Bondinho
- Views on views
- How Urca was made
- Capuchin monkeys
- Rock climbing
- Via ferrata
- Live samba and DJs

The Bondinho

Soar over Rio up to Sugarloaf and Urca Hill in the *bondinho* (aerial cable car). Named after the city's existing *bonde* (street cars), like the one in Santa Teresa, the *bondinho* was inaugurated in 1912 as the third aerial cableway in the world. Its first voyage carried 17 passengers to the top of Morro da Urca in around six minutes. A few months later, the 750m section between Urca Hill and Sugarloaf was completed.

PRACTICALITIES

Scan this QR code for prices and opening hours.

Today's *bondinhos* carry 65 passengers to the top in just three minutes and have resplendent views. Cars arrive at the station at **Parque Bondinho Pão de Açúcar** about every 20 minutes and cost between R$92 and R$185, depending on if you're a foreigner, local, student or senior.

The trip is fun in itself and includes a second leg up to 396m-tall Sugarloaf from the eastern edge of Urca Hill. There are always crowds, but it's still worth the visit.

Hike

Alternatively, hike up to Morro de Urca for free. Find the trailhead for **Trilha do Morro da Urca** along **Pista Cláudio Coutinho** – it's about 300m from Praia Vermelha. The trail is a steep climb for 20 or 30 minutes past lush forest and plenty of capuchin monkeys (resist the urge to touch or feed them). Once you're up, you'll still have to take the cable car to get to Sugarloaf, but Urca Hill is good enough in our opinion.

Climb & Via Ferrata

While hiking up Morro da Urca is simple enough, getting up to Pão de Açúcar without the cable car requires a guide and rock-climbing equipment. The iconic mountain has been pegged with more than 120 rock-climbing routes. Around for a quarter century, **Climb in Rio** (*climbinrio.com*) offers several options for accessing them, ranging from a mostly hiking trip for beginners to a 25m climb to the famous Via dos Italianos on the west face of the mountain for 5.9+/5.10 climbers. The certified instructors at Climb in Rio also offer guided climbs in and around the city, with proceeds supporting the nonprofit CEU, which provides free climbing instruction for underprivileged youth.

Another option is to climb up Sugarloaf via its lone via-ferrata route. Originally installed to rescue climbers in an emergency, the via ferrata doesn't have footholds – just rope – so prepare for a full-body workout. The climb is plenty of fun and you get awesome views the whole way. Thomas Arias of **EcotuRio** *(ecoturio.com, R$350)* is a qualified, English-speaking guide who can take you up (and take plenty of pics).

Samba

Every Sunday, catch live samba for sunset on Urca Hill from 3pm to 6pm. There are increasingly also live DJs on weekends and through Carnaval season.

Alternatively, book a romantic trip for Sunrise at Parque Bondinho. The R$550 experience takes you up in the cable car at 5am before it opens and includes breakfast at **Clássico Sunset Club** *(8am-7:30pm $$$)*.

Accessibility

Pão de Açúcar is one of the best places to travel in Rio for travelers with accessibility needs, including those in wheelchairs. Learn more about accessibility in the city on p236.

THE CREATION OF URCA

Urca was mostly mountains surrounded by sand as Mother Earth made it. But in the late 19th century, the city decided to make Urca into a neighborhood by adding landfill to expand the land to make a flat neighborhood.

Urca soon attracted Rio's elites who built stunning art-deco and Spanish-style houses. Celebs to have called Urca home include pop stars Carmen Miranda and 'King' Roberto Carlos.

TOP TIPS

- Travelers over 60, pregnant, with a child, with limited movement can skip the line for the *bondinho* at any stop.
- Don't feed the monkeys, and keep an eye out for them, as they love to steal food.
- There's a small museum about the history of the *bondinho* on Urca Hill beneath the station.
- There are pretty little forested trails on both Urca Hill and Sugarloaf where you can take a break from the crowds.
- Food is cheaper and better down below in Urca.

URCA ON FOOT

Meander Urca's shaded, military-secured streets, past dreamy architecture to sunset snacks and drinks on the *mureta*.

START	END	LENGTH
General Tiburcio Square	Bar Urca	2.4 km; 45 minutes

After visiting Pão de Açúcar (p128) and/or Praia Vermelha (p125), observe the dramatic war scenes at ❶ **Mausoleum of the Heroes of the Battle of Laguna**, a monument in the center of General Tiburcio Square.

Leave the busy tourist area and enter the calm, shaded streets surrounding ❷ **Praça Félix Laranjeiras**. Admire the adorable architecture and dream of what it'd be like o live here.

Exit via Rua Urandi to see the parked fishing boats floating in Baía de Guanabara and snap photos of Cristo Redentor from the ❸ **Rosa dos Ventos** viewpoint.

Stick to the coast and check out ❹ **Paróquia Nossa Senhora do Brasil**, a charming little church built in 1933 with curved double doors, winding staircases and beautiful blue tiles.

Take a dip at **Praia da Urca** (p125) and admire ❺ **Escola Eleva Urca**, a former casino (1933–46), TV station headquarters and now a bilingual school. Instead of walking under the school, head up the quiet street to 131 Av São Sebastião, ❻ **Carmen Miranda's House**, where the Brazilian star lived between 1937 and 1939.

Continue along Av São Sebatião to the staircase at the end, which will take you to Mureta da Urca (p125) and ❼ **Bar Urca** (p125).

Feira da Urca This neighborhood's weekly street market occurs every Sunday from 8am to 2pm.

Museu de Ciências da Terra Stone lions and birds guard this Portuguese-language earth and science museum.

Cláudio Coutinho Trail (p129) Get extra steps in on the paved 1.2km path at the base of Morro da Urca.

Baía de Guanabara
END
Av João Luís Alves
Praia de Fora
Alameda Floriano
R Otávio Correira
R Cândido Gaffrée
URCA
Praia da Urca
Pão de Açúcar
Av Portugal
R Marechal Cantuária
Enseada de Botafogo
Morro da Urca
R Osório Almeida
R Urandi
R Urbano Santos
Av Pasteur
Pç Euzebio Oliveira
Universidade Rio de Janeiro
START
Pista Claudio Coutinho
Pç General Tibúrcio
Praia Vermelha
Pista Cláudio Coutinho
0 400 m
0 0.2 miles

Humaitá

Humble Humaitá is but a few-block extension of Botafogo with a market, hidden park and a terrific restaurant and bar scene – but don't tell locals that. They're patriotic about their cute little neighborhood.

Indoor Wine & Gastronomy Market

Cobal do Humaitá

Once a former tramcar depot, **Cobal do Humaitá** (*@cobaldo humaita, 9am-7pm*) is now a thriving gastronomy and artisan market and the focal point of this tiny neighborhood. Find flower shops next to counters serving excellent snacks along with a few terrific restaurants. Can't decide? You can't go wrong with a Brazilian *bolo* (cake) from **Bolo Cecília** (*9am-7pm Mon-Sat, to 6pm Sun $*).

The real draw is the abundance of wine bottle shops – a rarity for Rio, which is hardly a wine city. Pick up a nice Malbec from **Espírito do Vinho** (*@espiritodovinho*) and complete your picnic with Brazilian crackers and cheeses from **Farinha Pura Emporium** (*@emporiofarinhapura*), a grocery store that often serves free samples. Outside in the parking lot of Cobal do Humaitá is another Rio rarity: an artisanal market that's on more than one day a week; Thursdays to Saturdays from 10am to 6pm. Here, you'll find plenty of jewelry, purses and women's clothing.

WHERE'S THE MARKET?

Street markets in Rio de Janeiro travel around to different neighborhoods every day of the week.

For instance, Saturdays there's one in Laranjeiras. On Sundays, there are markets in Ipanema and Glória. But don't stop there. Rio has many more street markets throughout the week, and they're the best places to find the freshest produce and the best artisanal products – often for much cheaper than in supermarkets or stores.

Scan the QR code for a list of street markets.

Block Party

Music, fun and food in Humaitá

After a tough day at the beach, you'll need a drink to relax, so follow the crowds to Humaitá for the perfect *pós-praia* (post-beach) atmosphere. A vortex of bars and restaurants at the intersection of Rua Visconde de Caravelas and Rua Capitão Salomão turns Humaitá into a mini-outdoor festival pretty much any night of the week except Mondays. Ice-cold beer flows, as do the fried snacks, but **Fuska** (*5pm-midnight Tue, from 11am Wed-Sat, to midnight Sun*) is usually the best place to grab a seat for live music. Check its Instagram (*@fuskabar2.0*) for its schedule, but you'll reliably find samba on Thursdays and Sundays.

DRINKING IN HUMAITÁ: OUR PICKS

Cirandaia: One of Rio's best cafes for coffee made with Aeropress, Chemex, espresso machine etc. *8am-6pm Mon-Fri, 9am-4pm Sat*

Petit S Bistro: Low lighting, vintage decor at this majestically ambient French bistro. *noon-midnight Tue-Fri, from 10am Sat, to 3:30pm Mon*

Meza Bar: Pop art and clever cocktails inspired by various countries, plus Brazilian regional cuisines. *6pm-1am Mon-Sat, 5-11pm Sun*

Alba: Photogenic gastro bar that transforms into a supper club at night. *noon-4pm & 7pm-1am Tue-Sun*

SIGHTS
1 Parque do Martelo

EATING
see 10 Bolo Cecília
2 Brota
see 10 Joaquina
3 Lasai
4 Tragga

DRINKING & NIGHTLIFE
5 Alba
6 Cirandaia
7 Fuska
8 Meza Bar
9 Petit S Bistro

SHOPPING
10 Cobal do Humaitá
see 10 Espírito do Vinho
see 10 Farinha Pura Emporium

Explore a Secret Park

Surprising Parque do Martelo

In a residential part of Humaitá, discover a hidden oasis unknown to even the majority of *cariocas*: **Parque do Martelo** *(Hammer Park)*. Administered by the local neigh-borhood association, Parque do Martelo spans dense Atlantic Forest, with strategic clearings where you'll find a spot to have a picnic, or forest bathe in serene tranquility among the rustling leaves. Take one of the paths deeper into the forest for quiet contemplation and to see some ruins. Compared with more manicured parks in Rio, the wildness of the foliage here is truly special. Along with being a calm break from city life, the park also functions as a community hub, complete with yoga, art lessons and kids programs. If you decide to hike deep into the park, wear good shoes and mosquito repellent.

Parque do Martelo is a remarkable symbol of community-led urban rewilding. For years, it was slated to become a real-estate development, but a 30-year community-led battle managed to convince politicians to leave the Atlantic Forest to do its thing.

EATING IN HUMAITÁ: OUR PICKS

Brota: Michelin Bib Gourmand with flavor-packed vegetarian dishes that won't leave you missing meat. *11am-5pm Tue-Sun* **$$**

Joaquina: One of the best options in Rio for home-style Brazilian plates. It's at Cobal do Humaitá. *noon-midnight* **$$**

Tragga: Argentinian steakhouse known for its tomahawk steak set ablaze at your table. *noon-4pm & 6pm-midnight* **$$$**

Lasai: Two Michelin-star destination from *carioca* chef Rafa Costa e Silva. Basque-inspired small plates. *8pm-midnight Tue-Fri, 7pm-2am Sat* **$$$**

BEST PARKS IN RIO

Parque Lage (p72): Manicured gardens and caves surrounding a mansion once owned by the wealthy Lage family.

Parque Nacional da Tijuca (p74): World's largest urban rainforest, with trails leading to waterfalls, coffee plantation ruins and Cristo Redentor.

Aterro do Flamengo (p136): Huge park and beach on Zona Sul's eastern flank, perfect place for running and working out.

Jardim Botânico (p68): Botanical gardens with thousands of plant species first established in 1808.

Parque Guinle (p142): Quiet park in Laranjeiras with murmuring waterfalls slipping into ponds surrounding the state governor's residence.

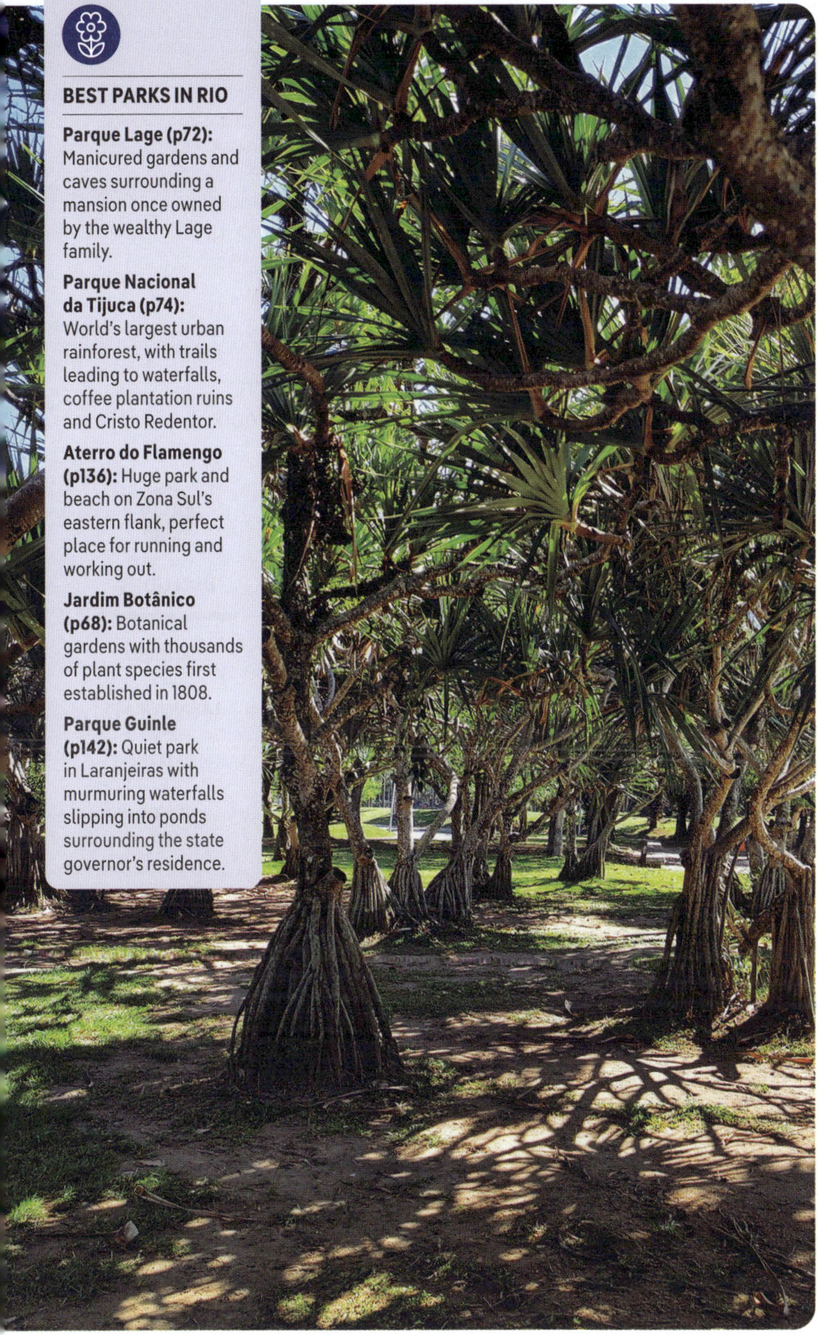

Aterro do Flamengo (p136)

Researched by Joel Balsam

FLAMENGO, LARANJEIRAS, CATETE & GLÓRIA

STREET MARKETS, HISTORY & CARIOCA LIFE

Leave the busy southern beach and hang out with the locals. You'll find Rio de Janeiro's liveliest Sunday market, cool nightlife, museums and history.

As Centro becomes Zona Sul, find the underrated neighborhoods of Flamengo, Laranjeiras, Catete and Glória. Formerly home to the Brazilian president and a popular retreat for urbanites, they lost their sheen as tourist attractions in the mid-20th century, due to the urbanization of Rio's southern beaches. But don't sleep on these neighborhoods. Or rather, do, as they're arguably some of the most convenient places to stay in Rio, especially during Carnaval. Wander quiet (for Rio), tree-lined streets, check out some amazing markets, work out and sip coconuts at a giant park/beach, see free art museums and check out an upstart nightlife scene.

INCLUDES

Feira de Laranjeiras (p140)

See p224 for places to stay in Flamengo, Laranjeiras, Catete and Glória.

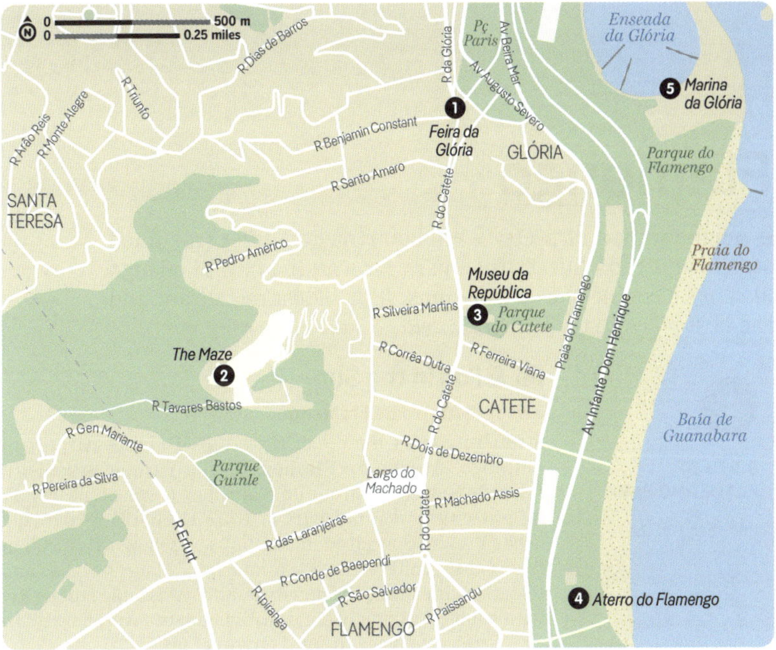
0 500 m
0 0.25 miles
R Dias de Barros
R da Glória
Pç Paris
Av Beira Mar
Av Augusto Severo
Enseada da Glória
5 Marina da Glória
R Triunfo
R Monte Alegre
R Arão Reis
R Benjamin Constant
1 Feira da Glória
GLÓRIA
Parque do Flamengo
R Santo Amaro
SANTA TERESA
R do Catete
Praia do Flamengo
R Pedro Américo
Museu da República
R Silveira Martins
3 Parque do Catete
Praia do Flamengo
Av Infante Dom Henrique
The Maze
2
R Corrêa Dutra
R Ferreira Viana
CATETE
Baía de Guanabara
R Tavares Bastos
R Gen Mariante
R Dois de Dezembro
Parque Guinle
Largo do Machado
R Machado Assis
R Pereira da Silva
R Erfurt
R das Laranjeiras
R Conde de Baependi
R Ipiranga
R São Salvador
R Paissandu
FLAMENGO
4 Aterro do Flamengo

FROM LEFT: JOEL BALSAM/LONELY PLANET; NAEBLYS/ALAMY

Highlights

❶ Feira da Glória
Shop at Rio's liveliest Sunday market, which has endless produce and prepared food. **p148**

❷ The Maze
Groove to jazz in a favela, with Gaudí-like decor and spectacular views. **p145**

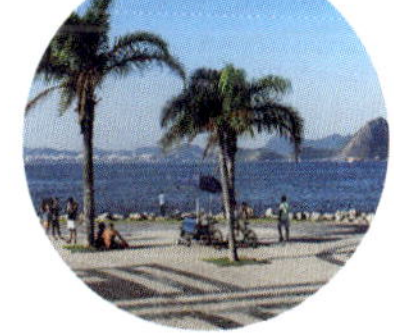

❸ Museu da República
Visit the former presidential palace with over-the-top decor and relaxing gardens. **p145**

❹ Aterro do Flamengo
Play in a huge urban park with a beach, grassy patches and museums (pictured above right). **p136**

❺ Marina da Glória
Watch breaching humpback whales during their migration, and learn to sail. **p148**

Getting Around

Metro
These neighborhoods are conveniently lined up along four stops on Zona Sul's single-line metro – Flamengo, Largo do Machado, Catete and Glória. Only Laranjeiras is far from the metro.

Bicycle
Rio's Itaú bike-share service is a great way to get around, and plenty of stations abound. Rent one with the bike Itaú app or through Uber.

Walking
Use your common sense and don't walk at night, but these neighborhoods are generally safe to walk around.

Flamengo

A neighborhood of pretty white apartments, quiet tree-lined streets and Rio's finest urban park for working out. Flamengo also has a couple of cool museums, Rio's oldest restaurant and the best place to try authentic *açaí*.

BIRTH OF FLAMENGO PARK

Before the 1960s, Aterro do Flamengo looked quite different than it does today. Back then, Santo Antônio Hill separated the neighborhood from Baía de Guanabara (Guanabara Bay). Incredibly, city workers whittled the hill down and used its residue to create the park and beach we see today.

To further beautify the park, teams of architects, urbanists, educators, sports and lighting specialists planted 17,000 trees and more than 240 species of Brazilian and tropical plants. They also added a couple of museums, a marina and a WWII memorial: **Monumento Nacional aos Mortos da Segunda Guerra Mundial**.

Fit & Fun in the Sun

Sweat in Aterro do Flamengo

Stretching from the domestic Santos Dumont Airport to Botafogo, **Aterro do Flamengo**, aka Parque Brigadeiro Eduardo Gomes or Parque do Flamengo, is one of the world's largest city parks and part of Rio's UNESCO-recognized urban design. Conceived in the 1960s by renowned Brazilian landscape architects Maria Carlota 'Lota' Macedo Soares and Roberto Burle Marx, the *aterro* (landfill) was added to the bay with rubble gathered from destroying Santo António Hill to give *cariocas* a place to get their sweat on.

Most of the park is beach, so order a coconut and enjoy breathtaking views of planes flying in front of Pão de Açúcar (Sugarloaf Mountain) before they land at the airport. Officially, it's safe to swim, but many locals don't trust the bay where the city dumps its sewage.

Elsewhere on the sand, join a game of volleyball, *futevôlei* (volleyball played without hands), beach tennis or workout in a cross-training course – most offer free intro classes.

Off the beach, there are some of Zona Sul's few basketball courts, as well as yoga and dance classes. You'll also see (and smell) plenty of locals grilling *churrasco* (meat) on weekends. On Sundays from 7am to 6pm, the curvaceous weaving avenues in the park close to traffic and fill with runners.

Fly Into the Future

Oi! Check out Oi Futuro

While many of Rio's best art galleries and museums are located in Centro, Flamengo's **Oi Futuro** *(oifuturo.org.br, free)* is a worthwhile visit, despite being off the map for many locals. Housed in a grand building with zigzagging staircases that climb up seven floors, the museum is dedicated to art technology, with multimedia installations that poke and prod at the meanings of modern architecture, urban design and the intersection between humanity and tech. You'll also find pop art, photojournalism and trippy videos. Don't miss the 6th-floor exhibit that delves into the history of technology, from telegraphs to floppy disks to Walkmans.

Before you climb up, register for the museum's hot-air balloon hyper-virtual reality experience. Waits can be an hour or more, especially on weekends. When it's your turn, you'll fly, virtually, above Flamengo to see epic views over Corcovado and Baía de Guanabara. Maybe skip this one if you're afraid of heights, as it feels very realistic.

Famous Food in Flamengo

Churrascaria, açaí and Rio's oldest restaurant

Flamengo is home to a few restaurants that should be on any food lover's list. **Assador** (*noon-11:30pm Mon-Sat, to 9pm Sun $$$*), in Aterro do Flamengo, is easily Rio's prettiest *churrascaria*. Views from the floor-to-ceiling windows are incredible, especially with planes landing; and *rodízio* (all-you-can-eat steak) with 16 cuts of meat is top quality. A connected restaurant, **Baleia Rios**, serves à la carte Mediterranean seafood.

Go to **Tacacá do Norte** (*9am-10pm Mon-Sat, to 8pm Sun $*) for Rio's most authentic *açaí* (blended Amazon berry

WHO REALLY INVENTED THE AIRPLANE?

If you ask most people, the Wright brothers achieved the first sustained flight in 1903. But ask someone in Brazil who invented the airplane and they'll probably say Alberto Santos Dumont (1873–1932).

As the argument goes, while the Wright brothers' flight created a buzz worldwide, few, if anyone, actually saw their Wright Flyer fly. Dumont, on the other hand, conducted the first public flight on the outskirts of Paris on November 12, 1906.

Dumont was distraught at how planes (his invention) were used as killing machines in WWI and committed suicide in 1932.

Brazil honors its proud son with the airplane-shaped design of its capital, Brasília, and the name of its domestic airport.

RECORDS/ALAMY

smoothie). Its *açaí* comes with or without sugar and tastes very different – and much healthier – than what you'll find at the beach. Also taste *tacacá,* a fermented fish soup from northern Brazil.

For a bite of history, try **Lamas** (*11:30am-midnight $$$*), which opened back in 1874. It serves Brazilian dishes over white tablecloths and has a street-facing cafe with Portuguese *natas* (custard tarts).

Learn About the Lady with the Fruit Hat

Museu Carmen Miranda in the park

At Aterro do Flamengo's southern curve, find a small, circular museum dedicated to Brazil's brightest star of the 20th century, **Museu Carmen Miranda** *(instagram.com/museucarmenmiranda, free).*

Born in Portugal, Maria do Carmo Miranda da Cunha, later known as Carmen Miranda (1909–55), moved to Brazil when she was young and became a popular radio star. Spotted by Broadway producer Lee Shubert in a Rio casino, Miranda

DRINKING IN FLAMENGO: OUR PICKS

Grão de Ouro: Coffee and Brazilian-style cakes at a family-run cafe close to the aterro. *8am-7pm Mon-Fri, to 1pm Sat & Sun*

Armazém do Chopp: Wooden, barnlike bar. Outdoor seating on a raised veranda; cooler (air-conditioned) seating inside. *11am-11pm*

Boteco Belmonte: Part of the popular Rio bar chain, this one's often lively, especially during football matches. *11am-2am*

Heróis e Cia: Servers dress as Captain America and other superheroes at this neighborhood burger bar. *11am-late Mon-Sat, to 10pm Sun*

Carmen Miranda, ***Week-end in Havana*** **cover**

was invited to perform in the US and audiences couldn't get enough. Bedazzled, bejeweled and with extravagant headwear – such as her signature faux-fruit hat – Miranda became a fixture in American theater, nightclubs and Hollywood movies. The way she danced – as in her famed 1941 song 'Chica Chica Boom Chic' – was nothing like most in the US had seen before. Of course, Brazilians knew she was dancing Afro-Brazilian-born samba.

In 1945, Miranda became the highest-paid entertainer in the US, earning $200,000 ($3.5 million today). Pressure over the years led Miranda to stimulants and sleeping pills, and she died of a heart attack at age 46.

Inside the small museum, see mannequins sporting the star's extravagant clothing and signature hats, trunks she carried her costumes in and rare photos. Information in English is accessed via QR code. If you're lucky, you may be treated to a show outside from Miranda's ever-extravagant devotees.

CARMEN CONTROVERSY

Carmen Miranda's legacy is a complicated one. While she reached heights of stardom and financial success in the US like no Brazilian ever had, she was criticized for perpetuating Latin American stereotypes. On a return to Brazil in 1940, she was booed off stage and spent 14 years outside the country in a self-imposed exile. Argentinians weren't happy with Miranda either, as her 1940 film, *Down Argentine Way*, was banned in the country for its insulting portrayal of Argentina. Miranda, a white woman, has also faced criticism for culturally appropriating samba, an Afro-Brazilian art form.

AT THE COPACABANA

Carmen Miranda, Groucho Marx and Steve Cochrane's 1947 film *Copacabana* was set at New York's club of the same name. Singer Barry Manilow also loved the club and wrote a song about it from a special hotel in Rio.

WHERE TO EAT IN FLAMENGO

Rango Sarado: Its healthy, protein-packed and vegetarian-friendly lunch plates are perfect for feeling your best on the beach. *noon-4pm* **$$**

Sushi Barcellos: Fresh sushi, cold beer and *yakisoba* (fried noodles) served on tables in a square. *9am-5pm Thu-Sun, 8am-3pm Wed* **$$**

Majórica: If you prefer your steak à la carte rather than buffet style, this steakhouse and seafood restaurant is a Flamengo classic. *noon-11pm* **$$$**

Alcaparra: The vibe at this Italian spot harkens to the area's luxury resort days. *8-10am & noon-midnight* **$$$**

Laranjeiras

Named after orange trees, Laranjeiras is a bookworm sort of neighborhood with a tight-knit community vibe. Join the neighbors at a street market, swaying to *chorinho* music and cheering on the soccer team, Fluminense.

BUY LOCAL

Rio is a city of entrepreneurs, where small businesses and brands are constantly popping up. Many get their start at street markets like Junta Local (*juntalocal.com*) a market brand that specializes in small, eco-friendly local brands that cater towards organic, vegan and gluten-free products. Not only food, Junta Local also has artisanal products.

Junta Local hops around Rio to markets like Feira de Laranjeiras. It's also planning to be part of a renovated Mercado São José, slated to reopen in Laranjeiras in the near future.

Hangout with Locals in the Market

Enticing Feira de Laranjeiras

The Saturday market, **Feira de Laranjeiras** (*7am-3pm*) is worth circling on your calendar to experience this tightly woven community. Sheltered by tall white apartments and trees along Rua Prof Ortiz Monteiro and inside Praça Jardim Laranjeiras, the market is a favorite for young and old, with a knack for attracting the finest artisans. Peruse an enticing lineup of produce and prepared food, such as purple potato bread, crusty focaccia, take-home pizzas, artisanal sausages and much finer cheeses than what you'll find at supermarkets. At the beginning or the end, you'll have the chance to fill up on Rio's marquee market snack: *pastel frito* (fried bread pocket, stuffed with a choice of meats, cheese or veggies) and *caldo de cana* (sugarcane juice).

Feira de Laranjeiras also has a great selection of artisanal clothing, such as handwoven baby slippers and trinkets to decorate your home, rather than the touristy souvenirs you'd find on the beach.

There's a live *roda de choro* (a more romantic, instrumental form of samba), in the middle of Praça Jardim Laranjeiras. Crowd around and enjoy it with a craft beer, wine or kombucha and fresh oysters (first Saturdays of the month only).

Jazz & Samba up the Hill

Party with Locals at Armazém Cardosão

The original **Armazém Cardosão** (*@armazemcardosao, music cover R$25*) was a mini-market and bar that first opened its doors in 1954. Revitalized in 2019, the bar lost none of its neighborly charm and now hosts some of the best weekly samba and jazz jam sessions in Rio de Janeiro.

Up a hill over Laranjeiras, Armazém Cardosão has live jazz on Tuesdays from 6pm to 9pm and samba on Thursdays from 7pm to 10pm. There's also samba starting at noon on weekends at the park next door. The vibe is fun, hip and rarely attracts short-term tourists from abroad. Of course, you may also go at other times to enjoy its enticing *petiscos* (snacks), such as

SIGHTS
1 Mirante do Pedrão
2 Mirante Dona Marta
3 Palácio Guanabara
4 Parque Guinle

SLEEPING
5 Casa Caminho do Corcovado
6 Jo & Joe

EATING
7 Cantina Orange
8 Ipiranga 138
9 Tasca da Mercearia
see 7 Trégua Cozinha

DRINKING & NIGHTLIFE
10 Armazém Cardosão
11 Capitu
12 Caruá
13 Symposium Vinhos

SHOPPING
14 Feira de Laranjeiras
15 Praça São Salvador

SEMINAL BRAZILIAN SCRIBE

Author Joaquim Maria Machado de Assis (1839–1908), of mixed Azorean Portuguese and Black heritage, lived in Laranjeiras and Cosme Velho. He had a knack for creating complex characters, who struggled with tragic views of life. Despite his pessimistic and existential leanings, Machado de Assis earned the respect of Brazil's upper classes and, in 1888, was declared a Knight of the Imperial Order of the Rose.

Today, he is a symbol of literacy and is considered one of Brazil's best writers. The Laranjeiras metro (former tram) stop Largo do Machado is named after him, and there's a cafe called Capitu (p142) that pays tribute to one of his most famous characters.

pastéis (fried dough) stuffed with shrimp and cream cheese, and *dadinho de tapioca (fried cassava balls)* with red pepper jelly. Full meals and *feijoada* (black bean and meat stew) are only available on weekends.

If going to a show, arrive early to snag a table outside. Otherwise, you'll be restricted to the crowd on the street and have to line up at the window to order. The window on the left is to pay, while the one on the right is to pick up your drinks. It's best to order a cab when coming and going at night, as the quiet, dark road outside the venue can be unsafe.

Shopping & Music in the Square

Multifunctional Praça São Salvador

In the heart of Laranjeiras, **Praça São Salvador** is a charming little square with a bandstand, a pretty fountain, plenty of places to sit and a children's play area. On weekdays, the park is a peaceful spot to chill and read a book, but on Sundays from 9am to 6pm it comes alive with one of the city's coolest street markets. Stalls sell art, jewelry, crafted goods and tasty food, while a *chorinho* (romantic, improvised samba) band plays under the bandstand. Praça São Salvador also beams around sunset on Thursdays with live jazz, Fridays for *forró* (couple's dance from northeastern Brazil) and on Saturdays for samba.

Read a Book in an Oasis

Chill in Parque Eduardo Guinle

As soon as you walk through sphinx-guarded gates into **Parque Guinle** *(24hrs, free)* from hectic Rua Laranjeiras, take a big inhale. Now breathe out. This public park is an oasis from busy city life, with gently flowing ponds, gawking swans and huge trees wrapped in lush foliage and sprouting flowers. No bikes are allowed in here, and no one is working out. This is a place to quietly read a book on a wrought-iron bench or quietly chat with your travel-mates to the soundtrack of a tiny waterfall.

Parque Guinle was once a garden owned by the billionaire Guinle family, which paid for Copacabana Palace. The Guinles used to live in the dramatic Palácio das Laranjeiras, which was built in 1914, but it was given to Rio de Janeiro state and it's now where its governor resides. Sadly, the palace isn't open to the public.

TRAIN TO CRISTO

The neighborhood of Cosme Velho, just west of Laranjeiras, is where you'll catch the train to **Cristo Redentor** (p66). See important tips and details about taking the train on p67.

DRINKING IN LARANJEIRAS & COSME VELHO: OUR PICKS

Caruá: Perfect for a cappuccino or a home-style lunch plate. Has vegetarian options. *noon-7pm Sun-Fri, 10am-4pm Sat*

Capitu: Cafe with plenty of lunch options, named after one of writer Machado de Assis' characters. *7am-9:30pm Mon-Sat, 8am-8pm Sun*

Armazém Cardosão (p140): Live music and atmospheric neighborhood bar. Great snacks and *pasteís*. *5-11:30pm Tue-Fri, noon-9pm Sat & Sun*

Symposium Vinhos: Bistro-style wine bar for true oenophiles. The menu is designed for the wine it will accompany. *6-11pm Mon-Sat*

RENATO NETO/SHUTTERSTOCK

Parque Guinle

See a Fluminense Match

Famed soccer stadium

Rio de Janeiro's Maracanã Stadium (p194), easily the world's most celebrated soccer stadium, is home to two teams: Flamengo, which is based in Leblon, and Fluminense which was founded in 1902 in Laranjeiras. Started by 22-year-old Rio-born British diplomat Oscar Cox after he learned about soccer while studying in Europe, Fluminense Football Club is now one of the most decorated teams in Brazil and an annual contender in national and continental leagues.

Fluminense, which also means someone from the state of Rio de Janeiro, used to play out of a small stadium in Laranjeiras but upgraded to Maracanã in 1950. Despite playing in Zona Norte, support for Tricolor – a nickname in honor of the team's distinctive maroon, green and white stripes – is particularly strong in Laranjeiras. Even if you can't make it to the stadium, it's a lot of fun to watch a game here in a neighborhood *boteco* (bar).

The best way to buy tickets is to get them from the official Fluminense Store in Copacabana (p103) – tickets go on sale to foreigners with a passport two or three days before match day. You can also buy them directly at Maracanã, however, if they're playing a big game, ie. against city rivals Flamengo, good luck, as club members usually eat up most of the seats. You may also be able to get tickets through your accommodation or local travel companies, but you'll pay much more than face value.

PRINCESS ISABEL

Born in Rio de Janeiro as the eldest daughter of Emperor Dom Pedro II and Empress Teresa Cristina, Princess Isabel (1846–1921) signed the single most important document in Brazilian history: Lei Áurea, or the Golden Law, which abolished slavery in 1888. Isabel's pivotal role in freeing four million enslaved people prompted backlash from rich farmers and the military, who sent her into exile in 1889.

For 24 years leading up to her exile, Isabel lived in Laranjeiras' **Palácio Guanabara** (formerly Paço Isabel), which is not open to the public. The extravagant yellow-and-white palace is now the official seat of the Rio de Janeiro state government.

Princess Isabel was baptized nearby at **Igreja de Nossa Senhora da Glória do Outeiro**, an impressive church on a hilltop with spectacular views of Baía de Guanabara. Learn the various, intriguing, ways to visit it (p152).

INTERNATIONAL SOCCER SHAME

For many Brazilians, July 8, 2014, was the darkest day of their lives. Brazil was hosting the 2014 FIFA World Cup and hoped to return to the glory that saw it win the international soccer competition five times – the most of any country. Without injured star Neymar, Brazil faced Germany in the semifinals and was utterly annihilated. Germany won 7-1, scoring five goals in the first 29 minutes.

After the game, boisterous Brazil fell into grieving silence and it's fair to say it hasn't recovered. The 7-1 loss is frequently used in taunts by rivals Argentina and Uruguay, and Brazil hasn't been able to silence its haters, losing in the quarter-finals at World Cups in 2018 and 2022.

Mirante Dona Marta

Vistas & Live Music

Well-known, and under-visited views

Many claim that **Mirante Dona Marta** offers the most perfect postcard view of Rio. This former helicopter-landing site sits 360m above sea level, offering uninterrupted views of Sugarloaf Mountain and Baía de Guanabara, Cristo Redentor, Maracanã and Lagoa. The site sits on the hill above the Santa Marta favela, so we don't recommend walking up. Instead, take a taxi; you'll follow the same road that takes you to Corcovado. During the day, the Mirante Dona Marta has security and is considered safe, but be careful at night.

Another great view is from **Mirante do Pedrão**, a little-known spot and upstart concert venue. Every Friday, Saturday and Sunday night around sunset, live bands play jazz, samba or *pagode* (popular samba music) on a small stage in front of a backdrop that includes Pão de Açúcar and Praia de Botafogo. If you visit between noon and 4pm on Saturdays and Sundays, a street cart serves *feijoada* and *moqueca* (seafood stew). You're going to want to take a taxi up and down to this one as well, as it's not safe to walk.

WHERE TO EAT IN LARANJEIRAS: OUR PICKS

Cantina Orange: Street cart making airy-crusted pizzas. Its red-checkered tablecloths deliver romantic vibes. *6-11pm Thu-Sun* $$

Ipiranga 138: A family home in a cute yellow historic building. Beloved neighborhood favorite for its daily lunch specials. *11:30am-6pm Mon-Sat* $

Tasca da Mercearia: Portuguese rice, codfish, *natas* in a stylish atmosphere near Praça São Salvador. *noon-midnight Mon-Sat, to 10pm Sun* $$

Trégua Cozinha: Chef couple Victor Lima and Ana Paula Souza do seasonal haute cuisine in an intimate bistro. *7:30-11pm Wed-Sat* $$$

Catete

A small grid of streets between two metro stops, Catete and Largo do Machado, Catete has a few worthy sights, including the former presidential palace and one of Rio's best jazz nights.

Tour the Former Presidential Palace & Gardens

Museu da República and Gardens

Catete's most imposing building, Palácio do Catete, now **Museu da República** *(museudarepublica.museus.gov.br, free)*, was initially built to showcase the obscene wealth of Antônio Clemente Pinto (1795–1869), a coffee baron responsible for bringing close to three million enslaved Africans to Brazil. In 1896, the palace housed the president of Brazil until leader Getúlio Vargas committed suicide here in 1954. Today, the palace and its gorgeous rear garden have been given back to the people as a free museum and park.

Everything you look at inside the palace is extravagant. Each room upstairs is decorated with painstaking (literally, as it was built before slavery was abolished) detail and in various styles, including Venetian and Moorish. The delicate wall carvings similar to *fleurs-de-lis* might just take the prize. On the ground floor, a Portuguese-only exhibition is dedicated to Rio's history in the early half of the 20th century.

Leave the museum to the left, and walk through the gate outside the south end of the building. Here, you'll walk into an impressive garden reminiscent of what you'll find in Europe, with tall palm trees, a gentle river with swans, and couples cuddling in the grass. The gardens also often host Junta Local (*juntalocal.com*) food and artisanal clothing fairs, featuring upstart small businesses specializing in vegan, organic and eco-friendly products.

Rio's Prettiest & Trippiest Jazz Venue

The Maze Jazz Views

Above Catete inside one of Rio's safest favelas, Tavares Bastos, **The Maze** *(@themaze_rio, R$15)* is simultaneously one of Rio's most amazing jazz venues and most spectacular viewpoints.

CARIOCA RENAISSANCE

Guide **Rafael Pavão** *(instagram.com/riofreewalkingtour)*, shares why he's feeling hopeful about Rio.

After it ceased to be the capital of Brazil in the 1960s, Rio de Janeiro fell into steep decline, with many of its previous problems being exacerbated and many new ones emerging. However, since the 2016 Olympic Games, I have seen new potential for the city finally emerging. The violence rates are much lower than I have ever seen in my lifetime, and the revitalization of previously abandoned areas of the city gives me hope of seeing Rio become a global city. We are at the beginning of a Carioca Renaissance and I'm very excited to see what the city will be 10 to 20 years from now.

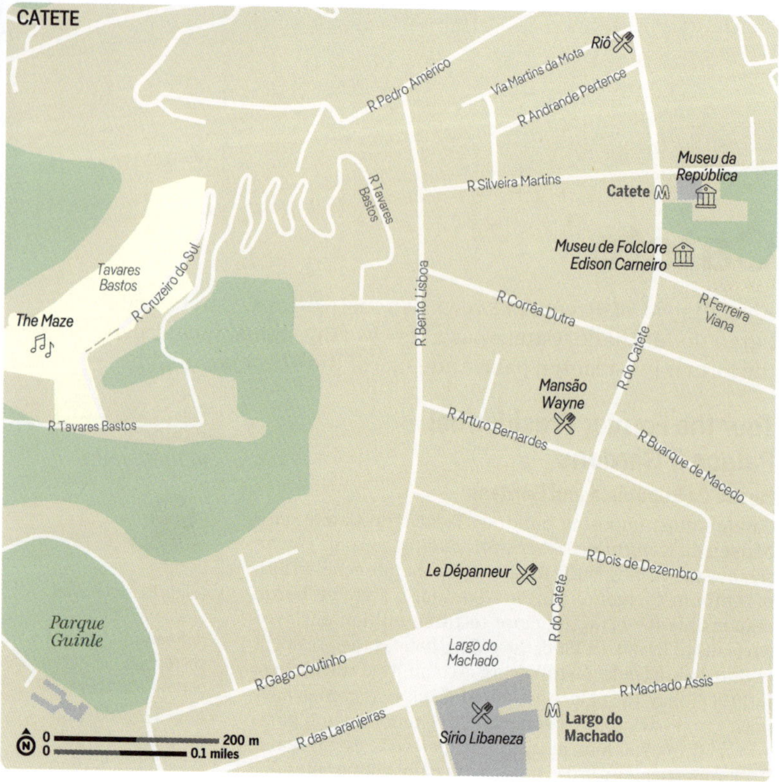

Founded in 1981 by the late British artist, filmmaker and journalist Bob Nadkarni, The Maze is filled with psychedelic tile decor that looks like something Antoni Gaudí would've dreamed up. Once a month, The Maze hosts a live jazz performance that attracts Rio's expats and bohemian crowd – don't miss it. Check its Instagram to see when it's happening. You can also visit during the day from noon to 5pm Wednesday to Saturday to see the artwork and soak in the views.

To get up, hire a motorcycle or ride the minibus from the entrance to the favela at the corner of Rua Tavares Bastos and Rua Bento Lisboa. Taxis and Uber cars won't go to the top. Follow signs through the tiny favela streets from there.

EATING IN CATETE: OUR PICKS

Sírio Libaneza: Always-busy mall counter doing amazing Levantine dishes like beef *kibe* and *kafta* for over 50 years. *8am-10pm Mon-Sat* $

Mansão Wayne: The random award goes to this resto-bar dedicated to 1960s *Batman* actor Adam West. *11am-late Mon-Sat, to 9pm Sun* $$

Le Dépanneur: Reliable French-inspired bakery, mini-market and restaurant with a little bit of everything (except wi-fi). *7am-11pm* $$

Riô: Kilo buffet with fresh salads, sushi and hot meals. All-you-can-eat pizza *rodízio* for dinner from 6-11pm. *11am-midnight* $$

LUCY NADKARNI

The Maze (p145)

Fascinating Folk-Art Museum

Museu de Folclore Edison Carneiro

Next to Museu da República, find an impressive museum showcasing folk art from across Brazil, especially the northeast. First opened back in 1968, **Museu de Folclore Edison Carneiro** (*gov.br/iphan/pt-br/unidades-especiais/centro-nacional-de-folclore-e-cultura-popular, free*) has a permanent exhibition that explores the myths and legends of Brazilian cultures, like Candomblé (Afro-Brazilian religion) as expressed through festival attire, ceramic figurines, dolls and carpets. There's also a cool little exhibit on graffiti in Rio de Janeiro. Check out the museum's shop for an amazing collection of folk art, clothing and traditional instruments.

When you leave the shop through the gardens, turn right to find more folk art from temporary exhibitions.

TWO SIDES OF GÉTULIO VARGAS

Few had more effect on Brazilian politics in the 20th century than Gétulio Vargas (1882–1954). Anointed interim president in 1930, Vargas ruled Brazil for 15 years and again from 1951 to 1954.

A savvy politician not easily classified as left or right, Vargas helped modernize Brazil by reforming the constitution, centralizing power and introducing social policies like a minimum wage, earning him the nickname Father of the Poor. Vargas also ruled as a dictator, banning political parties, imprisoning opponents and censoring journalists.

In 1945, the military removed Vargas from power, but he was reelected in 1951. A few years later, facing political turmoil, Vargas shot himself in his bedroom at Palácio do Catete.

AFRO-BRAZILIAN RELIGIONS

When enslaved Africans were transported to Brazil, they brought religious traditions that mixed with Christianity to become Candomblé and Umbanda. Often misunderstood and discriminated against, these Afro-Brazilian religions are resilient and fascinating. Learn more on p172.

Glória

Located on the dividing line between Centro and Zona Sul, Glória has a metro stop, beach access, and plenty of Carnaval parades. Experience its lively Sunday market, historic architecture and upstart bar scene.

BEST MARKETS IN RIO

Feira da Gloria (Sun; p148): If you go to one market in Rio, make it this one in Glória.

Feira de Laranjeiras (Sat; p140): Shuck oysters, sip wine and eat *pastel* (fried pastry) at this fun market in a quaint neighborhood.

Hippie Market (Sun; p80): Ipanema's market since 1975 has a great lineup of artisans, fruits and veg.

Feira de Antiguidades (Sat; p180): Hunt for antiques and thrift clothing at rock-bottom prices at this market in Centro.

Feira do Lavradio (Sat; p172): More than 250-year-old Rua do Lavradio has excellent artisanal finds. Stay for *baile charme* (coordinated dancing).

Rio's Liveliest Market

Sundays at Feira da Glória

Every neighborhood in Zona Sul hosts a weekly market, but **Feira da Glória** (*7am-4pm Sun*) is the king. Starting from the Glória metro stop, the market stretches north for several blocks and is packed with stalls selling everything you can imagine. There's fresher and cheaper meat, fish and produce than you'll find at supermarkets, and huge selections of cool shirts, dresses and artisanal finds – a keychain shaped like female genitals, anyone?

Come hungry, as the market serves food you won't likely find in Rio's restaurants, such as Afro-Brazilian *acarajé* (bean patties fried in palm oil and stuffed with dried shrimp), Chilean empanadas and spicy jollof rice from Rio's first Nigerian-food venue, **Cozinha Nigeriana da Latifa** (*@cozinhada.latifa*) – be prepared to line up. The market has become so big that it now has two columns of stalls, as well as a dedicated cooked-food market under a tent.

While there used to be *roda de samba* (a traditional form of samba) in the heart of the market, a recent crackdown by complaining neighbors have made schedules more erratic. If you're looking for music, there's a good chance there'll be some in **Praça Edson Cortes** through the market, and afterward in front of Monumento a Deodoro da Fonseca.

Whale-Watching & Sailing

Embark from Marina da Glória

From May until mid-August, more than 20,000 humpback whales make the 4000km journey from their krill-filled feeding waters in Antarctica to northeastern Brazil to breed. Along the way, these elegant 16m giants swim, jump and slap off the coast of Rio de Janeiro – watch them do so on a tour.

Whale-watching tours leave from **Marina da Glória** on a large comfortable cruiser. Book a six-hour tour with **Valeiro Sagarana** (*veleirosagarana.com*) via WhatsApp (*+55 21996*

SIGHTS
1 Igreja de Nossa Senhora da Glória do Outeiro
2 Marina da Glória
3 Monumento Nacional aos Mortos da Segunda Guerra Mundial
4 Museu de Arte Moderna
5 Quilombo Ferreira Diniz
6 Retrato Cultural

ACTIVITIES
7 Sail in Rio
8 Valeiro Sagarana

SLEEPING
9 Discovery Hostel

EATING
10 Braseirinho da Gloria
11 Casa da Glória
12 Cozinha Nigeriana da Latifa
13 Grégora Arte
14 Labuta Mar

DRINKING & NIGHTLIFE
15 Bar do Zé
16 Birosca
17 Fatchia
18 Isca
19 Ximeninho

ENTERTAINMENT
20 Bar do Zeca Pagodinho
21 Glorioso

SHOPPING
22 Feira da Glória

TRANSPORT
23 Plano Inclinado do Outeiro da Glória

RIO'S GHOST SHIPS

The water body where the Portuguese first entered this area has seen better days.

Polluted with an estimated 18 million liters of sewage per second, Baía de Guanabara is also home to around 50 ghostships that are left abandoned to rot in the water. Stripped of their engines and electronics, ships leak oil and further pollute the bay. They also pose a threat. In November 2022, a ship broke free and crashed into the Rio–Niterói bridge. Fortunately, no one was hurt and the bridge remained intact.

While the city pledged to clean up the boats before the 2016 Olympics, they remain, and probably will for years to come.

MAURO PIMENTEL/GETTY IMAGES

Whale-watching tour

524420, R$400). The tour is done in conjunction with **Projeto Baleia** *(baleiajubarte.org.br)*, a nonprofit conservation organization that has helped the humpback population off Brazil's coast bounce back after centuries of hunting. In 1990, four years after whale hunting was prohibited in Brazil, there were just 1500 individual humpback whales – today there are an estimated 35,000.

On the tour, you'll see vivid vistas of Pão de Açúcar, Corcovado and Copacabana beaches as well as, hopefully, humpback whales and dolphins. The trip includes snacks and nonalcoholic drinks. Outside of the whale-watching season, **Sail in Rio** *(sailinrio.com)* leads three-hour group excursions to enjoy the sunshine *(R$225)* or sunset *($R250)*. Or rent the whole boat for groups of up to 20 *(starting at R$2400)*.

Marina de Glória, a state-of-the-art marina built for the 2016 Summer Olympics, also has a lineup of excellent restaurants, and hosts festivals and concerts, including one of the most popular Carnaval *Blocos* (street parades), Sargento Pimenta *(@blocodosargentopimenta)*, which combines Beatles music with Brazilian rhythms.

EATING IN GLÓRIA: OUR PICKS

Labuta Mar: Fish sandwiches so good you'll be sad to finish, with tables stretching across to the park. *11:30am-11pm Tue-Sun* $$

Braseirinho da Gloria: Outstanding grilled *galeto* (spring chicken) and broccoli rice in a tiny restaurant. *11am-10pm Mon-Sat, to 6pm Sun* $$

Grégora Arte: Cute cafe with Santa Teresa vibes and a selection of homestyle dishes, such as quiche and cakes. *8am-10pm Mon-Sat* $$

Casa da Glória (p152): Dine or brunch in luxury outside a banker baron's estate. *noon-11pm Mon-Fri, from 10am Sat, 10am-4pm Sun* $$$

Go Out in Rio's 'Coolest Neighborhood'

Disco, pagode, samba and more

Glória is certainly on the up and up. To see for yourself, head to **Fatchia** (*7pm-midnight Wed-Sat, 5-11pm Sun*). Reminiscent of a hip bar in Brooklyn, Fatchia serves Detroit-style pizza, and DJs play disco upstairs in its low-lit lounge that has vintage furniture and vibrant art. Fatchia was cocreated by record-collecting owner DJ Facchinetti and the owners of eternally fashionable Rio bars Quartinho (p124), Chanchada (p124) and Suru (p169). **Isca** (*5:30-11pm Wed-Sat, 3-10pm Sun*), a Basque *pintxos* (gourmet snacks) bar on Rua do Russel facing Aterro do Flamengo (p136) is another sign of Glória's revelatory coolness.

For something more classic, head to **Bar do Zé** (*6pm-midnight Mon-Sat*), aka Britan Bar. At the bottom of a quiet residential hill formerly occupied by Brazil's elite, hence the colorful mansions, this bar has stone archways and wooden shelves topped with old bottles of *cachaça*. The party always spills onto the street, where you may see everything from live music to a pet pig. Another classic is **Ximeninho** (*noon-1am*), which does some of the cheapest *chopes* (pints) in Zona Sul and has plenty of outdoor tables.

Stretch those toes and be prepared to dance six nights a week at **Glorioso** (*@gloriosocultural, cover R$10+*). With an energy and decor similar to what you'll find in Centro, this open-air beer garden with graffiti and colorful lights hosts live music like *forró* and samba. Check its Instagram to see what's playing. Another spot to check out for live music is **Bar do Zeca Pagodinho** (*bfw.group/bar-do-zeca-pagodinho, R$20*). High-five a life-sized statue of Zeca Pagodinho, the contemporary singer who helped popularize the samba offshoot *pagode*, before entering the bar that often has live bands, food and drink.

Photo Gallery inside Urban Ruins

Retrato Cultural space and Birosca bar

For decades, the derelict, collapsed building behind the Moraes family's photography studio was a reminder of how far this once-luxe neighborhood had fallen since the Brazilian capital moved to Brasília in 1960. But where some might have seen fodder for demolition, Nana Moraes saw an opportunity. In 2017, she opened **Retrato Cultural** (*@retrato_espacocultural, free*) for events among the dramatic, photo-worthy backdrop of decaying walls slowly being consumed by trees and vines. After the COVID-19 pandemic, Retrato Cultural opened to the public as a gallery, a cultural event space and a bar, **Birosca** (*5-10pm Wed-Fri, from 1pm Sat & Sun*).

Over a few gallery buildings, evocative photographs hanging by thin wire become all the more tantalizing, due to their impactful setting on peeling brick, stucco and tile walls. Check Instagram for exposition information and events such as poetry, music and screenings on the giant projector. There's also live classical music on Thursdays from 7:30pm to 9:30pm.

PAGODE

The word *pagode* used to refer to parties among enslaved people, but in the 1970s it emerged as a rhythmic, country-style offshoot of samba. Often with instruments like a banjo and *tan-tan* hand drum and overly dramatic lyrics, *pagode* originated in Rio, with many crediting samba band Fundo de Quinta as its founding fathers.

After hearing Fundo de Quinta play, bossa nova singer Elizabeth 'Beth' Santos Leal de Carvalho helped usher them into the spotlight. Beth Carvalho also went on to work with Jessé Gomes da Silva Filho, aka Zeca Pagodinho, who is the most recognizable name in *pagode* today.

HOTEL GLÓRIA

A year before Copacabana Palace was built, another hotel from the very same French designer, Joseph Gire, attracted the glitzy and glamorous to Glória. Hotel Glória, built in 1922 for the centenary of Brazilian independence, looked similar to Copacabana Palace, with a bold white facade and eclectic accents inspired by French hotels. Stars of the day stayed in its 200 spacious rooms and danced in its popular nightclub. But as the attention moved to Rio's beaches, Hotel Glória fell out of favor and shut in 2008. The building is now owned by Abu Dhabi's sovereign wealth fund, who is transforming it into luxury condos.

See What's On at the MAM

Mesmerising Museu de Arte Moderna

With a prime location on the north end of Aterro do Flamengo, Rio's modern art museum, **Museu de Arte Moderna** (*mam.rio*) is an impressive piece of modernist architecture itself. Designed in the 1950s by architect Affonso Eduardo Reidy to contrast the contours of the city's hills with impressive landscaping from Roberto Burle Marx, the MAM has evocative works by international and Brazilian artists, including Bruno Giorgi, Di Cavalcanti and Maria Martins. The MAM also hosted a range of events, from talks to screenings to world leaders for the G20 in November 2024.

Mini-Pilgrimage to a Historic Church

Nossa Senhora da Glória do Outeiro

Records from French colonists in Rio tell of an indigenous Tupinambá (Tupi) village at the foot of a hill where Glória is located today called Kariók or Kariόg – inspiration for the name of Rio de Janeiro residents: Carioca. After the indigenous people were killed or enslaved and the French defeated, the Portuguese erected a church over Glória in 1739 to boast of their victory. **Igreja de Nossa Senhora da Glória do Outeiro** is a Brazilian baroque-style church with Portuguese blue tiles depicting biblical scenes and elaborate features like a wooden door and a handwashing basin. Portuguese royalty loved the church, and it's where Princess Isabel was baptized. Today, the church is off the radar for many visitors, but it's an underrated sunset spot, with views overlooking Baía de Guanabara.

One way to get up to the church is to make a mini-pilgrimage through the gate that faces the metro at Parque Municipal Lúcio Costa and walk up a short trail surrounded by lush foliage. Another is to head to Rua do Russell and ride the outdoor funicular **Plano Inclinado do Outeiro da Gloria** (*7am-7pm Tue-Sat, to 1pm Sun, free*). Don't worry, the funicular elevator isn't as old as it looks.

Alternatively, walk or drive up from Ladeira da Glória, a charming street that steers you past the striking spiraling silver decor of the ESPM Business School. If you go this way, be sure to stop for a drink or a romantic meal at Casa da Glória (p150). The bistro is on the poolside terrace outside a marvelously-restored bank baron's house built in 1770 and hosts live jazz on Fridays from 7pm to 10pm as well as weekend brunch. Unfortunately, the pool isn't open for customers.

A great time to visit Glória's church is in August when it celebrates a 10-day religious festival with ceremonies, processions and live concerts.

LAZYLLAMA/ALAMY

Igreja de Nossa Senhora da Glória do Outeiro

Eat Feijoada in a Quilombo

Resilient Quilombo Ferreira Diniz

Before slavery was abolished in 1888, African and indigenous peoples formed fugitive communities called *quilombos* based on community support, cultural preservation, sustainable agriculture and resistance. Like similarly fashioned maroons in the the Caribbean, *quilombos* have also persisted in Brazil and there are as many as 6000 today. One is just up the hill towards Santa Teresa and it welcomes visitors with open arms for *feijoada* (bean-and-meat stew served with rice) on Fridays.

Quilombo Ferreira Diniz *(@quilomboferreiradiniz)* was formed by two Afro-Brazilian families, Ferreira and Diniz, on the property of a 1912 hilltop mansion owned by the Lage family (the same ones who built Parque Lage (p72)). The tight-knit *quilombo* is a multigenerational community of around 70 people who live among rare tropical fruit trees that bear guava, papaya and acerola fruit, along with a pink millet tree the size of a 6-story building. Every Friday at noon, *quilombo* matriarch Tia Cida cooks up her famous *feijoada* as a live samba group plays in front of tables and chairs in the garden. The *quilombo* also hosts parties during Carnaval and other Brazilian holidays.

WHY I LOVE GLÓRIA

Joel Balsam,
Lonely Planet writer

After living across Zona Sul, my decision is clear: Glória is my favorite neighborhood in Rio de Janeiro. It conveniently has its own metro stop and is close to artsy Santa Teresa without being stuck up the mountain. It's near the vibrant culture and nightlife of Lapa, has much prettier architecture than Copacabana, and there's a beach where I love to run and play *futevôlei*.

With the arrival of hip new bars like Fatchia (p151) and renovations to Hotel Glória, this *Glórious* neighborhood is on its way back to its glory days. When it gets there, I'll be here to say I told you so.

Researched by Joel Balsam

SANTA TERESA & LAPA

STREET ART, MUSIC & PARTYING

Art is everywhere in these bohemian neighborhoods: outside on murals beneath historic facades, and inside in venues that shake through the night with samba.

Hilltop Santa Teresa got its start in 1629 when a chapel and later convent enticed believers to hike up. Soon after, the neighborhood attracted elites (who built European-style mansions), and later artists inspired to create in front of spectacular vistas. The neighborhood retains its bohemian community charm, with artwork and ateliers aplenty, along with a bevy of live music venues. On the edge of Centro, rough and tumble Lapa bears the scars of decades of neglect, but if you look past the decay, you'll find historical buildings, the ingeniousness of the Lapa Steps and Arches, and a nightlife scene that's the wildest in Rio.

INCLUDES

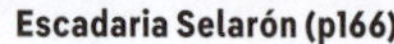

Escadaria Selarón (p166)

See p224-5 for places to stay in Santa Teresa and Lapa.

0 400 m
0 0.2 miles
Largo da Carioca
CENTRO
Feira do Lavradio 5
Bonde Station 3
Vaca Atolada 2
Av República do Chile
Av República do Paraguai
R do Senado
FÁTIMA
Av Mem de Sá
R do Lavradio
R Evaristo da Veiga
Av Rio Branco
R de Santa Luzia
Av Presidente Wilson
CINELÂNDIA
Pç Cardeal Câmara
Passeio Público
Pç Itália
Pç Deodoro
R Carlos Sampaio
R do Rezende
R Riachuelo
R Teixeira de Freitas
Av Infante Dom Henrique
Parque do Flamengo
LAPA
1 Escadaria Selarón
R André Cavalcânti
Pç Paris
Enseada da Glória
R Dias de Barros
R da Glória
SANTA TERESA
Ladeira do Castro
Av Beira Mar
Av Augusto Severo
R Cândido Mendes
R Monte Alegre
R Benjamin Constant
Largo dos Guimarães 4
GLÓRIA

Highlights

1 Escadaria Selarón and Arcos da Lapa
Marvel at two of Rio's most photogenic monuments, found in rough-around-the-edges Lapa. **p166**

2 Vaca Atolada
Dance to samba here into the wee hours of the morning for a spiritual experience. **p168**

3 Bonde
Ride the yellow tram from Centro up to Santa Teresa (pictured above right). **p156**

4 Largo dos Guimarães
Go for a walk around artsy Santa Teresa and dance to live music in this popular square. **p160**

5 Feira do Lavradio
Shop for artisanal treasures at this Saturday market and marvel at the historic street that hosts it. **p172**

Getting Around

Bonde
Hop on the historic yellow tram from the Bonde Station in Centro over the Lapa Arches to Santa Teresa. The lines can be long, so allow yourself plenty of time.

Taxi
Walking on your own, especially at night, isn't the best idea in these neighborhoods as phone theft is rife. Instead, hail a taxi. If you order an Uber, keep a good grip on your phone.

Walking
You should be safe to walk along Santa Teresa's main roads, especially when lots of people are around.

Santa Teresa

Hilltop Santa Teresa is still Rio's artsiest neighborhood, with murals and galleries galore. Head up via the yellow *bonde* (tram), and stay into the evening to eat and dance at a samba or jazz show.

FATAL BONDE CRASH

In 2011, the Santa Teresa Bonde was turning a corner when it derailed and overturned. Five passengers, along with the driver, died in the tragic accident, and another 56 were injured. The reason why so many people were injured was because, back in those days, people used to hang off the tramcar to ride for free.

Investigations found that a poorly maintained brake system was the culprit of the crash, and the Bonde stopped running for years – to the dismay of locals who'd lost their vital form of public transportation. After public protest, the Bonde returned in 2021 and there are plans to expand its service even further.

Ride the Historic Yellow Tram

Santa Teresa's unforgettable Bonde

Cute yellow tramcars known as the *bonde* began running up and down Rio's streets in 1859, first pulled by horses and then connected to electric tracks in the 1890s. The trolley transport system ran for 70 more years (anything with the name Largo was a tram stop) until cars pushed them off the road. Well, all but one.

Santa Teresa's 32-person **Bonde** *(visitesantateresa.rio/bonde, round-trip R$20)* rattles up the hill from the Bonde Station beside the Petrobras building in Centro – you can only buy tickets there, not in Santa Teresa. The tram runs from 8am to 5pm Mondays to Fridays, to 6pm on Saturdays and from 9am on Sundays. There are usually four trams running at a time that leave from the station every 20 minutes.

Riding the Bonde is pricey for visitors (it's free for locals), but it really is a lot of fun. Shortly after your departure, you'll be treated to the trip's most thrilling highlight as it glides directly over Arcos da Lapa (p166). The Bonde continues through winding residential streets up to the heart of Santa Teresa, Largo dos Guimarões (p160). You have views of the cascading favelas that surround Santa Teresa until the last stop, Dois Irmãos. There isn't much to do there, so we recommend staying in the Bonde and going back to Largo dos Guimarães to explore the neighborhood from there.

Art Shopping & Festivals

Galleries and ateliers galore

Art is everywhere you look in Santa Teresa. There are graffiti murals on concrete walls, telephone poles and beneath your feet, like painted ponds of fish, as you walk on the sidewalk. Chances are you'll see a top or up-and-coming artist creating while you're there.

Take home some art, and support local artists, by visiting the many ateliers, galleries and shops in the neighborhood. A good

A yellow *bonde* tramcar

place to start is **Domingos Cardoso Atelie** *(@ateliedomingoscardoso)*. The Brazilian artist from the state of Maranhão has been living in Santa Teresa and painting colorful favela scenes since the 1990s. Up the street, **Favela Hype** *(@favelahypeoficial)* is an ubercool shop from local designer Kananda Soares with fashionable shirts and an in-house bar.

Across from there, **Baobá Brasil** *(@baobabrasil)* by artist Tenka Dara sells stunning clothing that mixes African prints and other fabrics. Over at **Nau Cultural** *(@naucultural)*, find an amazing collection of *arte popular* – many of the pieces are from Black, female artists from the Brazilian northeast. The owners met many of the artists while driving in a Kombi (van) around the Brazilian north in 2019. Last but certainly not least is the artwork of Gétulio Damado and his son Victor at their Bonde-like stand **Bonzolandia Damado**. The instantly recognizable pieces like robots and painted hearts are all made from recycled materials. Find Bonzolandia Damado on the sidewalk on Rua Leopoldo Fróes, above the street where the trams pass. Text 021 98714-7730 if they're not there

A great time to see Santa Teresa art is during **Portas Abertas** *(@artedeportasabertasoficial)* – two weekends in September when artists open their studio doors to visitors. Or there's August's Festival de Arte Urbana de Santa Teresa or **Faust** *(visitesantateresa.rio/faust)*, which celebrated its first edition in 2024. Faust turns the neighborhood into a big art crawl with a provided map.

continued on p160

GÉTULIO DAMADO

Inside many of Santa Teresa's hotels, restaurants and shops are colorful robots and other artwork from the imagination of artist Gétulio Damado.

Born in Minas Gerais, Damado moved to Rio at 16 and lived in the Santo Amaro favela where he started making artwork for local kids using recycled materials. Damado moved to Santa Teresa and, along with his son Victor, made art out of bottle caps, cell phones, trashed metal – you name it. Damado's work has been exhibited in New York, London, Paris and Germany, and in Santa Teresa in the yellow *bonde* shop **Bonzolandia Damado** (p157).

The fact that the art is left overnight without it being stolen is proof how respected they are.

ART MUSEUM IN PORTO MARAVILHA

To see art from the comfort of a cool air-conditioned building, head to the **Museu de Arte do Rio** (p182).

SANTA TERESA
R do Oriente
R Cardeal Sebastião Leme
R Monte Alegre
R André Cavalcânti
Ladeira do Castro
R Paschoal Carlos Magno
R Triunfo
R Fonseca Guimarães
R Carlos Brandt
R Terezina
R Arão Reis
R Áurea
R Felício dos Santos
R Almirante Alexandrino
Ladeira do Meireles
R Bernardino dos Santos
Laurinda Santos Lobo
R Aprazível
SANTA TERESA
R Francisca de Andrade
R Leopoldo Fróes
Pizzaria do Hédi (700m)
Morro da Nova Cintra

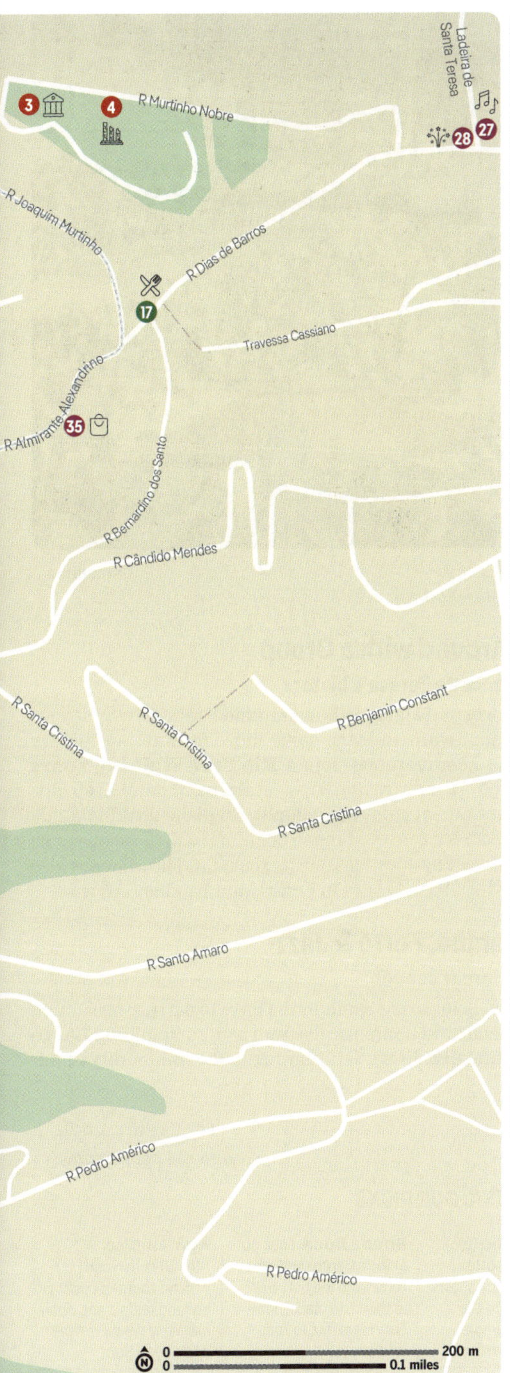

SIGHTS
1 Largo dos Guimarães
2 Museu Benjamin Constant
3 Museu da Chácara do Céu
4 Parque Glória Maria
5 Portas Abertas

ACTIVITIES
6 Samba dos Guimarães

SLEEPING
7 Casa Beleza
8 Castelo dos Tucanos
9 Chez Georges

EATING
10 Adega do Pimenta
11 Aprazível
12 Bar do Mineiro
13 Cafe do Alto
14 Casa Nossa
15 Nenete
16 Térèze
17 Zola

DRINKING & NIGHTLIFE
18 Agô
19 Bar da Fatinha
20 Bar do Gomes
21 Bonde Boca
22 Cultivar
23 Esquina Emporium
24 MGallery Hotel
25 Mô Café
26 Novooeste

ENTERTAINMENT
27 Bar do Serginho
28 Carmelitas
29 Casa Aprazível
see 17 Céu na Terra
30 Cine Santa Teresa
31 Solar do Mirante

SHOPPING
32 Bonzolandia Damado
33 Domingos Cardoso Atelie
34 Favela Hype
35 Vinil do Mustafá
36 Baobá Brasil
37 Nau Cultural

TRANSPORT
38 Bonde

SAFETY IN SANTA TERESA

Bohemian Santa Teresa shares its hilltop setting with several favelas. Extreme poverty plus international visitors – many carrying cell phones that cost more than many favela residents make in months – has made Santa Teresa rife for theft.

That said, things have been much better lately. Still, it's a good idea to take your phone out as little as possible when in Santa Teresa and to not wander off from the main strips of shops and restaurants along Ruas Almirante Alexandrino, Paschoal Carlos Magno and Aurea – especially at night.

It's also a safer bet to take the Bonde or a cab up instead of walking, especially at night.

ZUMA PRESS, INC./ALAMY

Carmelitas

continued from p157

Walk Around with a Group

Discover Santa Teresa's history

If you're worried about walking around Santa Teresa on your own, or just want to learn some more fascinating history about the neighborhood, join a **Rio Free Walking Tours** *(riofreewalkingtour.com, tips)* starting from Largo dos Guimarães on Saturdays at 2:30pm. English-speaking guide Rafael Pavão is a gem of a human being and will do whatever he can to answer any questions during your stay. The company also offers history-based tours in Centro and Paquena África.

Live Samba, Forró & Jazz

So many great venues

Aside from being artsy, Santa Teresa loves to party, especially on the weekends when samba calls from bars surrounding **Largo dos Guimarães**. Every Saturday night, the community center

DRINKING IN SANTA TERESA: OUR PICKS

Esquina Emporium: Craft beer is rare in Rio, but this place sells plenty of bottles. Enjoy one in its lovely garden. *11am-10pm*

Bar da Fatinha (p161): Vibrant bar that often hosts lively samba shows that spill out onto the street. *4pm-midnight Wed-Sat, 3-10pm Sun*

Bonde Boca: Look out at Rio's Centro and port zone from the balcony at this little place. *noon-5pm Mon-Thu, to 7pm Fri-Sun*

Agô: Art-filled Afro-Brazilian and African-themed cocktail bar and restaurant. *6pm-midnight Wed-Fri, from noon Sat & Sun*

Try its Africa mule with red peppercorns.

above the square becomes akin to a festival with **Samba dos Guimarães** *(@sambadosguimaraes, R$25)*, which has samba under a huge tent as well as an intimate indoor setting for *forró* (northeastern music and couples dancing). Down the hill, **Bar da Fatinha** *(@bardafatinha)* frequently hosts lively samba and *forró* shows on its bar terrace. Order an Antarctica beer from the bar and find a table, or watch from the street.

For 40 years, the cutest evening in Santa Teresa has been at **Bar do Serginho** *(@chorodaesquina)*. Every Monday night from 5pm to 8pm, the mini-market opens the terracotta-colored building across the street to unveil a gorgeous low-lit venue with stone walls and cool decor accents like wonky-framed mirrors and a hanging chair. Go early to snag a chair and be serenaded by *choro* music. Also known as *chorinho*, the genre was born in Rio in the 19th century and uses elements of jazz, like improv. It's R$30 to enter the venue, or R$10 donation from the street.

High above the city, **Solar do Mirante** *(@solar.do.mirante)* is another wonderful venue that hosts live music on Wednesday nights. The hollowed-out mansion has a spectacular vibe, and the music here, which tends to be chill jazz, is wonderful.

The music doesn't stop there. Look out for shows at **Casa Aprazível** *(@casaaprazivel)*, a mansion with unparalleled views over Rio, record shop **Vinil do Mustafá** *(@vinildomustafa)* and in the backyard of art gallery Nau Cultural (p157).

BAILE FUNK

You'll probably hear about Baile Funk favela parties during your visit.

Complete with Brazilian funk music, hip-hop and fireworks, Baile Funk can feel like a full-on concert when they happen every Saturday night. The thing is, Baile Funk parties are organized by drug gangs, and members carry their guns through the crowd.

The combination of booze and heavy arms is not something we can recommend to travelers in good conscience, so resist the temptation.

Carnaval Blocos in Santa Teresa

Some of the most famous blocos

Santa Teresa is one of the best places to party during Carnaval in February or March. There's something about tubas and drums blasting through small tree-lined streets that make *Blocos* (street parades) in Santa Teresa some of the most memorable of the season.

Carmelitas *(@blocodascarmelitas)* kicks things off as the official launch party on Friday. Try and come early or you'll end up way back with the sweaty crowds and unable to hear the band.

On Carnaval Saturday, Santa Teresa's **Céu na Terra** *(@blococeunaterra)* is another *Bloco* not to be missed. **Blocos de Rua** *(blocosderua.com/rio-de-janeiro)* has a list of the *Blocos* in Santa Teresa as well as elsewhere in Rio.

CARNAVAL 101

What's the difference between a *Bloco* and a parade in the Sambodrome? Learn everything you need to know about the world's biggest street party on p46.

DRINKING IN SANTA TERESA: OUR PICKS

Cultivar: Small cafe counter with *açaí* and arguably the best *pão de queijo* (tapioca cheese balls) in Rio. *8am-6pm*

Mô Café: Cute neighborhood cafe with a full menu connected to a vintage shop. *10:30am-7pm*

Novooeste: LGBTIQ+ cocktail bar on a busy corner with occasional live music. *6pm-midnight Wed-Fri, from noon Sat & Sun*

Bar do Gomes: Technically 'Bar Armazém São Thiago', former warehouse (1919) serving *chopes* and *petiscos*. *noon-midnight*

MARIELLE FRANCO

On March 14, 2018, Marielle Franco (1979–2018), a municipal councillor and activist from the Maré favela who'd spent her adulthood advocating for the rights of Black, LGBTIQ+ and poor people, was in a car when 13 bullets rained down, killing her and driver Anderson Gomes.

The assassination was a breaking point in a city and country plagued by inequality and violence, and protests broke out across Rio and the Brazilian diaspora.

Six years later, assassins Ronnie Lessa and Élcio de Queiroz were charged with 137 years in prison. Alleged masterminds, the Brazão brothers – former politicians and heads of Rio's Civil Police – were on trial at the time of writing.

BJANKA KADIC/ALAMY

Ruined Mansion Reborn

Architecture and views from Parque Glória Maria

Parque Glória Maria *(@parquegloriamaria, free)*, formerly known as Parque das Ruínas before it was renamed after a beloved Black female journalist, used to be owned by Laurinda Santos Lobo (1878–1946), a celebrated Rio socialite. From her Santa Teresa residence built at the turn of the century, Santos Lobo would throw huge parties filled with painters, poets, musicians and intellectuals. When she died, the palace fell into disrepair and turned into ruins, hence the original name.

A half-century after its owner's death, the building was elegantly revived for new generations of artists and art lovers by architects Ernani Freire and Sônia Lopes. With iron and glass on the ruinous brick palace, Parque Glória Maria is something special.

Visit the building and the back terrace, where there's a spectacular, nearly 360-degree view that stretches from the center of Rio across Guanabara Bay to Pão de Açúcar (p128). Parque Glória Maria also has a small art gallery downstairs and a performance theater.

At the end of the same street, find the home of another patron of the arts, **Museu da Chácara do Céu** *(@museudachacaradoceu, free)*. Museum of the Sky Farm in English, its

EATING IN SANTA TERESA: OUR PICKS

Cafe do Alto: Specialties from the northeast in a vibrant atmosphere. All-you-can-eat brunch on weekends. *9am-5pm Wed-Sun* $

Nenete: Fresh and delicious lunch specials – both vegetarian and meat – that taste homemade. *8am-3pm* $

Casa Nossa: Seafood served in a gorgeous setting with wrought-iron railings, live music and a huge tree in the middle. *noon-10pm* $$$

Bar do Mineiro: This classic bar is known for serving some of Rio's best *feijoada* (bean-and-meat stew served with rice). *11am-11pm Tue-Sun* $$

Museu da Chácara do Céu

art collection is from Raymundo Ottoni de Castro Maya (1894–1968), the first director of Rio's museum of modern art, Museu de Arte Moderna (MAM). Inside, find European art dating back centuries, including sculptures, maps and paintings by Henri Matisse and Nicolas-Antoine Taunay. Castro Maya's original home was (sadly) demolished in favor of this one in 1954.

Much more attractive than the building itself are the panoramic views from the balcony and the quiet, manicured gardens out back. The museum is open from noon to 5pm, Wednesday to Sunday and the gardens open up at 9am.

Father of the Brazilian Republic

See Museu Benjamin Constant

Wind back the clock to 1888 when Princess Isabel signed the most important law in Brazilian history, Lei Áurea (Golden Law), which finally brought an end to slavery. A year later, the military decided it was also time to abolish the monarchy, and Isabel was exiled in a nonviolent coup. On November 15, 1889, Brazil officially became a republic, and Benjamin Constant Botelho de Magalhães (1836–91) – a military man who'd fought in the Paraguayan War – is considered one of its founding fathers.

Santa Teresa's **Museu Benjamin Constant** (*museucasabenjaminconstant.museus.gov.br*, free), is the 1860

LOCAL FAVORITES

Letícia Santanna *(@santannalele)*, Master of Tourism, shares her top spots in Santa Teresa and Lapa.

Novooeste (p161)
Not only a LGBTIQ+ spot, but also a karaoke where hipsters from all over the world can sing along.

Bar do Serginho (p161)
If you are in town on a Monday, don't miss listening to *chorinho* – our national jazzy music made popular by Pixinguinha.

Rua Morais e Vale
Recently revitalized street on the corner of classic **Bar do Adalto** (p169) in Lapa, now a hub for cafes, art galleries and bars.

Panka (p172) or **Sabor Peruano** (p166)
If at some point, somehow, you get tired of Brazilian food, support new-wave immigrant businesses like these Peruvian restaurants.

EATING IN SANTA TERESA: OUR PICKS

Aprazível (p164): Romantic restaurant that tumbles down a lush hillside with enchanting views over the city. *noon-10pm Tue-Sat, to 5pm Sun* $$$

Pizzaria do Hédi (p164): Under-the-radar restaurant up a hill, with wine, thin-crust pizza and stellar views. *6-11pm Thu-Sat* $$

Zola: Neapolitan-style pizza and occasional live music inside a cavernous setting makes for a memorable date night. *6-10pm Wed-Sun* $$

Adega do Pimenta: German restaurant serving *currywurst* (curry-spiced sausage) and *schnitzel*. *noon-10pm Mon-Fri, to 6pm Sat & Sun* $$

DIVORCEE HANGOUT

Steps from Largo dos Guimarães, the site of Santa Teresa's five-star **MGallery Hotel** used to be a coffee plantation.

Later, it hosted a bar in the former enslaved quarters known as Bar dos Descasados (Bar of the Mismatched). The bar earned its name for its reputation of attracting a particular clientele: divorcees – the artsy neighborhood has long been freer than Catholic Brazil.

Bar dos Descasados still exists today, but is only open for private events. Ask the hotel door-attendant to take a peek when passing by, or make a quick visit during an evening that includes a meal at the hotel's decadent restaurant, Térèze (p164).

neo-classical-style estate where Constant lived for just a year before dying of illness, is dedicated to the republican positivist. Wander through the beautiful house and gardens to see furniture from Constant's family, who lived in the house until 1961 before it was transformed into a museum in 1982. Highlights include a painting of the scene at Campo de Santana, now known as Praça da Republica, where Brazil became a republic, as well as the intricately-designed toilet bowl.

The museum's exhibits also honor Constant's work as director of the Imperial Institute for Blind Boys (now the Benjamin Constant Institute) with temporary exhibits of pottery and ceramics made for people with visual impairments. Go ahead and touch the artwork for a sensorial experience.

When you're finished in the house, head down the back steps (facing north) to find ruins of an old *bonde* depot that was in use until 1908.

Catch a Movie

Cine Santa Teresa

If it's a rainy day or you just feel like taking it easy, see a film at **Cine Santa Teresa** *(@cinesantaoficial, Mon-Wed/Fri-Sun R$26/28)*. The former church in the heart of Santa Teresa's Largo dos Guimarães (p160) has just one screen and shows top international films along with independent and Brazilian movies. If you want to watch your movie in English, make sure it says *Leg* (subtitled) rather than *Dub* (dubbed).

Elevated Food from Elevation

Sublime settings for a meal

Santa Teresa's prime location atop the hill makes for spectacular views over this marvelous city. That view gets even better when you're digging into some great food.

Aprazível *(noon-10pm Tue-Sat, to 5pm Sun)* serves up both amazing views and cuisine from its hilltop restaurant, which cascades down onto romantic platforms that feel like a jungle maze. Dishes showcase the country's culinary highlights from the Amazon, Minas Gerais and out to sea with delectable options, such as *açaí* berry guacamole, *moquequinha* (seafood stew), roast pork with pineapple chutney and polenta, and house-made green-noodle vegetarian ravioli.

Another dazzling setting is **Térèze** *(7-11am and 6-10pm)* inside the 5-star MGallery Hotel. The haute French fine-dining restaurant has all the elements of a memorable dining experience, from the decadent menu to the suggested wine pairings and superb views. Start with some oysters before moving on to duck magret with spicy orange sauce, or steak frites, or beetroot gnocchi with coconut milk.

For a more budget-friendly meal with a view, head to **Pizzaria do Hédi** *(6-11pm Thu-Sat)*. It has tasty thin-crust pizza with wine, and occasionally invites bands to set the mood.

SANTA TERESA ART WALK

Wander through bohemian Santa Teresa's visitor areas, keeping your eyes open to see amazing artwork.

START	END	LENGTH
Mirante Jorge Salomão	Bar do Gomes	30 mins, 1.3km

Start with a beautiful vista over the city at ❶ **Mirante Jorge Salomão.** At the foot of the view is a mural of colorful fish, a yellow submarine and robots painted in 2024 by beloved neighborhood artist Gétulio Damado and his son Victor. Stop to photograph a multicolored mural of bespectacled Brazilian author Machado de Assis outside ❷ **Escola Municipal Machado de Assis** and continue to ❸ **Largo do Curvelo**, a beautifully decorated *bonde* stop. Check the clock at ❹ **Vinil do Mustafá** (p161) – it's time for Brazilian music! Peruse and find out when the record shop's next live show is happening. Pause at the ❺ **Bonde Mural** memorializing the fatal 2011 crash before entering Santa Teresa's busiest zone.

Shop-hop to ❻ **Largo dos Guimarães** (p160), on the lookout for the many murals of murdered politician Marielle Franco. Turn the corner to see ❼ **Mosaico Um Bonde para Santa Teresa**, a 2016–21 art project comprising 238 mosaics and 179 local and international artists and collaborators. Left on Rua Monte Alegre, you'll reach the end of this art journey, and perhaps the beginning of a new one involving beers and *bolinhos* (fried, stuffed balls) at neighborhood watering hole, Bar Armazém São Thiago aka 8) ❽ **Bar do Gomes** (p161).

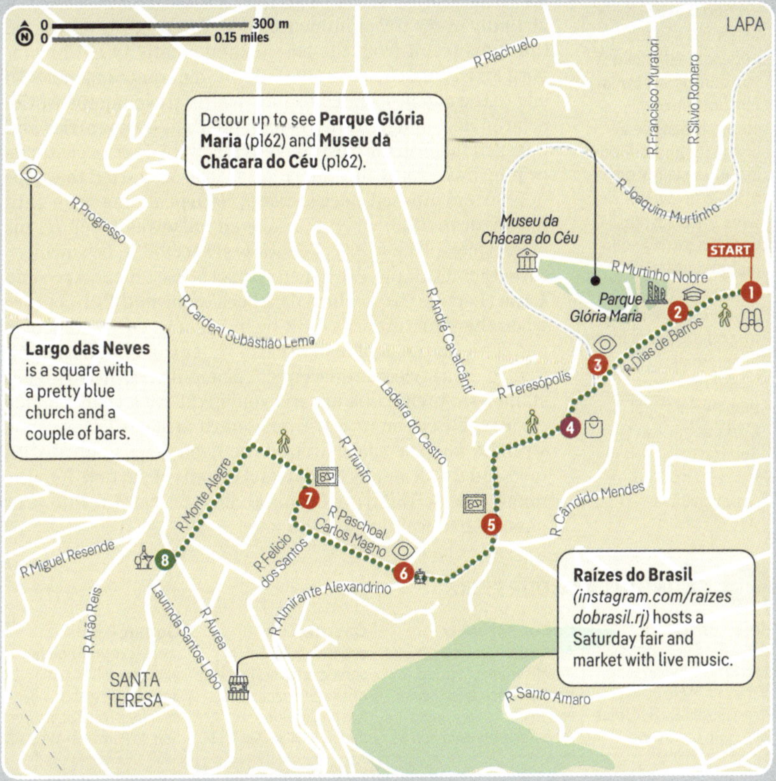

Lapa

The bohemian neighborhood of Lapa remains one of the best places to see live performances and party into the night. And while it bears the scars of centuries of neglect, there's beauty beneath the mess.

PHOTOGRAPHING THE STEPS

Visiting the Escadaria Selarón is a feat of patience, especially if you don't like crowds. The bottom of the steps always has a lineup for photos. Wait in line, or simply take a photo up higher. The huge Brazilian flag near the top is another picturesque spot.

If you don't want anyone in your photo, try coming first thing in the morning.

Need photo inspira- than the image of a grinning Jorge Selarón to the left of the entrance on Rua Joaquim Silva.

Photograph Lapa's Steps & Arches

Escadaria Selarón and Arcos da Lapa

Have you really been to Rio unless you've taken a photo on **Escadaria Selarón**? The Lapa Steps have become a symbol of Rio nearly on the level of Cristo, appearing in music videos like 'Beautiful' by Snoop Dogg and Pharrell and in the feeds of virtually every travel influencer. The 250 brightly decorated tile steps result from the passion and creativity of Chilean-born artist Jorge Selarón (1947–2013) who wanted to make an ode to the city he decided to stay in after traveling the world. Selarón accumulated tiles from more than 60 countries and installed them on the existing steps that were used for centuries by pilgrims to pray in Santa Teresa. Selarón started the steps in 1990 and finished a decade later. He kept adding them until his death in 2013, when his charred body was found on his masterpiece. The cause of death is suspected to be suicide.

Another much-photographed symbol of Rio are the **Arcos da Lapa** (Lapa Arches), which date back to the mid-18th century when the structure was built by indigenous enslaved people and served as an aqueduct to carry water from Rio Carioca to Centro. In a style reminiscent of ancient Rome, the 42 arches stand 64m high. Look up, and you might see a yellow Bonde (p156) cable car on its way from Centro to Santa Teresa. Look straight, and the space around the Lapa Steps is filled with food and drink stands that attract crowds of partiers into the night, especially during Carnaval. Be extra careful with your phone when walking around here.

EATING IN LAPA: OUR PICKS

Hoje Tem Curry: Indian food from Brazilian-born British-Indian son of the late Maze owner. *9am-9:30pm Fri-Sun, from 11am Mon-Thu* $

Sabor Peruano: Authentic Peruvian *ceviche* (raw fish), *chaufa* (fried rice) and *tacu tacu* (*rice and beans*). *noon-11pm Mon-Sat, from 6pm Sun* $$

Cazota: Cuts of expertly grilled meat served on a rooftop with drinks and occasional live music. *noon-midnight Wed-Sat* $$$

Gohan: Popular sushi spot with combo platters, grilled seafood and noodle dishes. *noon-midnight Thu-Sat, to 5pm Sun, to 9pm Mon-Wed* $$

SIGHTS
1 Arcos da Lapa
2 Escadaria Selarón
3 Santuário do Seu Zé Pelintra

SLEEPING
4 Casa Nova
5 Mambembe
6 Selina

EATING
7 Bar Brasil
8 Cazota
9 Cortiço Carioca
10 Gohan
11 Hoje Tem Curry
12 Panka
13 Refeittorio Gastromotiva
14 Sabor Peruano

DRINKING & NIGHTLIFE
15 Armazém Senado
16 Bar da Cachaça
17 Bar do Adalto
18 Rooftop Lapa
19 Suru
20 Vaca Atolada

ENTERTAINMENT
21 Beco do Rato
22 Carioca da Gema
23 Circo Voador
24 Clube dos Democráticos
25 Fundição Progresso
26 Rio Scenarium

SHOPPING
27 Feira do Lavradio

TRANSPORT
28 Bonde Station

CACHAÇA

Enslaved workers on sugar plantations are said to have made the first *cachaça*, Brazil's national spirit. Unlike rum, which is also made with sugarcane, *cachaça* is made using cane juice instead of molasses. *Cachaça* can come unaged (*branca* or *prata*) or aged (*amarela* or *ouro*), and in flavors like Gabriela, which is infused with ginger, cinnamon and cloves.

The most popular way to drink *cachaça* is in a *caipirinha* – a cocktail made with *cachaça*, sugar and limes. *Caipirinhas* may alternatively come with fresh fruit, such as passion fruit, mango or dragon fruit.

Pro tip: ask for *cachaça* brand Velho Barreiro instead of 51.

RIO SCENARIUM

Rio Scenarium

Drink Brazilian Booze

Bottoms up at Bar da Cachaça

When the sun goes and Rio's beaches clear out, the party shifts to Lapa, which fills up to the brim with both locals and international visitors. The epicenter is beneath the Lapa Arches, a seedy area with plenty of stalls to get fast food and sugary caipirinhas. Continue along Av Mem de Sá, to find bar after bar blasting music all night long.

Then head to the intersection of Avs Mem de Sá and Gomes Freire and walk up to the small counter **Bar da Cachaça** (*4pm-5am*) to try Brazil's potent sugarcane spirit. In true Lapa fashion, there are imitators on all sides, but Bar da Cachaça is the original. Choose from a long long list of *cachaça* infusions, including ginger, strawberry and chocolate with coffee. Definitely try jambu – a herb from the Amazon infused into *cachaça*. When you take the shot, hold it in your mouth as long as you can. When you swallow, you'll feel a tingling sensation that makes your mouth feel like leather. It's fun, we promise.

BRAZILIAN MUSIC

What is samba and how did it lead to bossa nova? And what's MPB and favela funk all about? Learn key points about Brazilian music on p253.

See Live Samba

Some of Rio's best venues

If there's but one bar that best exemplifies how music runs through the veins of *cariocas* it's **Vaca Atolada** (*4pm-4am Tue-Sat*). Inside this rundown *botequim* (traditional bar) named after a Brazilian stew of rib steak and cassava, you'll find a quintessential *roda de samba* (musicians playing in a circle) that feels like a spiritual ceremony. Bathed in awful white lighting and surrounded by activist posters, people of all colors, shapes and sizes sing at the top of their lungs, shake, twist and sweat out of their limited clothing.

Another legendary samba venue in Lapa is **Beco do Rato** (*becodorato.com.br, from R$20*). Meaning Alley of the Rat (you'll understand when you go), Beco do Rato hosts terrific samba shows, many of them involving female musicians (a rarity in Rio). Shows spill onto its wide patio where beer is served, as well as snacks like mountains of meat and fries. The party continues on Rua Morais e Vale, with vendors on all sides slinging drinks, blasting music or giving professional massages – you really never know what you'll get on a night out in Lapa.

Rio Scenarium (*rioscenarium.com.br, from R$22.50*) is a samba venue and so much more. Started in 1999 as a symbol of revitalization for the 18th-century residential street, Rua do Lavradio, Rio Scenarium is akin to a museum. Three floors of vintage decor include a photogenic wall of clocks and a metal elevator complete with an operator centered around a stage where performers play samba, *choro* (instrumental jazzy version of samba) and *pagode* (more romantic popular samba). Rio Scenarium also houses a more intimate venue called Dolores. Food is served and there's an all-you-can-eat *feijoada* (black bean stew) on Saturdays from 1pm to 4pm.

Last but not least is **Carioca da Gema** (*barcariocadagema.com.br, from R$30*), a chandelier-lit venue, bar and restaurant that hosts live shows, usually samba, from Tuesday to Saturdays.

MADAME SATÃ

A persisting symbol of Lapa's bohemian edginess is that of João Francisco Dos Santos (1900–76), a drag queen known as Madame Satã (Satan).

Born in Pernambuco in the Brazilian northeast with 16 siblings, Madame Satã became a Lapa fixture as a performer, petty thief and street fighter. Madame Satã would fight police and Johns in defense of sex workers as well as for less valiant reasons, and spent years in prison – legend has it that he participated in 3000 fights and had a razor blade in his shoe.

See Madame Satã and other Lapa figures in a mural on the corner of Ruas Teotônio Regadas and Lapa.

Catch a Concert

Venues Circo Voador and Fundição Progresso

When big-name international and Brazilian acts come to town, they might play at either **Circo Voador** (*circovoador.com.br*) or **Fundição Progresso** (*fundicaoprogresso.com.br*), both located next to Arcos da Lapa.

Circo Voador got its start in a circus tent near Arpoador as an improvised space where theater, dance and music troupes could practice and perform. Then, a project called Rock Voador transformed the venue into sacred ground for the youth of the era, and it became the platform for launching the rock-and-roll movement in Brazil that eventually led to Rock in Rio. The Circo was moved to Lapa at the end of 1982, where it remained open until 1996 when the mayor forced its closure and demolition. In 2002, after a long judicial fight, supporters of the Circo won the right to rebuild the venue, which operates to this day as one of the most coveted venues in Rio.

DRINKING IN LAPA: OUR PICKS

Bar da Cachaça (p168): Tiny bar slinging tinier shots of flavored *cachaça* in a party zone of Lapa. *4pm-5am*

Rooftop Lapa: Rooftop bar above Selina, a hostel in a gorgeous, restored Lapa building, with occasional DJs and good vibes. *4-11pm*

Suru: Hipper-than-thou pink-walled bar with tasty cocktails, *petiscos* and sandwiches. *noon-2am, from 7pm Mon, to 8pm Sun*

Try its Mangaleta cocktail with mango and ginger foam.

Bar do Adalto: Tiny dive bar with writing and photos all over the tables and walls. Good for a late-night drink and sandwich. *7am-4am, to 10pm Sun*

THE NEW MPB

Música popular brasileira or MPB technically means popular Brazilian music, but the word is generally used to refer to music from the late 1960s and 1970s, which included artists from the *tropicália* movement who criticized Brazil's 1964–1985 military dictatorship.

Musicians who sang during that time launched into the stratosphere of stardom and remain in Brazil's pantheon today. They include Gilberto Gil, Jorge Ben Jor, Gal Costa, Caetano Veloso, Maria Bethânia, Novos Baianos and Tom Zé.

Lately, a new generation of MPB artists has come into fashion, led by the sons and grandson of Gilberto Gil: Gilsons. Other new MPB musicians to listen to : Luedji Luna, Julio Secchin and Silva.

JOHN MICHAELS/ALAMY

Across the street in an old foundry, Fundição Progresso is one of the largest independent cultural centers in the country, where art, culture, education and environment come together for positive social effect. The foundry was also saved from demolition, and functions as both a venue and community space where theater, circus, dance groups and musicians can practice and perform. The space offers a range of courses and workshops and has a hanging garden that's used as a laboratory for urban agriculture.

Dance Forró

Clube dos Democraticos

Travelers who've spent time in other Latin American cultures may hope to come to Brazil and dance salsa or bachata. Unfortunately, you're likely out of luck in Brazil. There is, however, *forró*.

Born in northeastern Brazil and popularized by musician Luiz Gonzaga, *forró* is a musical genre commonly played with an accordion, *zabumba* (African drum) and metal triangle; and like salsa, it is danced in pairs with a leader and follower. If you know how to dance *forró* or hope to be swept off your feet, head to **Clube dos Democráticos** *(@clubedosdemocraticoslapa)* on Fridays starting at 9pm for its weekly *forró* night. Established in 1867 as a Carnaval club with money won in the lottery, Clube dos Democráticos is a mural-filled mansion with an enormous dance floor and a long stage that gets covered with musicians.

Clube dos Democráticos

Lunch for Social Good

Eat at Refeittorio Gastromotiva

Lapa has seen better days, with many living on the streets and buildings falling into ruin after the capital of Brazil was moved out of Rio de Janeiro to Brasília in 1960. Instead of turning its back on the neighborhood, a group of chefs, entrepreneurs and a journalist turned a building in Lapa into a training ground for local chefs and a place to support its houseless population.

Started just ahead of the 2016 Summer Olympics in partnership with Italian nonprofit Food for Soul *(foodforsoul.it)*, **Refeittorio Gastromotiva** *(11:30am-3pm Mon-Fri, R$45)* serves a 3-course lunch cooked by a rotating cast of local and international chefs. Fixed-menu lunches have a vegetarian or meat option and are picked up on a tray, cafeteria-style, to be eaten on long tables or on auditorium-style steps in the back. At 5pm, food is then served to 72 unhoused individuals.

Prayer Site for Afro-Brazilian Religions

Santuário do Seu Zé Pelintra

In the shadow of Arcos da Lapa on a seedy side-street (Ladeira de Santa Teresa), there's a sanctuary in honor of Umbanda saint Zé Pelintra. **Santuário do Seu Zé Pelintra** features a statue of the stylish Panama hat- and white-linen-suit-wearing

RUA DO LAVRADIO

Linking Lapa and Praça Tiradentes, 700m Rua do Lavradio started in 1771 by Marquês do Lavradio, former vice-king of Brazil, as Rio's first residential street.

It was home to elites, politicians and artists, and the design of the buildings is spectacular, featuring blue tile and finely carved cornices. After falling into steep decline for decades, Rua do Lavradio was saved by local businesspeople – many of them owners of antique shops – who proposed a weekly market.

The plan worked, and Rua do Lavradio is now a beacon of urban preservation in Rio. It's also a symbol of what could have been if the city had done more to save its historic buildings.

CAPOEIRA CLASS

Learn how to play capoeira, an Afro-Brazilian dance, martial art and game on Fridays in Lapa and on Mondays and Wednesdays in Leme. There are also *rodas* (circle games) under the Lapa Steps. Find out where and when on p114.

RELIGIOUS FREEDOM

Religions with links to Africa have faced discrimination since arriving in the Americas and, despite Brazilian laws protecting freedom of religion since 1946, practitioners of Afro-Brazilian religions Candomblé and Umbanda are frequently attacked.

Fundamentalist evangelical groups, including Brazilian drug gangs that have adopted Christianity, accuse Afro-Brazilian religions of being 'witchcraft' or 'satanism' and launched a 'holy war' against them. In 2023, Candomblé priestess Mãe Bernadete was murdered, and violations of religious freedom are on the rise.

The issue spilled over into the mainstream in May 2024 when Brazilian pop star Anitta, a practitioner of Candomblé, shared photos of herself in religious clothing and said she lost 200,000 followers.

man in a glass case over a white tile platform adorned with candles. Believers will come to light a candle and call upon Seu Zé for guidance in issues of health, business and family. The site was declared a Rio heritage site in 2022.

Umbanda is an Afro-Brazilian religion that started in Rio de Janeiro in the early 20th century that has its roots in Candomblé, a similar religion practiced more commonly in the northeast of the country, which in turn has its roots in African traditions. Both Umbanda and Candomblé believe in *orixás* (spirits) and incorporate elements of Roman Catholicism, which was initially a way for enslaved Africans to practice without angering Portuguese colonists. A difference between the two religions is that Candomblé practitioners believe *orixás* occupy bodies as mediums during ceremonies, while Umbanda believes ancestors' souls occupy bodies, including that of their beloved Zé Pelintra. Similar versions of these religions are found across the Americas, including Cuba's Regla de Ocho (Santeria) as well as Voudou, or Voodoo, in Haiti and New Orleans.

Shop in History

Feira do Lavradio

Every Saturday, one of Rio de Janeiro's best-preserved streets turns into a fun open-air market with some of the best artisanal shopping you'll find anywhere in the city. The street's glorious 18th-century buildings become a living installation as **Feira do Lavradio** *(@feiradolavradio)*, also known as Feira do Rio Antigo, lines the whole street with stalls selling antiques, clothing and crafts. Food stalls, samba bands and the occasional capoeira on the first Saturday of the month at 10am add to the festive atmosphere. The market runs from 10am to 7pm. From 3pm to 11pm, dance to world pop tunes at the *baile charme* (coordinated line dancing) on Rua do Rezende.

Feira do Lavradio got its start in the late 1990s after a group of the street's business owners figured a street market would be a good way to convince the city to preserve the historic street. After infrastructure work finally managed to stop sewage from overflowing onto the street during rainy days, the market was born and has become the place to be on Saturdays.

PARTY NEARBY

When you're finished shopping at Feira do Lavradio, head over to perpendicular Rua do Senado for a samba party in front of **Armazém Senado**. The street also has one of Rio's best restaurants.

EATING IN LAPA: OUR PICKS

Cortiço Carioca: Brazilian dishes like *mexido* – mixed meat and rice plates. *noon-midnight, to 6pm Sun & Mon* $$

Refeittorio Gastromotiva (p171): Three-course fixed menu lunch by rotating local and international chefs. *11am-3pm Mon-Fri* $$

Bar Brasil: One of Rio's oldest establishments (1907), serving German sauerkraut and wurst. *11am-midnight, to 2am Fri & Sat, to 5pm Sun* $$

Panka: Lapa is blessed with not one, but two excellent Peruvian restaurants. This one's always full. *noon-11pm Mon-Sat, to 6pm Sun* $$

ROGER CANNON/ALAMY

Santuário do Seu Zé Pelintra (p171)

Researched by Marisa Megan Paska

CENTRO & ZONA NORTE

URBAN SPRAWL WITH HISTORY, ART, MUSIC

The artsy and edgy neighborhoods of Centro, Porto Maravilha and Zona Norte are home to samba, the church of football, unique artistic movements and Afro-Brazilian history and culture.

When the Portuguese began construction of their first South American colony, the south zone of the city didn't exist. It was in the modern-day Centro neighborhood that Rio de Janeiro – and the entire country of Brazil – got its start. Built on land taken from the Tupinamba indigenous group and on the backs of enslaved Africans, colonial-era houses and palaces were erected, and informal communities, destined to become the city's first favelas, began to take hold. Today, the palaces have become museums and galleries, and, thanks to the Porto Maravilha renovations, Afro-Brazilian history has been uncovered and preserved. Delve into samba, Carnaval and football – and learn about Brazil beyond white colonialism.

INCLUDES

Carnaval, Sambódromo da Marquês de Sapucaí (p188)

See p225 for places to stay in Centro and Zona Norte.

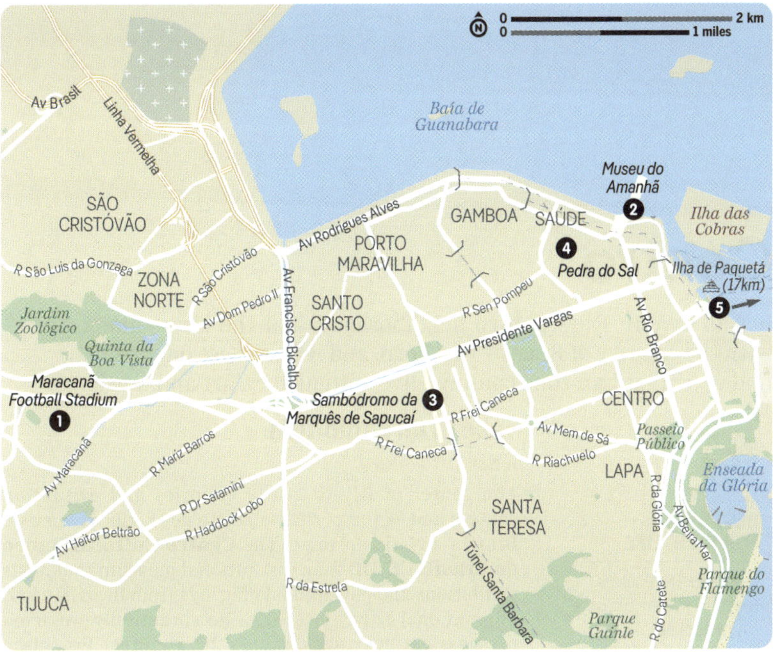

Highlights

❶ Sambódromo Marquês do Sapucaí

Marvel as this 700m-long runway comes alive with light, color and music during Carnaval season. **p188**

❷ Museu do Amanhã

Explore the exhibitions at this LEED-certified architecturally unique museum that asks us to think about tomorrow. **p182**

❸ Maracanã Football Stadium

Catch a game at Brazil's largest football stadium and watch a game with the faithful. **p194**

❹ Pedra do Sal

Get your groove on at the cradle of Rio's Afro-Brazilian culture, with lively samba events every Monday. **p186**

❺ Ilha de Paquetá

Jump on a ferry to this small island (pictured above) with no motor vehicles that feels like stepping back in time. **p196**

Getting Around

Public Transport

These zones have infinite transportation options, which seem to be constantly improved – arrive by bus, metro, VLT or train.

Taxi or Rideshare

Taxis and rideshare cars are an easy and inexpensive way to get around, and always recommended if you're going somewhere after dark.

Walking

Although these areas are a bit gritty, walking during the day is fine, just take care of your phone if you're using maps. When in doubt, hop in a taxi.

Centro

It was here in Rio's Centro neighborhood that the city – along with the country of Brazil – was born, and where these days you'll find a gritty urban zone coming alive with history, art and music.

BEST SPOTS FOR NIGHTLIFE

D-EDGE: São Paulo's legendary nightclub gets a new address along Rio's Pier Mauá. Three stories with rooftop views deliver incredible electronic all-nighters.

Wells Beer & BBQ: Artisanal beer and BBQ bar in the center of Rio that's home to all-night samba and street parties.

Nova Gafieira: The place to go if you're serious about dancing. Every night offers a different musical style, spotlighting samba and *forró*.

Rua de Cerveja: This development project on Rua Carioca is creating a pedestrian street lined with craft-beer bars that's quickly becoming Centro's new hot spot.

The Home: This full-on techno and house club is a go-to for the gay crowd. Opens every Saturday at 11:59pm.

Take In an Exhibition

A dose of culture

The center of Rio is full of galleries and exhibition centers and is the perfect place to get a global view on Brazil's artistic universe. The **Centro Cultural Banco do Brasil (CCBB)** is an institutional museum that hosts exhibitions and educational offerings from Brazilian and international artists, located inside a beautifully preserved neoclassical building designed by architect Francisco Joaquim Béthencourt da Silva in 1880. In the 1920s, the building became the headquarters for Banco do Brasil, which it remained until 1989, when the bank turned the space into a cultural center and art museum. The CCBB has been named one of the most-visited art museums in the world, and is one of the country's central sites for seeing international artists. Or check out smaller hot-spots like **A Gentil Carioca**, a contemporary gallery founded by a a few artists that features up-and-coming artists and is a key driver of the artistic conversation in the city.

Architectural Library of Dreams

Real Gabinete Português de Leitura

In 1837, 43 Portuguese immigrants got together and decided to dedicate themselves to the creation of a library –to improve access to reading materials both for members of the group as well as for other Portuguese immigrants in the country. Over time, their project grew, and they decided to build a formal house for their books. Architect Rafael da Silva Castro designed the Neo-Manueline style building (a Portuguese architecture style reminiscent of the Renaissance Gothic style) that would become the **Real Gabinete Português de Leitura** *(realgabinete.com.br; free)* built between 1880 and 1887. The facade was inspired by the Mosteiro dos Jerónimos in Lisbon, while the rooftop stained-glass window laid in iron was the first of its style to be built in Brazil.

CENTRO

0 400 m
0 0.2 miles

D-EDGE (900m)
Av Venezuela
R Sacadura Cabral
Morro de São Bento
R Dom Gerardo
Baía de Guanabara
Ferry to Palacio da Ilha Fiscal
R do Jogo da Bola
Pç Major Valô
São Bento
R Viscon de Inhaúma
R Sen Pompeu
R Acre
Av Rodrigues Alves
R Camerino
R da Conceição
R Teófilo Otoni
Pç Pio X
Ferry to Ilha de Paquetá
Ferry to Niterói
Praça XV
Candelária
Av Presidente Vargas
Av Marechal Floriano
Uruguaiana
R do Rosário
R do Ouvidor
Pç XV (Quinze) de Novembro
Presidente Vargas
R dos Andradas
R da Conceição
Av Passos
R da Alfândega
R Uruguaiana
R Gonçalves Dias
Pç Marechal Âncora
R Dom Manuel
Colombo
R da Assembléia
R São Jose
Av Erasmo Braga
Saara
R de Buenos Aires
Largo de San Francisco de Paula
Sete de Setembro
Tiradentes
Av Nilo Peçanha
R Mal Aguinaldo
R da Carioca
R da Constituição
Carioca
R Visconde do Rio Branco
Largo da Carioca
Av Almirante Barroso
Av General Justo
R Pedro I
Av República do Paraguai
R México
Av Graça Aranha
Aeroporto Santos Dumont
Av República do Chile
Pç Floriano
R do Senado
Av F Roosevelt
Bonde Station
R Ubaldino Amaral
R da Relação
R do Lavradio
R Evaristo da Veiga
R de Santa Luzia
Antônio Carlos
R dos Inválidos
Av Gomes Freire
R dos Arcos
Av Presidente Wilson
Av Beira Mar
Santos Dumont
Arcos do Lapa
R do Passeio
Av Infante Dom Henrique
Parque do Flamengo
Av Mem de Sá
Prodigy Santos Dumont (200m)
R do Rezende
R Jardel Jercolis
R Riachuelo
LAPA

SIGHTS
1 A Gentil Carioca
2 Centro Cultural Banco do Brasil
3 Queerioca
4 Real Gabinete Português de Leitura
5 Teatro Rival
6 Theatro Municipal

SLEEPING
7 Vila Galé

EATING
8 Café Tero
9 Casa Paladino
10 Confeitaria Colombo
11 Govardhana Harí
12 Hachiko
13 Kim Pocha
14 Labuta Bar
15 Lilia

DRINKING & NIGHTLIFE
16 Mauacba Skate and Coffee Shop
17 Nova Gafieira
18 Rua de Cerveja
19 The Home
20 Wells Beer & BBQ

SHOPPING
21 Feira de Antiguidades
22 Saara

EATING IN CENTRO: OUR PICKS

Lilia: Creative and chic without pretension; a lunchtime favorite for those in the city's center. *11:30am-3pm & 7:30-10:30pm Mon-Sat* $$$

Café Tero: An oasis of charm, offering homemade, artisanal pastas and mock- and cocktails. *noon-6pm Mon-Thu, to 7pm Fri-Sun* $$

Confeitaria Colombo: Known as much for its resplendent, old-world decor as its cakes and pastries. *11am-6pm Mon-Sat* $$

Labuta Bar: Mouthwatering bar fare enjoyed on bar stools and beach chairs on the street out front. *11:30-8pm Mon-Sat, noon-5pm Sun* $$

FAMOUS & HISTORIC BUILDINGS OF CINELÂNDIA

See some of Cinelândia's most famous, ornate and unique buildings in this culturally insightful walking tour.

START	END	LENGTH
Catedral Metropolitana de São Sebastião	Museu de Belas Artes	1.6km; 23 mins

Start off at the ❶ **Catedral Metropolitana de São Sebastião**, a 75m-tall cone-shaped catholic cathedral, thought to be inspired by the Mayan Pyramids, that architect Edgar de Oliveira da Fonseca designed in the 1970s, before walking over to the ❷ **Teatro Riachuelo**, which occupies a listed 1890s building where the first sound feature film was played in 1920. Pass by another famous theater – the ❸ **Cine Odeon**, an early 20th-century cinema immortalized in the song 'Odeon', before heading to the ❹ **Centro Cultural da Justiça Federal**, a belle-epoque construction once home to the country's supreme court; it's since been turned into a cultural center *(noon-7pm Tue-Sun; free)*. Make your way to the ❺ **Palácio Pedro Ernesto**, a 1923 building that's the seat of the city's municipal government, and learn about its politics, architecture and history on a free tour *(10am-3:30pm Mon-Fri)* – although note that tank tops, flip-flops and shorts aren't allowed. Just across the street you'll find the ❻ **Biblioteca Nacional** *(National Library)*, another ornate building with free guided tours *(10am-5pm Mon-Fri)* that's also considered by UNESCO to be one of the 10 largest national libraries in the world. Finally, end your stroll at the ❼ **Museu Nacional de Belas Artes**, where you'll find a 20,000-piece collection of 19th-century paintings and sculptures in an ornate 1908 listed building.

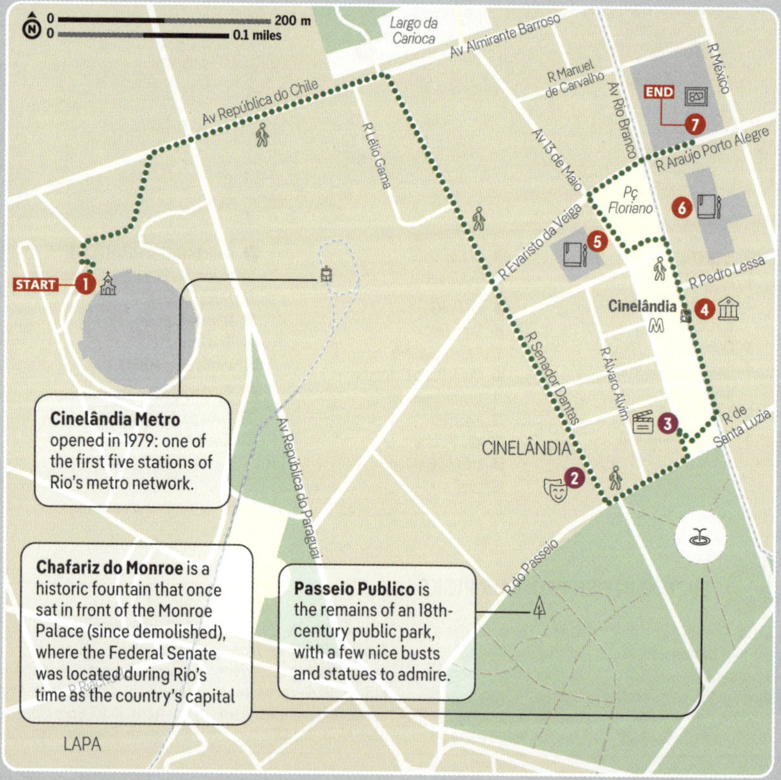

Cinelândia Metro opened in 1979: one of the first five stations of Rio's metro network.

Chafariz do Monroe is a historic fountain that once sat in front of the Monroe Palace (since demolished), where the Federal Senate was located during Rio's time as the country's capital

Passeio Publico is the remains of an 18th-century public park, with a few nice busts and statues to admire.

ROBERTHARDING/ALAMY

Theatro Municipal

One of Brazil's Most Beautiful Theaters

A diamond in the rough

Campaigning for the **Theatro Municipal** *(theatromunicipal.rj.gov.br)*, the headpiece of the Cinelândia square, began soon after Brazil's declaration of the Republic in 1889 (the end of the monarchy), although it wasn't until 1905 that construction on the French-style theater designed by Brazilian Francisco de Oliveira Passos and Frenchman Albert Guilbert began.

The building was completed in just 4½ years – possibly a Brazilian record – and opened in 1909 with a capacity for 1739 spectators (later expanded to 2361). It still has opera, ballet, classical concerts and theater productions, and even occasionally offers tickets for R$2 to R$10 (watch its Instagram). You can also visit for a guided tour Tuesday to Friday *(R$20, no prebooking)*.

Where Drag Dreams are Born

Teatro Rival's concerts and shows

Head over to the **Teatro Rival** *(teatrorival.com.br)*, a small, subterranean theater open since 1934 for a concert, a play or one of its famous drag shows. Under the leadership of Américo Leal, the theater became a symbol of resistance in the 1970s during the dictatorship; and later, a stage for many greats, such as Arlindo Cruz, Beth Carvalho, Zeca Pagodinho and Elza Soares in the '90s. The theater, which celebrated its 90th birthday in 2024, continues to have a full schedule of events.

THE WOMEN OF DRAG

In the 1980s, the Teatro Rival was the site of what would become nationally famous drag shows with 'transvestite drag' queens, launching the careers of divas like Rogéria, Jane di Castro and Divina Valéria, among others. The group revolutionized thinking about sexuality and gender roles and challenged morals of the era – a big task in the middle of a repressive military dictatorship.

The journey of this unique group to stardom became the topic of a 2016 documentary, *Divinas Divas*, directed by Leandra Leal.

In kind, the Teatro Rival continues to provide space for this type of alternative theater – two of its main attractions these days are an event and contest called Drag Star and Gongada Drag.

SKATE CENTER

Praça XV is also the unofficial center of street skateboarding in Rio de Janeiro, after a movement by local skaters, entitled I Love XV, challenged a law prohibiting skateboarding in the square, and managed to win permission from the city government to use Praça XV (and the nearby Praça Marechal Âncora) for skateboarding. To celebrate, the group, which renamed itself Coletivo XV, built a 5m-long skateboard statue called 'Piskate', designed by skater and graphic designer Jorge Cupim, and installed it at Praça XV on International Skateboarding Day in 2015. The collective is often found at the nearby **Mauacba Skate and Coffee Shop** *(@mauacba skatecoffee)*, located right in front of the VLT's ticket office in the square.

ZUMA PRESS, INC./ALAMY

Shopping, Saara

Myriad Mazelike Shopping Streets

Extreme outdoor shopping

Just near the Uruguaiana metro station, you'll find more than 1000 small shops along 12 streets that make up one of Rio's most unique commercial zones. **Saara** (Sociedade de Amigos e Adjacências da Rua da Alfândega) got its start in the 19th century, when Portuguese merchants set up shop to sell fabrics and foodstuffs from Portugal. It remains an important commercial zone, supporting small local commerce typically owned by immigrant or minority groups. Find everything from fabrics to flowers to notebooks and home goods on sale. It's also the place to be pre-Carnaval, as Saara has everything you need to put together the perfect costume.

One of Latin America's Largest Antique Fairs

For treasure hunters

Every Saturday morning from 8am to 2pm in Praça XV, stands stretch out from just in front of the Paço Imperial nearly to the ferryboat terminal, selling all kinds of antique rugs, furniture, records, knickknacks and secondhand clothes at **Feira de Antiguidades** *(Antique Fair)*. There are officially 366 stalls and just over 600 sellers registered for the event, although there are numerous unofficial sellers on the scene, as well as a number of stalls selling snacks, meals and drinks. Go early for the best finds.

EATING IN CENTRO: BEST INTERNATIONAL EATS

Govardhana Hari: Vegetarian Indian food in a simple, incense-infused dining room. Exceptionally loyal clientele. *11:30am-3:30pm Mon-Fri* **$$**

Kim Pocha: Following street-fair success with its contemporary-Korean food, this Korean family opened a *botequim*-style spot. *11:30am-3:30pm Tue-Sat* **$$**

Casa Paladino: Over 100-year-old shop/snack bar known for its overstuffed sandwiches, omelets and fritters. *7am-8:30pm Mon-Fri* **$**

Hachiko: Japanese fusion restaurant serving modern flavors in a charming loft-style space. *11:30am-11pm Mon-Sat* **$$$**

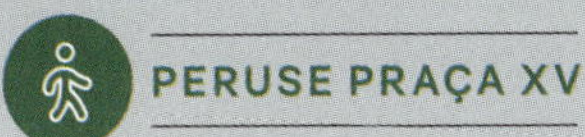

PERUSE PRAÇA XV

Wander down some of Rio's first streets, where you'll find the perfect blend of history and contemporary culture.

START	END	LENGTH
Praça VX de Novembro	Casa França-Brasil	1.1km, 15 min

Start off at ❶ **Praça XV (Quinze) de Novembro**, a central square that's been around since the 16th century. The square – which was renamed in honor of the November 15, 1889, the day Brazil proclaimed itself a Republic – hosts numerous open-air markets and events, and is also the jumping-off point for ferry transfer to the islands and Niterói. Flanking the square you'll find the ❷ **Paço Imperial**, an 18th-century former residence to Rio's governors that's now a museum and art-exhibition space *(free entry)*.

From there, walk under the ❸ **Arco de Teles** along the Travessa do Comércio, past ❹ **Casa Carmen Miranda** (her crumbling former home), until you hit the ❺ **Rua Ouvidor**, one of the city's first streets that's lined with bars, restaurants and home to a lively Saturday afternoon samba.

Turn onto the Rua do Mercado, where the ❻ **Junta Local** has built their headquarters, before continuing along the waterfront to the ❼ **Espaço Cultural da Marinha**, a nautically themed museum run by the navy that's an awesome stop if you're with kids.

Then, head over to visit the ❽ **Casa França-Brasil**, an 1820s construction that was the first neoclassical building in the city, and served as the customs house for more than a century. It was restored in the 1980s and turned into a contemporary arts center in the 1990s, which it remains today.

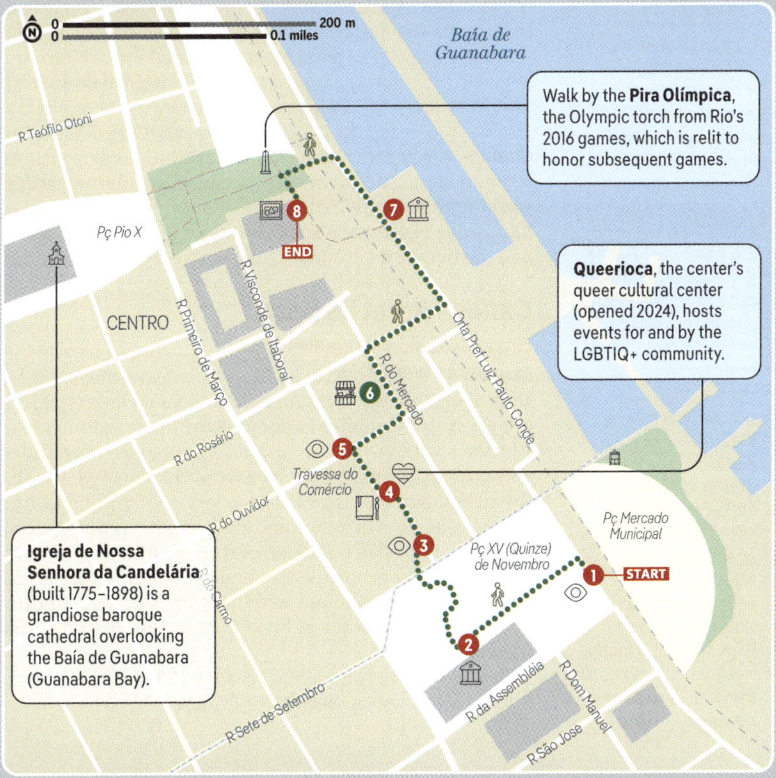

Walk by the **Pira Olímpica**, the Olympic torch from Rio's 2016 games, which is relit to honor subsequent games.

Queerioca, the center's queer cultural center (opened 2024), hosts events for and by the LGBTIQ+ community.

Igreja de Nossa Senhora da Candelária (built 1775–1898) is a grandiose baroque cathedral overlooking the Baía de Guanabara (Guanabara Bay).

Porto Maravilha

Rio's most recent urban-renovation project has created a new touristic zone in the city's center that keeps growing and changing, while simultaneously uncovering and preserving some of the country's most important history.

PRAÇA MAUÁ HISTORY

During Brazil's early colonial period, what is now the Praça Mauá was once a small beach, aptly named Prainha. Up through the 19th century the water lapped against the modern-day Pedra do Sal, which is where the dockworkers unloaded salt and other goods, until the city realized its need for a port that could receive larger ships.

In the beginning of the 20th century, the Pier and Praça Mauá were built where the old Largo da Prainha once stood, and named after the Baron of Mauá, a pioneering entrepreneur responsible for creating the Bank of Brazil. A statue, inaugurated in 1910, still stands in the square in his honor.

Get Interactive at Museu de Amanhã

Time to think about tomorrow

Rio's **Museu do Amanhã** *(Museum of Tomorrow; museudoamanha.org.br; 11am-6pm Tue-Sun, R$30 timed entry, online reservations recommended)* is an interactive science museum that raises the question: what will our world look like 50 years from now? The jewel of the renovated Praça Mauá, the museum's extraordinary structure was designed by Spanish architect Santiago Calatrava, is covered in photovoltaic panels and was LEED certified by the Green Building Council. Permanent and temporary exhibitions help visitors to understand the effect that humans have on the natural world and our potential role in changing the outcome of tomorrow. The space also hosts numerous events, concerts and parties on its grounds, which are very worth visiting.

Carioca Art at its Best

Museum dedicated to Rio

Museu de Arte do Rio *(MAR; museudeartedorio.org.br; 11am-6pm Tue-Sun, adult/under 5 or over 60 R$20/free)* is a unique, 6-story building connecting the historical Dom Jõao VI Palace with an old bus terminal via a modern sky bridge and terrace, purpose-built as part of the Porto Maravilha urban renovation project. The eclectic, historic building serves a huge exhibition hall with eight unique spaces, featuring both short- and long-term exhibitions (although all are temporary); while the modern building focuses on educational courses and activities for the surrounding communities, in what is known as the Escola do Olhar (school of seeing).

There's free entry for all on Tuesdays. There is also an art library on-site open Tuesday to Friday.

SIGHTS
1 Mural Etnias
2 Museu de Arte do Rio
3 Museu do Amanhã

ACTIVITIES
4 AquaRio
5 Rio Star

EATING
6 Café Ateliê Benoliel
7 Café do MAR
8 Shukran Moujab

DRINKING & NIGHTLIFE
see 8 Quintal do Porto Bistrô

The Waterfront Wonder of Pier Mauá

Making the center more marvelous

The waterfront warehouse spaces of Pier Mauá host everything from tech conferences like **Rio Innovation Week** to festivals, conferences and even ranging parties, all with views of Baía de Guanabara. External walls are decorated with street-art murals (like the Guinness-record-winning **Mural Etnias**) and integrated with the VLT tram for easy access.

Towards the end of the pier you'll find the **Rio Star** observation wheel (Rio's giant Ferris wheel) and the port for arriving cruise ships – all part of the urban revitalization project undertaken in the area, better known as the Porto Maravilha.

EATING AT PRAÇA MAUÁ: OUR PICKS

Café Ateliê Benoliel: This crowded gastronomic museum cafe sits inside the Museu de Amanhã. *10am-6pm Tue-Sun* $$$

Café do MAR: Specialty coffees and desserts shine; and the lunch plates aren't bad, either. On MAR's ground floor. *10am-6pm Tue-Sun* $$$

Shukran Moujab: Middle Eastern cafe inside Portinho *mercado* serves sandwiches, snacks and meze platters. *9am-6pm Mon-Fri, 11am-6pm Sat & Sun* $$

Quintal do Porto Bistrô: Burgers, plates and bar snacks served with love at Portinho *mercado*. *10am-6pm Mon-Sat* $$

PORTO MARAVILHA

The **Porto Maravilha** project, which began in 2009, works to revitalize a 5-million-sq-meter area of Rio's central port zone, specifically in and around the Pier Mauá.

The 30-year, R$8-billion initiative has already seen the pier restored to use; two new museums built (the MAR and the Museu de Amanhã); and several new transportation links installed, including the VLT train, tunnels and a network of bicycle lanes. Excavations related to the project also unearthed a surprising amount of Rio's Afro-Brazilian history, including the uncovering of the now-UNESCO-protected Valongo Pier, which is thought to have received more African enslaved people than any other port in the Americas.

DENI WILLIAMS/SHUTTERSTOCK

AquaRio

South America's Largest Aquarium

Underwater Love

This 26,000 sq meter **AquaRio** *(aquariomarinhodorio.com.br; adult/under 21, over 60, students/age 3-11 R$120/75/70)* is South America's largest aquarium, if you're measuring by liters of *água* (water). The five-floor, 28-tank exhibition takes you past 4.5 million liters of saltwater, where nearly 10,000 animals of 350 different species from all four oceans reside.

The main event is a 7m-tall tank with a plexiglass tunnel passing through, giving you the feeling of being immersed in the ocean as rays and reef sharks pass over your head. The private institution located at the north end of Pier Mauá also features the largest solar roof installed in any urban area of Brazil; the 6000 sq meters of panels cuts the aquarium's energy costs up to 30%.

Book your tickets online for a discount (and to skip the lines).

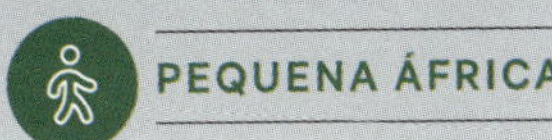

PEQUENA ÁFRICA

During the Porto Maravilha project, some of Rio's most important Afro-Brazilian sites were 'unearthed' and now form a part of the city known as 'Little Africa'.

START	END	LENGTH
Largo de São Francisco da Prainha	Instituto dos Pretos Novos (IPN)	2.1km; 30 mins

Start off at the 1 **Largo de São Francisco da Prainha**, where you'll find a 2 **statue of Mercedes Baptista** (1921–2014), the first Black ballerina of Rio's municipal theater (1948). Climb the stairs up to the 3 **Morro da Conceição**, one of the city's first communities where some still-surviving Portuguese-style houses mark the history, before heading to 4 **Valongo Observatory**, an astrological teaching observatory founded in 1881.

Walk down through the 5 **Jardim Suspenso do Valongo**, a 20th-century garden restored by the Porto Maravilha project, which occupies the space once belonging to *casas de engordo*, where enslaved people were brought to be fed before being sold into slavery. Head to the 6 **Praça Jornal do Comércio**, where an educational and artistic memorial remembers the enslaved Africans brought over during the colonial period, then walk across the square to the UNESCO 7 **Cais do Valongo** (Valongo Pier). According to informal records, the pier, which was uncovered in 2011 by the Porto Maravilha project, was the site of arrival for more than a million enslaved Africans – the most of anywhere in the Americas.

Finally, continue to the 8 **Instituto dos Pretos Novos (IPN)**, an Afro-Brazilian cultural center that also houses the Cemitério dos Pretos Novos, a former cemetery for enslaved people discovered in 1996 under the historic mansion.

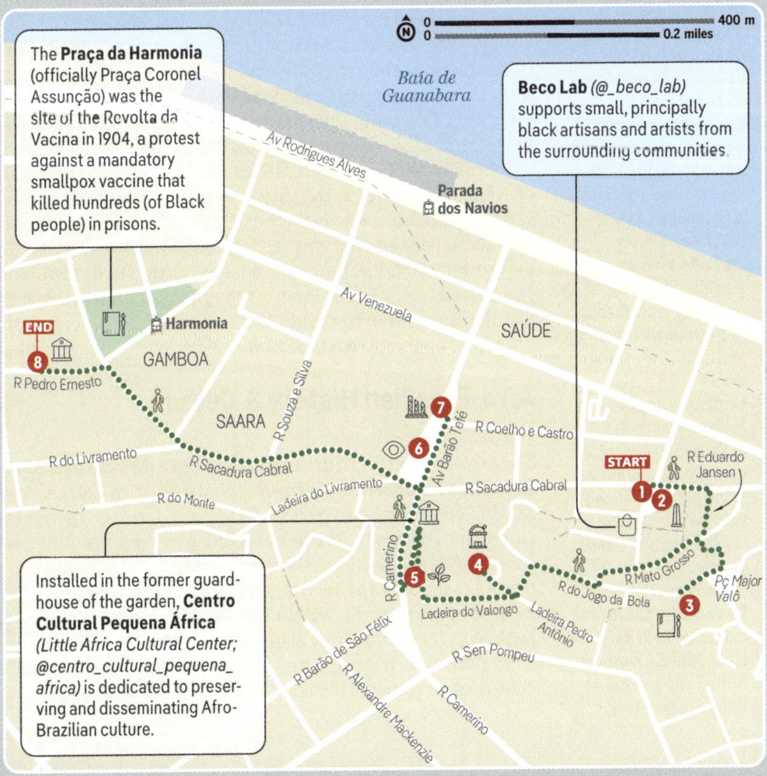

The **Praça da Harmonia** (officially Praça Coronel Assunção) was the site of the Revolta da Vacina in 1904, a protest against a mandatory smallpox vaccine that killed hundreds (of Black people) in prisons.

Beco Lab *(@_beco_lab)* supports small, principally black artisans and artists from the surrounding communities.

Installed in the former guardhouse of the garden, **Centro Cultural Pequena África** *(Little Africa Cultural Center; @centro_cultural_pequena_africa)* is dedicated to preserving and disseminating Afro-Brazilian culture.

Saúde, Gamboa & Santo Cristo

Rio's original port district is known as the birthplace of samba, the epicenter of Little Africa and the heartbeat of Rio's Carnaval; while being peppered with urban art, music and counterculture.

TIA CIATA

Hilária Batista de Almeida, better known as Tia Ciata, was a Bahian-born mãe de Santo from the Candomblé religion, who, after moving from Salvador da Bahia to Rio, became a grande dame in the city's Black community. Tia Ciata's house was already a central meeting place, thanks to the religious events and celebrations she would hold, but it cemented its place in history when Tia Ciata began to open her home to *sambistas* in the post-abolition years when playing samba was prohibited by law.

Her former home – **Casa da Tia Ciata** *(tia ciata.org.br)* in Rio's Little Africa – has been turned into a museum that tells her story.

Learn About the Birthplace of Samba

Epicenter of African culture

Pedra do Sal was once a meeting point for the dockworkers of Rio, as well as the main access to the Morro da Conceição, one of the city's first informal residential areas for the lower class (aka, favela).

When the city was first built, the waters of the Baía de Guanabara reached the cove, and its name – Salt Rock – came from the salt shipments unloaded there from arriving ships. In the 1860s, following the Paraguayan War, the region became so concentrated with an Afro-Brazilian population that it was unofficially baptized Little Africa, and became the epicenter of African culture in the city. From here, the first *carioca* sambas were born and even the first Carnaval samba schools.

In 2005, Pedra do Sal was recognized as an Urban Quilombo by the Fundação Palmares, and soon after its descendants were given rights to the land, although there is an active fight against the church to secure their heritage. You can visit the animated open-air *roda de samba* held every Monday evening.

Afro-Brazilian History & Culture

Historic museum

The 2024-reopened **Museu da História e da Cultura Afro-Brasileira** *(Museum of Afro-Brazilian History and Culture, MUHCAB; rio.rj.gov.br/web/muhcab; free)* is dedicated to telling the story of the enslaved Africans brought over by European colonists, their lives and their effect on the development of Brazil and the Americas. The museum, which is located in the historic Colégio José Bonifácio (a *palacete* dating back to 1877), counts over 2500 items in its collection, ranging from paintings to sculptures to photographs from across the centuries. It's open Thursday to Sunday, 10am to 5pm.

HIGHLIGHTS

1 Sambódromo Marquês do Sapucaí

SIGHTS

2 Casa da Tia Ciata
3 Fábrica Bhering
4 Museu da História e da Cultura Afro-Brasileira
5 Pedra do Sal

EATING

6 Armazém 04
see 6 Bar da Dulce
see 6 Casa Porto
see 6 Dois de Fevereiro

Visit an Artists' Factory

Artistic warehouse of Fábrica Bhering

Don't miss a stop at the **Fábrica Bhering** *(@fabrica.bhering; free)*, a six-story 15,000-sq-meter warehouse that was once a candy and chocolate factory. Transformed in the early 2000s, it gained popularity when it was added to the official ArtRio circuit in 2011. These days, there are nearly 50 artist ateliers on site, alongside 40 plus entrepreneurs running small businesses inside of what is now a protected building. Beyond art, you'll find a secondhand clothing store, handmade furniture from demolition wood, a sweet shop and cafe, a bistro, a rooftop terrace and even a used-book store. The factory, which opens from 9am to 6pm Monday to Friday and 10am to 7pm on Saturdays, also has a monthly 'open house' event and frequently hosts a lively samba group on Saturday afternoons.

EATING IN THE LARGO DA PRAINHA: OUR PICKS

Armazém 04: Retro venue with huge variety of bar snacks and over 100 *cachaça* brands. *11am-midnight Mon-Thu; 11am-1pm Fri & Sat* $$

Casa Porto: Two-story hot spot. Lunch at huge bay windows overlooking the praça. *noon-10pm Tue & Wed, to 1pm Fri & Sat, to 9pm Sun* $$

Dois de Fevereiro: Expect Bahian favorites like *bobó, moqueca* and *baião dos dois. 11:30am-5pm Tue-Thu & Sun, to 10pm Fri & Sat* $$

Bar da Dulce: Corner *botequim* serving typical bar snacks and ice-cold beers in typical *pé-sujo* style. *8am-11:30pm Tue-Sun* $

BYDRONEVIDEOS/SHUTTERSTOCK

TOP EXPERIENCE

Sambódromo da Marquês de Sapucaí

The Sambódromo da Marquês de Sapucaí is the home of Rio Carnaval's spectacular samba parades, and the 700m-long runway is renowned for both its architecture and its history. It was designed by Brazilian architectural legend Oscar Niemeyer – also famous for designing the United Nations Headquarters in New York City – on the same site where the samba schools already held their annual parade.

DON'T MISS

- The Concentration
- A Curva
- Velha Guarda
- A Bateria
- Comissão de frente
- Alegorias
- Ala das Baianas
- Ala das Passistas

Construction

An anomaly in Brazil, the Sambódromo was constructed in just 120 days, with three shifts of workers working around the clock to ensure the site was ready for the 1984 parade (it was, just barely).

Three years later, the site gained its official name, the Passarela Professor Darcy Ribeiro, in honor of the well-known anthropologist who was one of the main drivers of the project, and it was Ribeiro himself who gave the Avenue it's popular nickname – Sambódromo – which combines samba with the Greek term *dromo* meaning an avenue or corridor used for

PRACTICALITIES

Scan this QR code for more information.

running (although you'll also hear it referred to as the Avenida or the Sapucaí as well).

Of the 700m Sapucaí, 560m are parade grounds, which the samba schools of the Carioca Special Group are expected to parade down in all their glory in 75 minutes or less, to avoid a time penalty.

Parade Parts

Of Rio de Janeiro's more than 70 registered samba schools, 12 make up what is known as the Grupo Especial, who perform on the Sunday, Monday and Tuesday night of Carnaval. Here are some of the elements to watch out for.

Concentration

Also called the *esquenta*, or warm up, the concentration is the moment before everything gets underway. While one school is parading, the next school will be in their *esquenta*, just off the Av along one of the city's main freeways, getting ready for their turn.

Grito de guerra

When it's time for a parade to begin, the announcer will present the school and their theme over the microphone. The moment is marked by fireworks – in 2023, schools used silent fireworks in respect to members of the crowd with autism and/or other mental disabilities – and the *grito de guerra*, or war cry (each school has its own) is repeated among the ranks as the cars begin to move.

The Curve

To enter onto the Av, schools have to make a 90-degree turn known simply as a *curva* (the curve). It's a very technical moment, during which 9m-tall parade cars topped with dancers need to turn in time to the music without falling over. For anyone who has paraded, it's also considered to be one of the most emotional moments of the night, when you first see the Av's blazing lights and colors.

School Divisions

Comissão de frente

The Comissão de Frente (commission of the front) is the first line of the parade, consisting of 10 to 15 people who perform an elaborate choreography meant to introduce the school's theme. Their performances are often very theatrical and can last several minutes.

Alegorias

The Alegorias are the parade cars, which are essentially moving sculptures that can reach up to 9m, 80cm tall (but no taller, so as not to hit the TV cameras), and are elaborately decorated to fit with the theme of the year. The cars are moved by human power only – motors are not allowed, due to fire risk – and are topped with dancers in elaborate costumes known as the *destaque* and *semi-destaque*.

TYPES OF TICKETS

If you want to watch what *cariocas* call the best show on earth, you'll need to plan ahead to get tickets. *Arquibancada*, or the bench seats, are the cheapest but sell out exceptionally quickly (currently sold on Ticketmaster), while the Camarotes, or VIP boxes, which are more expensive, will often include free food and drink and still have availability closer to the event. Carnaval ARARA *(@carnaval daarara)* is a favorite.

BEYOND SAMBA

Between bench seats and VIP Boxes, the Sambódromo has room for over 80,000 spectators. Outside of Carnaval season, the site also hosts concerts and events – ranging from motorcycle races to operas to evangelical conventions – and even held the archery and marathon events during the 2016 Olympic Games, as well as archery for the Paralympics. In 2021, the Sambadrome was declared Historic and Artistic Patrimony.

TOP TIPS

- Even those who aren't members of a samba school are able to purchase a costume and join the parade.
- Most samba schools have a website where you can choose an available costume (beware of the hot and heavy ones), although they're a bit difficult to use, and you'll be on your own getting to and from the Av.
- If you've got the cash, Carnaval-specific agencies like **Experience Carnival** *(experiencecarnival.rio)* can get you in on the action – even on top of the parade floats themselves –with transport, photography and even samba classes included.

Mestre-sala e porta-bandeira

The *mestre-sala* (dance master) and *porta-bandeira* (flag-bearer) are a couple who present a special dance, while graciously carrying their school's colors. Their costumes are typically Carnavalized versions of 18th-century gala-clothes.

Bateria

One of the most important elements of the parade is the *bateira* (percussion) orchestra. The *bateria* is responsible for setting – and keeping – the pace of the parade and the music, while the entire school – even technical members – sing that year's samba at the top of their lungs for 75 minutes straight. *Baterias* from the Grupo Especial typically have between 250 and 300 members, are led by the master conductor, and often have a *Rainha de Bateria (*samba queen), representing them.

Ala de passistas

The *passistas* are the school's principal samba dancers. These elaborately dressed, seminude women are one of the best-known images of Carnaval, and their role is to dance the traditional samba-no-pé nonstop during the parade.

Ala das baianas

Considered to be one of the most important parts of a samba school, the *baianas* represent the past on which samba was built. The group of white-clad women, dressed in typical Bahian outfits, remind us of the women who formed the first groups of samba in Salvador.

Velha-guarda

The *velha-guarda* is a group of the oldest *sambistas* in the school who walk along during the parade dressed in colorful formal-wear, waving to the crowds. Members of the *velha-guarda* are typically aged in their 70s or above and are often founders of the schools themselves, but usually retired from holding any other positions in the parade. They tend to be samba legends, and are generally the most revered group in the parade.

Zona Norte

The zones around the Maracanã, São Cristóvão and Benfica you'll find some of the coolest cultural sites in the city, along with plenty of amazing places to dance, eat and celebrate.

The Northeast Comes to Rio

Feira de São Cristóvão

Officially called the Centro Luiz Gonzaga de Tradições Nordestinas, the **Feira de São Cristóvão** is the largest open market and fair dedicated to northeastern Brazilian food, music and traditions, located in the heart and center of Rio de Janeiro.

The open-air market, comprising nearly 70 stands, brings the traditional flavors of the Northeast to Rio, while the stage hosts live acts that play a variety of northeastern music – from *forró* and *baião* to *arrasta-pé* and *maracatu*. The pavilion that hosts the Feira da São Cristávão was designed by architect Sérgio Bernardes and built in the 1950s to house an international industry and commerce fair, and the 156,000 sq-meter covered space won an architecture award in 1958 in Brussels for innovation.

The building later became storage space for the samba schools, until 2003, when it hosted its first Northeastern fair – a move that quickly became permanent. It's open 10am to 6pm Tuesday to Thursday *(free entry)*, 10am to 4am Friday and Saturday *(R$10)*; and 10am to 8pm Sunday *(R$10)*.

FORRÓ

Forró is a music style born in Pernambuco, in Brazil's northeast, that's exceptionally popular in the region, and with the migration of its residents, across the country as well. The music is traditionally played by a trio of instruments – the accordion, *zabumba* (a type of bass drum) and triangle – and the style is broken down into a number of genres, like *baião*, *arrasta-pé* and *xaxado* (although most foreigners can't tell the difference).

Forró's dance, called xote, is a dance for pairs. The step is simple: two to the left, two to the right (with a little hop in between), although note that if someone asks you to dance, you're typically quite close to your partner.

Shop at CADEG

Central market dreams

The **Centro de Abastecimento do Estado da Guanabara** *(CADEG; cadeg.com.br)* is a little piece of Lisbon covered with flowers. Beyond being the place to stock up on plants and garden ware – its flower market may be the best in the city – this three-story central market has a huge concentration of restaurants and shops featuring gastronomic offerings from Portugal. Visit for some of the best (and cheapest) shopping around – home goods, clothing, regional specialties, wine, cheeses and more – or simply for some incredible bolinhos de bacalhau, an ice-cold beer and to soak in the atmosphere. The city's Municipal Market is open 24 hours a day, although individual shop and restaurant hours may differ. The flower market opens from 2am to noon Monday to Saturday.

HIGHLIGHTS
1 Maracanã Football Stadium

SIGHTS
2 BioPark Rio
3 Quinta da Boa Vista

ACTIVITIES
4 Maracanã Tour

EATING
5 Aconchego Carioca
6 Adegão Português
see 11 Barsa
7 Casa do Sardo

DRINKING & NIGHTLIFE
8 Bar da Frente
9 Bar do Omar
10 Bode Cheiroso
see 8 Noo Cachaçaria

SHOPPING
11 CADEG
12 Feira de São Cristóvão

Discover the Soul of the Dance

Samba on Mondays

On Mondays, the **Renascença Clube** *($30 entry; $15 students & seniors)* in Andaraí is the place to be for samba lovers. Come rain or shine, the house will be packed from 4pm to 10pm for one of the most traditional samba presentations in the city, led by legend Moacyr Luz. It's truly the soul of what samba is all about – positive energies, harmony and joy resonate across the club's huge outdoor patio where everyone dances and sings together until well after the sun has gone down.

Escape to Nature

Sprawling Parklands

This huge **Quinta da Boa Vista** in São Cristóvão is the largest public green space in Rio's Zona Norte. The nearly 155,000-sq-meter park is topped by the São Cristóvão Palace, the former residence of the King of Portugal and the Emperors of Brazil, which later housed the Museu Nacional, the oldest scientific institution in the country, until an untimely fire broke out in 2018 and destroyed nearly everything beyond the building's facade. Although nearly 90% of the museum's collection was lost, restoration attempts of both the building and its scientific undertakings are underway.

Another one of the park's main attractions is the zoo, the oldest in Brazil, which reopened in 2019 under new management as the **BioPark Rio**, with a strong conservation, education and research ethos. The small but well-maintained city zoo is worth an hour's visit if you're in the area.

Besides the park's larger attractions, the lake, artificial caves, sports fields and rolling green hills are a hot spot on weekends for picnics, get-togethers, family gatherings or simple relaxation.

Arrive by train or metro to the São Cristóvão station or via rideshare.

SÃO JORGE

Although, technically, Rio has a different patron saint (here's looking at you São Sebastião); *cariocas* know that their real patron is São Jorge, a horse-riding, dragon-slaying soldier, whose red cape is perpetually floating in the wind.

On April 23, the entire state stops to celebrate him – starting at 5am with a fireworks display and parade at the Igreja Matriz de Quintino, in Zona Norte.

Meanwhile, around town, samba groups are warming up and numerous *feijoadas* are being cooked in São Jorge's honor – the black bean is the traditional food offered to Ogum, who is the synchronistic saint to São Jorge in Candomblé and Umbanda Afro-Brazilian religions.

EATING & DRINKING IN ZONA NORTE: OUR PICKS

Bode Cheiroso: Unpretentious bar next to the Maracanã. Known for its *feijoadas*, meat pies and mouthwatering bar food. *11:30am-10.30pm Tue-Sat; 11am-6pm Sun*

Bar da Frente: Retro bar with creative snacks, artisanal beers and a very bohemian vibe. *Noon-10pm Wed-Sat, to 5pm Sun*

Bar do Omar: Enjoy your *petiscos*, beers and *caipirinhas* with a side of samba and expansive views from the terrace. *5pm-Midnight Thu-Fri; 3pm-Midnight Sat; 3-11pm Sun*

Noo Cachaçaria: Cocktail bar with long list of special *cachaças*, colorful *caipirinhas*, sumptuous bar snacks. *Noon-11pm Wed-Sat, 9:30am-5pm Sun*

Adegão Português: Opened in 1964, well-loved Iberian food joint is the go-to Portuguese and Spanish classics. *11am-5pm Mon-Thu, to 6pm Fri-Sun* $$

Casa do Sardo: A success since 2012, this Mediterranean restaurant has its roots in Sardinia. *noon-10pm Tue-Sat, to 4pm Sun* $$

Aconchego Carioca: Northern-Brazilian-style dishes served in this colorful, women-owned bar. *noon-11pm Tue-Sat, to 5:30pm Sun* $

Bar do Momo: Modest *boteco* known for its exceptional – and award-winning – bar food. *noon-11pm Mon-Sat, to 6pm Sun* $$

CELSO PUPO/SHUTTERSTOCK

TOP EXPERIENCE

Maracanã Football Stadium

The Maracanã was inaugurated June 16, 1950, and has been the heart and soul of *carioca* football ever since. Football is more than a religion in Brazil – it's a way of life. The country virtually stands still when the national team plays in the World Cup, and similarly, the city stops when its top clubs go head to head, when all eyes turn to the Maracanã.

DON'T MISS

- Locker Rooms
- Warm-up Rooms
- Press Room
- The Pitch
- Torcidos
- Players' Benches

The Church of Football

When it was built, the Maracanã was the largest stadium in the world, capable of holding nearly 200,000 spectators. Its first World Cup match was played a week after its inauguration, with Brazil beating Mexico 4 to 0. The stadium has gone on to host the Final of the Confederations Cup in 2013, the 2014 World Cup and the opening and closing ceremonies of the 2016 Olympics, as well as concerts by the Rolling Stones, Tina Turner, Coldplay and Madonna, plus two outdoor masses led by Pope John Paul II in 1980 and 1997. The stadium is also set to host the opening and closing games of the 2027 Women's World Cup.

PRACTICALITIES

Scan this QR code for more information.

Modernization

Prior to the 2014 World Cup, the Maracanã was modernized to fit FIFA's standards, substituting the standing-room style seating for stadium chairs and reducing spectator capacity to just under 80,000 people. Although it remains the largest stadium in Brazil, the move created plenty of controversy, as it eliminated the cheapest spectator sector – making it more difficult for the lowest income fans to afford tickets – and decreased capacity for important games. However, the modernization also improved the safety of the stadium, making games a more attractive outing for local families.

Management

In 2019, the city's government canceled the Maracanã's management contracts, and the administration was turned over to the city's two largest football clubs – Flamengo and Fluminense. The pair created a management society, Fla-Flu SA, which is now responsible for managing the stadium and it's complex.

Game Day

There are matches year-round, generally on weekend afternoons or on Wednesday or Thursday evenings. Tickets for matches are available online or at the door, although prepurchase gives you more seating options, and is basically a requirement if you're going to a much-awaited game.

The *torcidos*, (fan clubs), congregate behind their respective goals for nonstop singing, drumming and heckling (sectors E&F or C&B – the cheapest seats), while the East (Section D) and West sections (A) offer a relatively calmer experience and have better views of the field. Maracanã Mais tickets are box sectors on the West side of the stadium that include a buffet meal, and start around R$150. Bring beer money and plenty of sunscreen, as not all sections are in the shade.

Stadium Tour

You can visit the stadium outside of game days on a **Maracanã Tour** *(tourmaracana.com.br; $R75/37.50 adults/students & seniors)*, which is a great way to get to know this piece of history without having to go head on with the crowds. Daily, 45-minute long tours are offered by bilingual guides, taking you through the locker rooms, warm-up rooms and the press room before heading out onto the field itself to see how the players feel on the pitch. There is also a small on-site museum where you can see the number 7 jersey worn by Garrincha in the 1962 World Cup; the ball that scored Pelés thousand goal; and the story of Zico, still the Maracanãs top scorer to this day.

MARACÃ-WHAT?

The stadium's official name is the Estádio Jornalista Mário Filho, in honor of the late Pernambucanos journalist, who was jokingly called the 'stadium's boyfriend' during the era of its construction for all the help he gave the project. However, it's always been known as the Maracanã, a Tupi-Guarani word that means 'rattle-like', in reference to the sound made by the birds who lived in the area.

TOP TIPS

- Watching football is always done with other members of your *torcida* (fan club), so as to avoid potential conflict.
- Certain bars will be taken over by those cheering for Botafogo (black and white) and other bars for those cheering for Fluminense (red and green), however it's mostly the iconic red-and-black jerseys of Flamengo that you'll see around, because even in soccer-obsessed Brazil, Flamengo can lay claim to the largest fan base in the country.
- If you're ever unsure of what to wear on a night out, sporting your team's jersey will always be in fashion.

Ilha de Paquetá

A short ferry ride from the city's center takes you to an adorable, exceptionally safe little island in the middle of the Baía de Guanabara that feels worlds away from the chaos of the Marvelous City.

ISLAND FESTIVALS

The island also hosts a few major events throughout the year – the Festas de São Roque, held the weekend after August 16th in honor of the island's patron saint, is easily the biggest, attracting revelers from across the city to celebrate.

The next most important event on the island is the celebration of São Pedro, the patron saint of fishers, on June 29th.

Then of course there's Carnaval. Paquetá has its own *Blocos* (street parties), along with a few 'invaders', like Pérola da Guanabara and Boto Marinho, which leave from Praça XV in Rio's center, party on the ferryboat then spend all day parading through the island's streets (until the trumpeters run out of air, that is).

Exploring the Island

No cars, no problems

Accessible only by a 40 minute ferry ride from Praça XV, the quiet, safe, bucolic **Ilha de Paquetá** has pastel-colored colonial facades lining dusty streets where bicycles, electric golf-carts and even horse-drawn carriages roam – petrol-powered vehicles are prohibited on the island, turning Paquetá into a peaceful little paradise. But that doesn't mean you'll have nothing to do.

The island's few thousand residents form a tight-knit community, regularly hosting events, film screenings and live-music nights, all easily found via the island's well-updated online portal *(ilhadepaqueta.com.br)*.

Casa de Artes Paquetá

Artistic community

If you're looking for a more intellectual offering, head down to the **Casa de Artes** *(House of the Arts; casadeartespaqueta.org.br @casadeartespaqueta; 10am-5pm Sat-Sun; free entry)*, the island's de-facto cultural center, for a closer look at Paquetá's artistic community.

Start off at the Centro de Memória (Center of Memory), the Casa's permanent exhibition on the history of the island, complete with historic photos and accounts of Paquetá's early life, before heading to check out any temporary exhibitions, literary encounters or musical events that might be on the calendar.

The Casa de Artes, which first opened in 1999, is also home to a music school and a beautiful garden with a Gaudí-inspired mosaic staircase, which brings you up to a lovely terrace with lovely views over the São Roque beach and the bay.

Enchanted Water

No cars, no problems

Once upon a time, there was a well. The **Poço de São Roque** was, at first,the primary well of the São Roque Farm, although it soon became the most important well in the area, due to

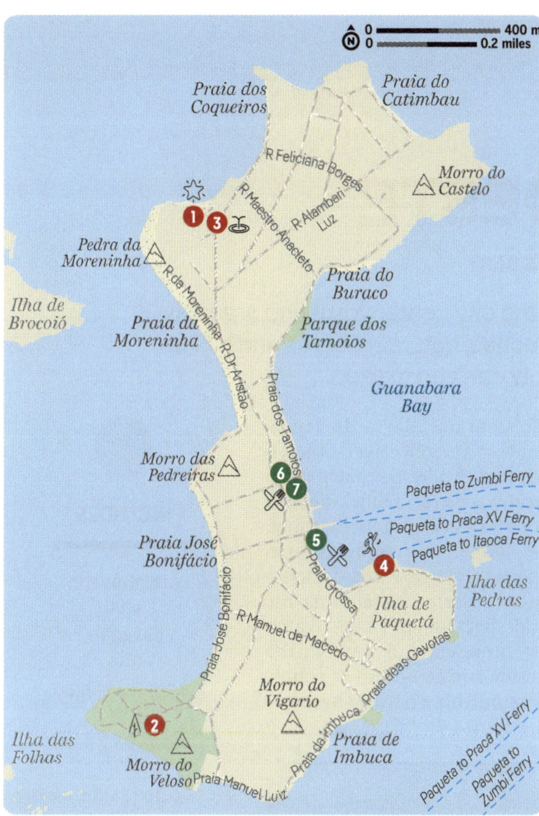

SIGHTS
1 Casa de Artes Paquetá
2 Parque Municipal Darke de Mattos
3 Poço de São Roque

ACTIVITIES
4 Paquetá Yacht Club

EATING
see 1 Casinha Amarela
5 Confeitaria Bodega
6 Tia Leleta
7 Zeca's

the seemingly endless quantity and high quality of its waters.

The well, however, was much more than just a place to get a drink. Many considered its water's enchanted, capable of making your crush fall in love with you, or even of curing debilitating illnesses.

Although now closed, the island's residents are fighting for its reopening to maintain the legends of Paquetá alive, and the well still sports an old inscription that speaks to its magic qualities.

FREE EVENTS

You'll also find free outdoor events at the **Parque Municipal Darke de Mattos**, as well as dance parties at the **Yacht Club.**

EATING IN PAQUETÁ: OUR PICKS

Zeca's: Headed by the charismatic *Vovô* (grandpa) Zeca. Classic homemade Brazilian dishes. *11am-5pm Wed-Thurs, to 10pm Fri-Sat, 11am-9pm Sun* $$

Casinha Amarela: Weekend only favorite spot for *boteco*-style meals with views over the Baía de Guanabara. *noon-6pm Sat & Sun* $$

Tia Leleta: Down-to-earth bar/restaurant, where the beer is ice-cold and dishes for two easily feed four. The *moqueca* shines. *9am-9pm Thu-Tue* $

Confeitaria Bodega: Enjoy afternoon coffee and freshly made sweets with views of the ferryboats and the Bay. *11:30am-7:30pm Wed-Sun* $

Researched by Marisa Megan Paska

ZONA OESTE

WHERE NATURE IS AT ITS BEST

Outside the chaos of the city center you'll find arguably the most beautiful beaches, nature reserves and hiking trails in Rio. They simply can't be missed.

The neighborhoods of São Conrado, Barra da Tijuca and Recreio dos Bandeirantes are collectively known as Zona Oeste (West Zone), and they're the place to go to get your fix of natural beauty, or grab a much-needed adrenaline kick. Adventurous types can practice surfing, kitesurfing, skateboarding, paragliding, hang gliding, stand-up paddling and serious trekking; while the more laid-back travelers will enjoy deserted beaches, rustic oceanfront restaurants and spectacular views. Watch the sunset from a mountaintop, catch a wave in the early morning, dance until the sun comes up or simply slow down and enjoy Rio's astonishing natural beauty – away from the crowds.

INCLUDES

Hang-gliding, São Conrado (p200)

See p225 for places to stay in Zona Oeste.

FROM LEFT: RENATA BARBARINO/SHUTTERSTOCK, JULIO MACIAS/SHUTTERSTOCK

Highlights

❶ Pedra Bonita
Climb up a mountain for the amazing views, or so you can hang glide your way down. **p200**

❷ Ilha da Gigóia
Catch a boat to a little island (pictured right) at the beginning of Barra; the perfect place for a lazy, waterfront lunch. **p204**

❸ Sitio Burle Marx
Take a tour of the UNESCO-protected former residence of Brazil's most famous landscape architect. **p218**

❹ Prainha
Spend a day at an Atlantic-rainforest-backed little beach that many consider to be Rio's most beautiful. **p212**

❺ Museu Casa do Pontal
Explore this free, sprawling museum, considered the most complete record of Brazilian folk art. **p212**

Getting Around

Metro
In 2016, Rio's metro was extended to include stops in São Conrado and Jardim Oceânico. The line connects to Zona Sul, Centro and Zona Norte.

BRT
If you're continuing west past Jardim Oceânico without a car or taxi, you'll need the BRT – Rio's overground answer to the Metro.

Bicycle
One of the most beautiful ways to travel the zone is by bicycle. There is an oceanfront bicycle path that runs from Leblon to Recreio, at the far end of Zona Oeste.

São Conrado

This upscale beachfront neighborhood has high-rises, hillside houses and a chic shopping mall hiding a laid-back, white sandy beach where surfers play and hang gliders land. Oddly enough, it's all backed by Brazil's largest favela.

ROCHINA

One of Latin America's largest favelas occupies a giant swatch of hillside just behind São Conrado, back-to-back with Gaveá in the south zone.

It's estimated that **Rochina** has over 130,000 residents (its the second-largest informal community in the country), and its proximity to the incredibly wealthy neighborhoods provides a poignant look at Brazil's social inequality.

The neighborhood is large enough to be insular – it has its own library, sports complex, health center and even a TV channel – and has a number of social projects working to provide access to sports, art, culture and job training to the local residents.

Unfortunately, safety remains an issue – stray bullets are still relatively common here.

Bonita Bonita

The prettiest little mountaintop

Perhaps the most accessible peak hike in the city is **Pedra Bonita** (beautiful rock), a relatively easy, meandering uphill trek that rewards you with exceptional views across both Zona Sul and Zona Oeste. The 40-minute trek ends at an expansive granite peak, where you'll find plenty of space to spread out and picnic, or to enjoy the views in peace. The trailhead is easily reachable by car or rideshare from São Coronado – however, be aware of the wait to enter. The site is also the launching point for paragliders and hang gliders, meaning there can be quite a bit of traffic on the one-way road up to the trailhead on a clear, sunny day. On your way down, stop at the launching ramp – even if you're not looking to soar, it's still exciting to watch the flyers jump off the cliffside.

Flying High

Para- and hang-gliding

As you're sitting on the sands of São Conrado beach looking up, you're likely to see a strange type of bird in the air. When the weather is clear, Pedra Bonita, which sits as a backdrop to the beach, becomes the go-to launching spot for para- and hang gliders – and the stretch of sand furthest west, known as Praia do Pepino, doubles as a landing pad for those who are flying down. If you're keen to get in on the action, book a flight with **Flying Guru** *(@flyinguru; R$880, including insurance, minimum age 14)*. Instructors are both friendly and highly certified, and the equipment is well maintained, with all safety norms in place for a double flight. You'll spend between eight and 20 minutes in the air, depending on the conditions that day, and launching is, of course, weather dependent.

Beach Clubbin'

Get your groove on

São Conrado beach is an anomaly when it comes to the beaches of Rio de Janeiro – unlike its neighbors in Zona Sul, the sands of São Conrado are clean, safe, and relatively free of beach vendors. While this invites you to have a much more laid-back

beach experience, it also means that when it comes time to eat, you'll have to get off the sand. Luckily, the strip is lined with some excellent kiosks; many of which, like QuiQui (p201), offer full-on gastronomic experiences. For those looking for an after-beach party vibe, check out Soga Beach Club (p201) at the far west corner of São Conrado; with delicious food and regular DJ attractions, there's no better place to be on a Sunday afternoon when the sun goes down.

Tucked-Away Beach with Dramatic Cliffs

Tempting but tiny Joatinga

In between São Conrado and Barra de Tijuca is one of the loveliest little hidden beaches in Rio. Set at the foot of dramatic beachfront cliffs, **Praia da Joatinga** is located inside a condominium of houses in a neighborhood called Joá. It's a tiny little beach, with only 300m of sand that virtually disappears at high tide, but it's a favorite for its exceptional beauty and relative exclusivity. Access to the beach is through the condominium, which not everyone realizes is open to beachgoers, and as relatively few public-transport options pass there, the crowds are limited, making for a more laid-back beach day.

EATING ON THE STRAND: BEST KIOSKS

Soga Beach Club: Chic beachside hut good for lunch and sundowners. Live DJ sets are the weekend are a specialty. *9:30am-6:30pm Tue-Fri, to 10pm Sat & Sun* $$

QuiQui: Gastro-bar where classic cocktails and seafood snacks are the perfect combination. *noon-7pm Wed & Thu, to 11pm Fri & Sat, to 9pm Sun* $$

Gávea Beach Club: Seafood-focused Italian food with good wines. Waves lapping at your feet. *5-11pm Tue-Wed; 1-11pm Thu-Fri; noon-11pm Sat & Sun* $$

Barthô Praia: While the bar food is delicious at this beachfront kiosk, it's the cocktails that really shine. *noon-midnight Wed-Sun* $$

CYCLE TOUR

São Conrado to Pontal

In 1986 Brazilian musical legend Tim Maia released his love song to Rio entitled '*Do Leme ao Pontal*', a distance that these days can be traveled by bicycle. While you don't have to cycle the whole route, it's definitely worth it to experience the beauty Maia so passionately sang about by following this coastal trail through the West Zone of Rio.

1 Praia de São Coronado

Begin at **Praia de São Coronado**, a flat stretch of sand where you can pick up an orange Itaú Bike from the station to start your trip.

Across from the bicycle station you'll see the 2019-reopened Hotel Nacional, an iconic structure from the 1970s that was designed by architect Oscar Niemeyer, and whose gardens were conceived by landscape architect Roberto Burle Marx. Continue southwest along the beach, enjoy a quiet cycle with plenty of blue views.

The cycle: It's approximately 4km to get from São Coronado to Barra, crossing the Elevado do Joá, a floating, oceanfront road with a bicycle lane (reopened 2024) that has views for days.

2 Quebra Mar

When you've arrived in Barra da Tijuca, the elevated cycling lane will end, taking you down to the asphalt where a red painted bicycle path will guide you to Barra's oceanfront road. From there, head left until you hit the pier, aka **Quebra Mar**, and if it's a calm day, make your way all the way to the end for exceptional views.

ZUMA PRESS, INC./ALAMY

Praça Duó skate park (p206)

Top tip If you decide to cycle back, try to time your trip so that you hit this spot for an absolutely superb sunset.

The cycle: Continue along Barra's beachfront past Praia do Pepê – where the kiteboarders gather on windy days – on your left, and a bit further on you'll see the Praça Duô skate park on your right. It's approximately 5km along a flat, beachfront road to the next stop.

3 Classico Beach Club

The beaches of Rio are lined with informal restaurants that sit on the strand called kiosks, and while some have a more rustic vibe, **Classico** has turned their kiosks – of which there are a few across the city – into full-on beach clubs with elaborate lunches, luxury lounge chairs and plenty of space to sprawl out on the sand. It's an ideal spot to grab a coconut, an ice-cold beer or take a full lunch break while resting your legs on a lounger.

The cycle: After you've rested up, continue along the cycling lane through Praia da Reserva, an unspoilt beach backed by a wetlands preservation zone, until you hit the beaches of Recreio dos Bandeirantes.

4 Praia da Macumba

At the far end of Recreio beach, right at Post 12, you'll see a giant rock that seemingly grows out of the water – welcome to the Pedra de Pontal.

Continue on to the other side of the stone where you'll find the Praia da Macumba (p212), a magnet for surfers and laid-back surf culture. You can leave your bicycle at the Itaú station, then grab a drink from a beachfront kiosk.

If you've got energy left, consider hiking to the top of the Pedra for sunset.

Barrinha

In between the neighborhoods of Joá and Barra de Tijuca is an area called Barrinha, best known for its islands, canals and alligators. It's an exceptional escape to nature in the middle of the city.

SERTÃO CARIOCA

Prior to Portuguese colonization, the area of Barrinha, like the entire coastline from São Paulo's Litoral Norte up to the Região dos Lagos in Rio was inhabited by the *Tamoio* (or Tamoyo) indigenous group. It was estimated their population reached upwards of 70,000, and some of their cultural traditions in the Barrinha region were recorded in a series of articles written by historian and illustrator Armando Magalhaes Corrêa in the early 1930s – a series that also spoke of the life of the settlers who lived in the region, along with the native flora and fauna. The book, which is still in publication, offers a unique insight into life during Barra de Tijuca's very early days.

Island Hopping

Jungle-covered islands in the city

Barrinha is best known for its set of nine small islands divided by a series of canals, often lovingly called the Carioca Venice. Accessible only by boat taxi (which you can find just behind the Jardim Oceânico metro station near the 'lagoa' exit, or next to the Shell gas station at the Barra Point shopping center – approximately R$3 to R$8), a visit to the islands will make you feel as though you've left the city behind and entered into another world.

The most well-known island is **Ilha da Gigóia**, which has a few thousand inhabitants, as well as a small number of cafes, restaurants and even some guesthouses if you want to spend the night (**Casanova Residence** is quite a nice choice).

Hop on a boat and grab lunch or a sunset beer at one of the canal-front venues; or negotiate a tour with one of the boaters to visit all nine islands (usually around R$40), where alligator spotting is a favorite pastime.

Time the Tide for Praia dos Amores

A secret beach

At the very beginning of Barrinha you'll find one beautiful, tiny secret beach sitting underneath the Joá overpass, known for its white sand and translucent turquoise waters. **Praia dos Amores** is a shallow, calm beach that forms where the canal meets the islands of Barrinha. The only catch is timing your visit – to get the perfect experience, you'll need to consult a tide chart. The small swatch of sand disappears at high tide, and the crystal-clear waters can change to brown and murky if you arrive when the tide is going out, so make sure to time your visit with an incoming tide (when the water is coming into the canal from the ocean), and preferably, on a full or new moon, when the tide change will be the highest. If you get it right, the rewards will be more than worth it.

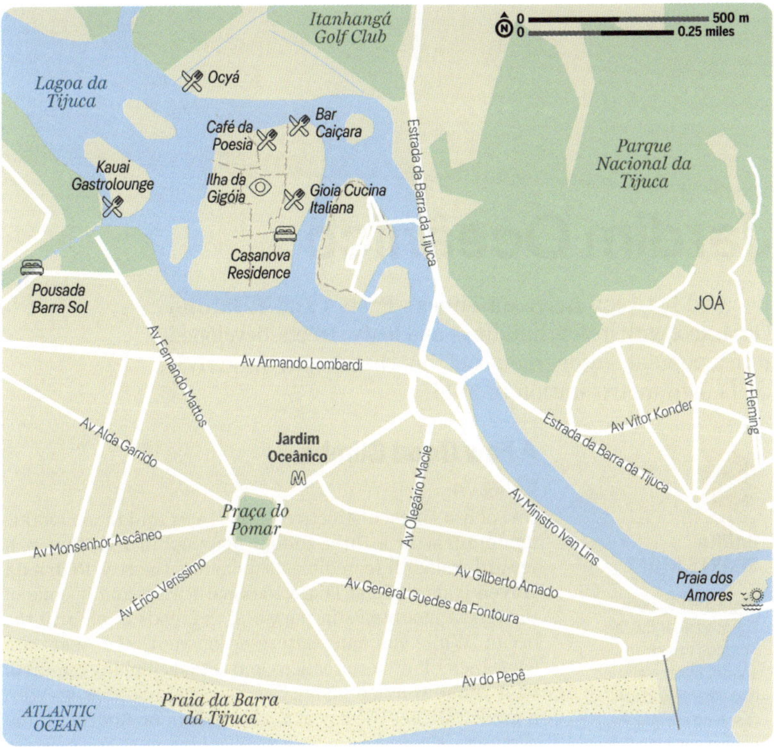

Coffee & Poetry

Getting away from it all

Bookworms and café aficionados will love an afternoon getaway to the **Café da Poesia** *(@cafedapoesia99)*, where you'll feel worlds away from the city's chaos. This adorable café founded by a poet-and-baker Argentine couple is the perfect place to immerse yourself in the smells and tastes of fine artisanal coffee, freshly baked treats and the literary gems that line the walls. Located on a quiet, narrow, footpath on Barrinha's Ilha de Gigoia, arriving at the café is enough of a journey to disconnect from the outside world – and after an hour or two tucked away in a cozy café corner, it's easy to forget that it even exists.

EATING ON THE ISLANDS: OUR PICKS

Ocyá: High-end seafood restaurant on Ilha Primeira. Make a sunset reservation. *noon-6pm Wed & Thu, to 10pm Fri & Sat, to 8pm Sun* **$$$**

Gioia Cucina Italiana: Italian-style cuisine, delicious cocktails. Spacious, waterfront patio. *12:30-6pm Wed, to 11pm Thu-Sat, to 7pm Sun* **$$**

Kauai Gastrolounge: Gastrobar on the Ilha do Ipê for Brazilian bar-food classics and live music. *6pm-midnight Thu, 8pm-5am Fri & Sat; 6pm-2am Sun* **$$**

Bar Caiçara: One of Gigóia's most classic stops. Ideal for a *moqueca*, *pastels* and ice-cold beers. *Noon-7pm Wed & Thu, to 10pm Fri & Sat, to 8pm Sun* **$$**

Jardim Oceânico

Located between Barra da Tijuca's Posts 1 and 4, Jardim Oceânico, with its low buildings and leafy streets, developed into a popular, autonomous neighborhood with the arrival of its own metro station in 2016.

BARRA SPORTS STOPS

Yoga Surf School: Located near Barra's Posto 3, this sports school has developed its own method for teaching surfing – yoga plays a big role.

K08 KiteSurf Club: A kiosk/beach club has kitesurfing lessons on Praia de Pêpe – choose from five, 10 or 20-hour packages.

KitePoint Rio (K7): Owned and run by kite champion Marcelo Cunha, this kitesurfing school also offers Jet Ski and stand-up paddleboarding when the wind is down.

Gaia Surf Feminino: The largest female-focused surf school on the sand, Gaia supports women learning and improving their surfing, between posts 7 and 8.

A Few Good Climbs

Going Up

One of Rio's most distinctive peaks is a 844m-tall monolithic mountain with a three-to-four-hour uphill trek that will reward you with incredible views across the city. **Pedra da Gávea** is part of the Tijuca National Forest, and it's one of the tallest mountains in the world that ends directly in the ocean. While you can venture up on your own, there are some incredibly steep sections and actual climbing required, so if you're worried about your physical abilities, go with a guide (Michel Nicolay *@michelnicolay* or Rodrigo Indio *@guiarodrigoindio* are both excellent options). You can also opt to stop at the lower-down Garganta do Céu, a unique viewpoint that sits between Pedra da Gávea and Pico dos Quatro, accessible by the same trail (no rock-climbing required here). Whichever you choose, be sure to bring plenty of water, leave early to avoid the heat, and reward yourself with a stop at the waterfall near the start of the trail on your return.

The Best Skate Park in Rio

Practice at Praça Duó

Located in Praça São Perpétuo (better known as Praça do Ó), the **Praça Duó skate park** is a skaters' dream. This old amphitheater was transformed into a beachfront skate-park in 2018, and subsequently added to in 2022 to permit the park to host international events. The skate park is free to enter and great for all levels; it includes a large transition bowl, a street skate zone and a park zone; and has adequate illumination to allow for nighttime skating – plus, its just a 15-minute walk from the Jardim Oceânico metro station.

There are a number of small skate schools offering lessons at the park – just ask if you're looking to learn, show up to skate with friendly locals or watch one of the competitions hosted here during the year.

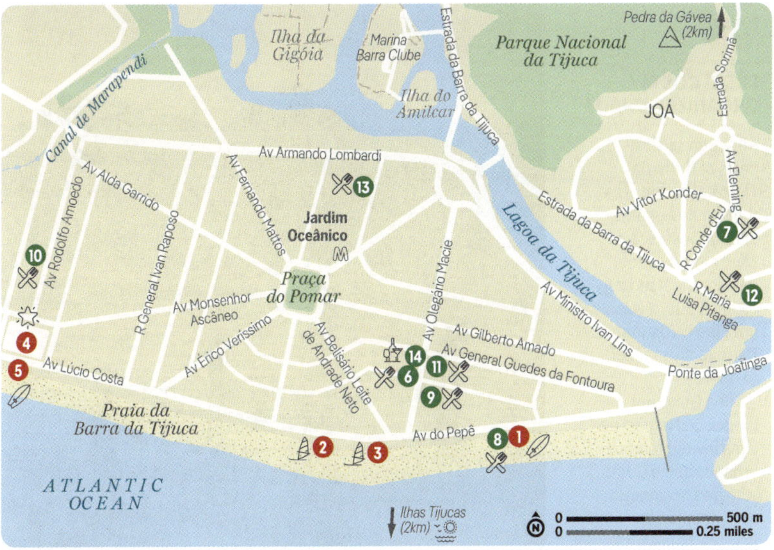

ACTIVITIES
1 Gaia Surf Feminino
2 K08 KiteSurf Club
3 KitePoint Rio (K7)
4 Praça Duó Skate Park
5 Yoga Surf School

EATING
6 .Org Bistrô
7 Bar do Oswaldo
8 Bondai Praia
9 Caffé Olé
10 João Padeiro Fermentação Natural
11 Mana Poke Barra da Tijuca
12 Pura Rio
13 Skinna

DRINKING & NIGHTLIFE
14 Boteco Rios
see 6 Seu Bar

Enjoy Nightlife on Av Olegário Maciel

Barra's Little Miami

Although it's only 750m-long, this little street in Barra packs a punch when it comes to nightlife. Av Olegário Maciel, which runs perpendicular to the beach at the beginning of Jardim Oceânico, has enough bars, clubs, restaurants and *botecos* to keep you going until the early morning. A few of Zona Sul's renowned hot-spots – like Bar do Adão, Brewteco and Canastra Bar – have outposts here; while other locals are purely Barra born. **Seu Bar** is one such establishment, with ample indoor and outdoor seating and a drink list to match, while **Boteco Rios** is an ideal place to go if you prefer to pair your creative cocktail or ice-cold beer with a *picanha* or a barbecue dinner.

EATING IN JARDIM OCEÂNICO: OUR PICKS

Bondai Praia: Beach bar where water sports, live music, delicious healthy dishes and spectacular sunsets set the scene. *9am-8pm* $$

Bar do Oswaldo: Traditional *padaria* (bakery), opened since 1946, famous for its *batidas* (tropical milkshakes, often in cocktail form). *noon-1am Sun-Thu, to 3am Sat & Sun* $$

.Org Bistrô: Modern, vegetarian restaurant with plant-based Brazilian favorites in cozy, colorful cafe-style dining room. *noon-3:30pm Mon-Sat* $$

Pura Rio: Small, laid-back vegan restaurant in Barrinha with mouth-watering, creative dishes. *noon-4pm Fri, 9am-5pm Sat & Sun* $

LÚCIO COSTA/ ORGANIZED CHAOS

Although several parts of Barra da Tijuca – like the area that would become Jardim Oceânico – were already under development as early as the 1930s, it wasn't until the 1970s that Barra really started to boom.

Then Governor Francisco Negrão de Lima invited famous urbanist Lúcio Costa, who had designed the pilot plan for Brasília, to create a development plan for the 120-sq-km area that would become Barra. Unfortunately, Costa's innovative plan would suffer so many alterations over the decades that the urbanist himself declared that the development had nothing to do with the plan he had provided, and he abandoned the group responsible for the plan's implementation.

MARIA ADELAIDE SILVA/ALAMY

Paddleboarders, Ilhas Tijucas

Water Adventures on Ilhas Tijucas

Offshore activities

Known for their crystal-clear waters and abundance of marine life, the **Ilhas Tijucas** (Tijuca Islands) are a favorite outing for water lovers. Sitting in between Barra da Tijuca and São Conrado just 2km off the coast (leaving from the Joatinga canal), you can visit this watery paradise by boat, stand-up paddleboard, Jet Ski, kayak or even – for the quite fit – swimming.

Choose a day when the ocean is calm and the wind is down to have the best experience, and expect about a 45-minute paddle each way, if you're going by paddleboard or kayak.

EATING IN JARDIM OCEÂNICO: OUR PICKS

João Padeiro Fermentação Natural: Delicious artisanal bakery set in a beautifully renovated, house, offers coffee, meals, snacks, and incredible fresh bread all day. *9am-9pm Tues-Sat; 9am-5pm Sun* $$

Caffé Olé: Charming, family café with a romantic atmosphere and delectable dishes. Not cheap, but very much worth it. Reservations recommended *(via WhatsApp +55 21 991 208990). 6-11pm Tues, 12:30-11pm Wed &Thurs, 12:30 pm-midnight, Fri & Sat, noon-6pm Sunday* $$$

Skinna: Down-to-earth seafood restaurant (there are meat and children's options) with plenty of charm and surprisingly good service in a family-friendly environment. *noon-midnight Tues-Sun* $$

Mana Poke Barra da Tijuca: Simple, colorful and healthy do-it-yourself Poke bowls – the perfect post-beach snack or pre-game for a night on the town. *11am-10:30pm daily* $$

Barra da Tijuca

This sprawling suburb of Rio de Janeiro modeled after Miami in the US is known for its shiny condos, shopping centers and nightlife – along with its breathtaking 14.4 km of white sandy coastline.

Artistic Offerings Galore

The vast Cidade das Artes

Cidade das Artes *(City of Arts; cidadedasartes.rio.rj.gov.br)* is a huge, 97,000-sq-meter space dedicated to a multitude of artistic offerings, ranging from theater performances and exhibitions to ballet, concerts, symphonies and Broadway musicals.

The space, which was inaugurated in 2013, has one of the largest exhibition halls in Latin America – and for the little ones, the complex also displays the largest LEGO model in Latin America, a 947,000-piece masterwork replicating 25 of the most famous points in Rio de Janeiro – including Pão de Açúcar, Cristo Redentor, Arcos da Lapa and the Maracanã.

Before heading out, be sure to stop at the delicious **Abry Gastrobar,** best known for its Sunday brunches.

Take a Lesson at Campo Olímpico de Golfe

Get ready to swing

Built for the 2016 Rio Olympics, this 18-hole, 7000-yard **Campo Olímpico de Golfe** *(rioogc.com)* golf course has become a magnet for afternoon get-togethers – both on the green, and at the sunset-view bar.

Unfortunately, the course was built within the bounds of the Marapendi Natural Reserve, however thankfully it wasn't made exclusive – post-Olympics, the golf course was open to all, and even offers three free lessons with a golf pro for anyone interested in learning the sport (offered at 11:30am and 12:30pm on weekends and holidays with prior reservation).

You can also book a helicopter tour of Zona Oeste with **Blue Sky Tours**, leaving from the golf grounds themselves.

ECOLOGICAL CONSERVATION: RESERVA DE MARAPENDI

Historian and professor Armando Magalhães Corrêa, author of the article series *O Sertão Carioca* (one of the first historical accounts of early Barra de Tijuca, published in the 1930s) was the first person to propose the creation of a bio-reserve in Barra da Tijuca.

Year later, his dream was realized with the creation of the Marapendi Natural Reserve in 1991.

Not even a decade after its creation, the Praia da Reserva became the second beach in Rio de Janeiro to receive recognition by the Foundation for Environmental Education in Denmark for its exemplary management of a protected coastal zone and creation of sustainable tourism offerings.

SIGHTS
1 Bosque da Barra
2 Parque Natural Municipal de Marapendi
3 Praia da Barra da Tijuca
4 Praia da Reserva

ACTIVITIES
5 Campo Olímpico de Golfe

EATING
6 Carlota's Beach House
7 Muah Gastrobar
8 Olívia & Cia
9 Quiosque do Alfa

DRINKING & NIGHTLIFE
10 021 Lounge Bar
see 10 All In Lounge
11 Padano Sertanejo & Bar
12 Up Turn
see 10 Vitrinni Lounge

ENTERTAINMENT
13 Cidade das Artes

Take Refuge in Bosque da Barra

Under-the-radar forest park

The 50-hectare **Bosque da Barra** park is a favorite getaway for Barra families, as well as a refuge for the local fauna – you'll find plenty of birds, butterflies, capybara and caimans lounging around the lake. For the human species, the park offers a jogging path, a playground and nearby bicycle rentals, as well as football and volleyball courts, bathrooms and a limited amount of car parking (so arrive early if you want a spot). You can also easily arrive by bus to the Alvorada station, or by BRT to the Bosque da Barra station. Unfortunately, bike lanes connecting the park are limited. Note that there are no snack bars on site, so bring your own picnic to enjoy the afternoon.

A Trip to the Beach

Sprawling beaches of Barra and Reserva

Although nowhere near as crowded as Ipanema or Copacabana, the **Praia da Barra da Tijuca** still sees a lot of action, especially on weekends around Posto 8. If you're looking for more laid-back vibes, stick to Postos 6 or 4; or to really get away from it all, head out west to Reserva. **Praia da Reserva**, officially known as the Praia da Reserva de Marapendi, is an 8km-long stretch of sand that marks the coastline of the **Parque Natural Municipal de Marapendi**, a 665.62-hectare preservation zone in between Barra de Tijuca and Recreio dos Bandeirantes. The white sandy beach, featuring crystal-clear water, is backed by lakes, wetlands and Atlantic rainforest and is divided into 26 'islands', each marked by a rustic beach kiosk. The main road, Av Lúcio Costa, follows the entirety of the beach, making parking relatively easy at any point on the route (beware of traffic on weekends and holidays).

PRAINHA

The first beach to receive recognition by the Foundation for Environmental Education for exemplary management of a protected zone was **Prainha** (p212), a paradisiacal cove just west of Recreio dos Bandeirantes

BEST NIGHTLIFE IN BARRA

All In Lounge: This stylish nightlife venue, where electronic music, *pagode* and samba reign, is almost always packed to the brim.

Up Turn: This longest-standing Barra nightclub is a laid-back, open-minded joint that's popular with the LGBTIQ+ crowd.

021 Lounge Bar: This 1600-sq-meter nightclub with a huge live-music stage is the place to be on Friday nights.

Vitrinni Lounge: On Friday nights, Vitrinni is where the party's at. Live samba and *pagode* and DJs playing funk and *sertanejo* set the scene.

Padano Sertanejo & Bar: *Sertanejo*-themed nightlife spot, where the country-style music plays into the wee hours of the morning.

EATING IN BARRA: BEST BEACH KIOSKS

Muah Gastrobar: This Mediterranean restaurant is an outpost of Muah Gastronomia, a culinary sensation from Rio's North Zone. *noon-10pm* $$

Quiosque do Alfa: Traditional seafood and hearty beach platters are easy to agree on. *8am-midnight Tue-Sun; 10am-6pm Mon* $

Olívia & Cia: Simple beach snacks (sandwiches, *tapiocas* and omelets), hearty lunches; try the seafood *moqueca*. 9am-8:30pm Wed-Sat, to 7pm Sun-Tue $

Carlota's Beach House: Sushi, Italian-inspired seafood and beachy cocktails. A neighborhood favorite. *noon-midnight* $$

Recreio do Bandeirantes

One of the farthest afield neighborhoods of the west zone, Recreio do Bandeirantes still has houses and is free of skyscrapers – and it's probably one of the least expensive place to live or stay in the city. Ideal for nature lovers.

BEST SURF SCHOOLS

Longboard Paradise: Recreio's longboard clubhouse also has an on-site surf school – ideal if you want to learn longboarding.

Recreio Sharks: Surf coach Gabriel Concato and his team offer regular classes on Macumba Beach for surfers looking to improve their skills.

Escola De Surf Jeronimo Telles: This well-known Recreio surf school has been offering lessons to all ages and levels since 1992.

Marítimas Surf Feminino (@as maritimas): Rio's only surf school with an all-female teaching staff and development classes geared towards female surfers.

Bailarinas do Mar (@bailarinasdomar): A longboard surf-gal crew whose meetups and surf trips are soul affirming and open to all.

Brazil's Largest Folk-Art Museum

Ecologically impressive Museu Casa do Pontal

The largest museum for folk art in Brazil, the **Museu Casa do Pontal** *(museudopontal.org.br; free, R$20 donation recommended)* is a reference in Brazilian culture and considered by UNESCO to be one of the most complete anthropological offerings of Brazilian folk art. The museum sits inside an ecological reserve, with gardens designed to integrate into the landscape – picnic-friendly – and in 2022, it became the first museum in the country to produce 100% of the energy it consumes. Beyond 5000 sq meters of exhibitions, the museum also has theatrical guided visits (booked in advance) and has a full calendar of events. It's open Thursday to Sunday, 10am to 6pm.

Embrace Surf Culture

Waves galore in the west

The West Zone is a magnet for surfers, with long, uncrowded coastlines and some of the best waves in Rio. It's no surprise that surf culture is thriving, with projects popping up across the zone to support the surfing community. At **Praia da Macumba**, longboarding culture reigns, and **Small Riders** is ground zero. It has an on-site restaurant, a gallery and a coworking space, along with plenty of live-music events on weekends. Need a surfboard for your trip? Check out **Caio Teixeira Surfboards** *(@caioteixeirasurfboards)* for classic longboards and retro shapes; or write to Suzana Till, the creator of **Mulheres Fazendo Pranchas** *(Women Who Shape Surfboards; @womenwhoshapesurfboards)*, whose elegant surfboards are enviable in the water.

One of Rio's Most Beautiful Beaches

A tiny, hidden beauty

This tiny cove of white sand backed by protected Atlantic Rainforest is a favorite weekend getaway for *carioca* surfers and beach lovers alike. **Prainha** sits inside a 147-hectare preservation zone, meaning there's no public transport to arrive and limited car capacity – so you'll need to arrive early if you want to come by car or be ready to walk the 2km up

SIGHTS
1 Cachoeiras da Mucuíba
2 Museu Casa do Pontal
3 Parque Estadual da Pedra Branca
4 Praia da Macumba
5 Prainha
6 Small Riders

ACTIVITIES
7 Bailarinas do Mar
8 Escola De Surf Jeronimo Telles
9 Longboard Paradise
10 Marítimas Surf Feminino
11 Recreio Sharks

SLEEPING
see 9 Longboard Paradise Hostel

EATING
12 Asa Rio
see 12 Donna Madalenna
13 Kaçuá
14 Natural do Recreio

SHOPPING
15 Caio Teixeira Surfboards

PARQUE ESTADUAL DA PEDRA BRANCA

One of the largest urban nature parks in the world, 12,394-hectare **Parque Estadual da Pedra Branca** protects more than half of the city's native Atlantic rainforest.

It's also home to the city's highest peak, Pico da Pedra Branca, as well as two colonial-era churches – the chapel of São Gonçalo do Amarante, built in 1625, and the Church of Nossa Senhora de Montserrat, dating back to 1776.

The park, which was created in 1974, sits on land that was already inhabited by three *quilombo* communities (the best known being Quilombo do Camorim), which were given legal status by the Cultural Palmares Foundation in 2014 and 2017.

ROBERTHARDING/ALAMY

Prainha beach (p212)

and down hills to get to the beach from the park's entrance. Behind the beach there bathrooms and showers, parking, surf racks, a playground and a few beach kiosks where you can grab a bite, as well as a well-maintained, 2km trail that takes you to the top of the Mirante do Caeté, where you'll get exceptional views stretching across the coastline.

Swim in Pools & Waterfalls

Fresh water escapes

Surrounded by lush Atlantic rainforest, the **Cachoeiras da Mucuíba** (Mucuíba waterfalls) lie inside the Parque Estadual da Pedra Branca and are easily accessible by car and a short hike. The trail takes you past four pools for swimming – each with a small waterfall – with the first and the fourth being roughly 20 minutes apart. Follow the main trail directly to the first pool, frequently full of families, then continue on to the second pool, where there's a nice little waterfall and dwindling numbers of bathers. The third pool has an even nicer little waterfall, while the trail to the fourth pool is a little overgrown but very worth the effort. There's no bus, taxi or rideshare service in the area, making moto-taxis the easiest way to arrive and leave if you don't have your own transport.

EATING IN RECREIO: OUR PICKS

Natural do Recreio: Pay-by-kilo restaurant features fresh ingredients. Pet- and surfer-friendly. *11:30am-4.30pm Mon-Fri, noon-5pm Sat & Sun* $

Asa Rio: Laid-back lunchtime or after-beach go-to, where grilled dishes, sandwiches and fresh juices feature. *11.30am-midnight* $

Donna Madalenna: Long-standing, slightly upscale *boteco* known for pizza, overloaded traditional plates and ice-cold draft beer. *11.30am-10pm* $$

Kaçuá: Hearty northeastern dishes served in unpretentious dining room. *noon-midnight Thu-Sat, to 7pm Sun & holidays* $$

Barra de Guaratiba

This waterfront neighborhood in the far western reaches of Rio is a combination of hilltops houses, pristine beaches and riverside stops. Trek and explore the mangroves, as well as the renowned gastronomy scene.

A Rest in the Restinga

Blissful private beach

In the far west reaches of Rio, you'll find an exceptional preserved natural area that's infrequently visited – even by *cariocas*. The **Restinga de Marambaia** is a long, thin private beach that's backed by a a maze of rivers and mangroves that stretch out to the sea – perfect for exploring by paddleboard, kayak or on a boat tour.

The blissfully peaceful area entices you to relax and enjoy – expect superb sunsets and sea-turtle visitors. If you're not staying overnight, you can book day-use at the upscale hotel **Le Relais de Marambaia** *(lerelaisdemarambaia.com.br)*, which includes pool access, stand-up paddleboard use and lunch options; or at **Camping Guaratiba** *(campingbarradeguaratiba.com.br)*, with its pool, bar and ocean-view deck that combine to make it a perfect place to catch a magical Marambaia sunset.

Headland Hiking

Over the hill and through the woods

Grumari Beach and its surroundings make the the **Parque Natural Municipal de Grumari** *(Grumari Natural Park)*, an 805-hectare area that includes the neighboring beaches Praia do Inferno, da Funda, do Meio e Praia do Perigoso – all accessible by the **Praias Selvagens hiking trail** – or by boat.

The trails can be picked up from the most western end of Grumari Beach or from Barra de Guaratiba. There are also a number of other trails that take you through the Atlantic rainforest to spectacular lookout points and hilltops – like **Pedra do Telégrafo**, a mini-mountaintop that's claimed plenty of social-media fame for the unique pictures you can take 'hanging' off the cliff.

If you're planning a hike, download your maps on *wikiloc.com* prior to heading out, as there's little to no cell-phone reception in the area, and not all of the trails have excellent signage.

PICA-PAU AMARELO

While Europe had the Brothers Grimm, Brazil had Monteiro Lobato (1882–1948), primarily a children's-book writer whose works were often set at the Sítio do Pica-Pau Amarelo (Farm of the Yellow Woodpecker).

The farm and its fabled residents were brought to life in a wildly popular television series by Rede Globo made between 1977 and 1986. Its filming took place in Guaratiba, on a full farm that was designed and built to host the project. The farm even had gardens designed by Roberto Burle Marx himself.

The Sitio *(@antigacasadositio)*, Located on the Estrada Burle Marx, was later restored and is now open for nostalgia-filled visits for those who were fans of the program in their youth.

HIGHLIGHTS
1 Sítio Burle Marx

SIGHTS
2 Pedra do Telégrafo
3 Praia de Abricó
4 Praia de Grumari
5 Restinga de Marambaia

ACTIVITIES
6 Praias Selvagens Hiking Trail

SLEEPING
7 Camping Guaratiba
8 Le Relais de Marambaia

EATING
9 Baixo Grumari
10 Bira
11 Restaurante Tropicana
12 Tia Penha

The Sandy Paradise of Grumari Beach

Undeveloped coastal beauty

In between Recreio and Barra de Guaratiba the undeveloped **Praia de Grumari** is a dream in and of itself, and visiting is like being transported to a sandy jungle coastline far away from city life. In contrast to Rio's more central beaches, Grumari is a very safe, long and clean stretch of sand – you can generally leave your belongings and go for a swim without worrying. While there isn't much in the way of services, there are a few beach vendors on weekends, as well as restaurants on either end of the beach.

Note: at the end of the beach closest to Recreio, the **Praia de Abricó** is the only nudist beach in the area.

There is no public transport in the area, so you'll have to arrive by car, taxi, rideshare or, if you're feeling fit, by bicycle.

Fishmonger, Guaratiba

ROBERTO BURLE MARX

Self-taught botanist, accomplished multi-disciplinary artist and storied landscape designer, Roberto Burle Marx (p218) is internationally recognized as the creator of the modernist tropical garden.

Born in São Paulo to Brazilian-German parents, Burle Marx studied in Berlin and then Rio, where his career as a landscape artist took off, thanks to his mentor Lúcio Costa and collaborations with renowned architect Oscar Niemeyer (p220). He also undertook numerous expeditions into the Brazilian rainforest, and ended up with 13 plant species named after him.

Caiçara Cuisine

Lunch all day long

Known for its incredible seafood, the *caiçara* cuisine in Guaratiba has become a tourist attraction in its own right.

Typically, you'll find traditional fisher recipes perfected over years being served in rustic settings surrounded by mangroves, with the ocean off in the distance. Eating in Guaratiba feels a bit like being transported to a small fisher's town in rural Brazil – dishes are always served with a smile, without a rush, and with enough food for three: just beware – lunch can all too easily turn into a daylong event.

TRANSCARIOCA

The **Transcarioca Trail** (p76), which runs across the entire city of Rio, starts here in Barra de Guaratiba. The first stretch of the trail takes you across the headlands, past the unspoiled beaches to Grumari.

EATING IN GUARATIBA: OUR PICKS

Tia Penha: One of the pioneer restaurants on the Guaratiba gastronomic route serves mouthwatering seafood. *11am-5pm Mon-Fri, to 6.30pm* Sat & Sun $$

Bira: The most famous of Guaratiba's restaurants has both exceptional seafood and breathtaking views. *noon-5pm Thu-Sun* $$$

Restaurante Tropicana: Popular *caiçara* seafood dishes plus plant-based takes for vegetarians/vegans. *11am-6pm Mon-Fri, to 7pm Sat & Sun* $$

Baixo Grumari: Expect lovely people, great food, delicious *caipirinhas* and a festive atmosphere. *11.30am-6.30pm* $

Casa do Roberto

TOP EXPERIENCE

Sítio Burle Marx

Sítio Burle Marx was once the home, laboratory, atelier and workplace of internationally renowned Brazilian landscape artist Roberto Burle Marx. The property, now UNESCO listed and managed by the state, has one of the most important collections of living tropical plants in the world, and continues to be a botanical research space, museum and cultural center.

DON'T MISS

- Casa do Roberto
- Atelier
- Loggia
- Capela Santo Antônio da Bica
- Graziela Barroso Greenhouse
- Cozinha da Pedra
- The Gardens

History

In 1949, brothers Roberto and Guilherme Siegfried Burle Marx bought the first plot of land destined to become the Sítio Roberto Burle Marx em Guaratiba, in the West Zone of Rio. The location was chosen for its rich soil, extensive native vegetation and its location at the edge of the Parque Estadual da Pedra Branca, a protected stretch of Atlantic rainforest that would save the zone from real estate speculation. Two neighboring plots were added in 1952 and 1960, respectively, creating the site we see today.

PRACTICALITIES

Scan this QR code for prices and opening hours.

Casa do Roberto

This restored colonial-style house was the artist's home during the last 20 years of his life. It was remodeled as a museum and open to visitors in 2019, hosting curated exhibitions giving insight into Roberto Burle Marx's personal life, persona and work. Besides the living room, dining room, kitchen and guest room, the house also has a ceramics room, music room, prayer room and a small atelier, and hosts expansive collections of religious, African, Mesoamerican and South American art.

Atelier

The main atelier is really a multiuse space where Burle Marx both worked and held an array of events, ranging from concerts to courses to exhibitions. The building itself was built overtime, starting in the 1970s when Roberto managed to acquire a neoclassical facade from a demolition site (although it was only installed a decade later). The spacious building has a number of large-size works by the artist, purpose-made for the space.

Loggia

This 60-sq-meter building in between the main house and the chapel is decorated with exceptional contemporary tile work done by the artist, and adorned with an extra long, solid wood table where Burle Marx used to work.

The Chapel

Originally built in the 18th century, the Capela Santo Antônio da Bica was part of the original Fazenda da Bica bought by the Burle Marx brothers. They restored the chapel upon purchasing the land, and again in the 1970s. It's still used for religious ceremonies and masses, as well as the annual St Anthony's Day procession.

Gardens & Greenhouses

Unsurprisingly, the gardens are spectacular. They also host more than 3500 tropical and subtropical species in greenhouses and gardens, while harmoniously preserving 405,000 sq meters of native vegetation. The main greenhouse was named after Graziela Barroso, a great friend of Burle Marx who was also the first woman to become a naturalist at the Botanic Gardens of Rio in 1946.

Cozinha da Pedra

One of the more interesting buildings on-site, the outdoor kitchen is where Burle Marx used to hold the lunches, dinners and parties for which he became renowned. The stone floor, concrete-awning-covered open space, which was designed by architects Rubem Breitman e Haroldo Barroso Beltrão and decorated with a huge tile panel done by Burle Marx, won an award from the Institute of Brazilian Architects in 1963 under the name 'Pavilhão Roberto Burle Marx'.

PRESERVATION

The property has been a national preservation site since 1985, and in 2021, it became the first modern tropical garden to be inscribed on the UNESCO World Heritage List, for its artistic, environmental and cultural importance. Burle Marx donated his home to the federal government, with the condition it continue a research center, a wish executed upon his death in 1994.

TOP TIPS

- The Sítio is open from Tuesday to Saturday (closed holidays).
- The 1½-hour tours (offered in Portuguese or English) are by reservation only, taking place at either 9:30am or 1:30pm, and cost R$10 (cash only; half price for students and 60+, under 5 are free).
- Only 140 visitors are allowed each day to minimise the effect on the ecosystem. The online reservation system *(sitio-roberto-burle-marx.reservio.com)* will tell you which days have openings, as well as what language tours will be available each day.
- Accessibility adaptations are available, and should be requested upon booking.

Day Trips from Rio de Janeiro

Cross the bay to Niterói to see Oscar Neimeyer architecture and to the mountainous German-designed village of Petrópolis.

Places

> **OSCAR NEIMEYER**
>
> Born in Laranjeiras, Oscar Neimeyer (1907–2012) studied architecture in Rio and, at 29, helped design the headquarters of Brazil's Ministry of Education and Health. Neimeyer's architectural style was influenced by European modernism of the 1930s–1960s, which featured flat roofs, open floor plans and minimalism.
>
> In 1940, Niemeyer met Belo Horizonte Mayor Juscelino Kubitschek and designed the ambitious Pampulha Architectural Complex. Kubitschek went on to become Brazil's president and asked Neimeyer to design the new capital in Brasília, forever solidifying the architect's legacy. Neimeyer also designed buildings in New York, London, Paris and Caracas.

If you've climbed Pão de Açúcar (p128) or walked to the eastern banks of Zona Sul you've seen it – Niterói, a mirror of Rio with tall white apartments overlooking pretty beaches. A separate municipality within Rio de Janeiro State, Niterói is home to eight structures by world-renowned modernist architect Oscar Neimeyer, including his saucerlike contemporary art gallery. See them on a 11km coastal walk and dine in some of the city's destination restaurants, including a seafood market that grills fish straight from the market stand. Then, go to one of the area's finest beaches.

Further afield is Petrópolis, the former summer residence for Brazilian royalty with a surprising density of German-style architecture.

Niterói

TIME FROM RIO DE JANEIRO: **20 MINS**

Architecture from Oscar Niemeyer

Cross Baía de Guanabara to Niterói by ferry, taxi/Uber or bus to see Brazil's second-largest collection of Oscar Neimeyer architecture. Walk left from the **Araribóia** ferry terminal to find the curvaceous **Teatro Popular Oscar Niemeyer** (*@teatropopularniteroi*), a 460-person theater that was finished in 2007. The complex, which includes two more Neimeyer buildings, is only open on weekends and you can't go inside unless it's hosting a concert.

Continue along the 11km coastal multiuse path, Caminho Neimeyer, to the architect's saucerlike **Museu de Arte Contemporânea** (*culturaeumdireito.niteroi.rj.gov.br/mac, adult/senior R$16/8*). Completed in 1996, Niterói's MAC hosts temporary exhibitions of photography, sculpture and textiles, though it's hard to beat the views out its 360-degree windows.

A chill beach and mountain climb

Technically a different municipality than Niterói though nearby, **Praia de Itacoatiara** is one of the finest beaches in the area. Cleaner than Niterói's beaches on Baía de Guanabara, Itacoatiara is surrounded by pointy peaks sprinkled with palm trees and has soft, squeaky sand.

Get better views by walking up Rua das Papulas to the trailhead of **Parque Estadual da Serra da Tiricica** (*meio*

CARLOS.MENESES/SHUTTERSTOCK

Museu de Arte Contemporânea

ambiente.niteroi.rj.gov.br/parque-estadual-da-serra-da-tiririca-peset). The state park has two easy, 30-minute hiking trails: Enseada do Bananal, which takes you to a cliff's edge overlooking the sea; and Costão de Itacoatiara, which climbs 208m up a steep (and slippery) rock face to overlook Praia de Itacoatiara below.

Petrópolis

TIME FROM RIO DE JANEIRO: 1½ HRS

German architecture and history

A town filled with German-style buildings is probably the last thing you'd expect 40km north of Rio – but that's Petrópolis. Founded in 1845 by Emperor Dom Pedro II as a mountain retreat for the royal family to escape Rio's infamous summer heat, the town attracted German immigrants from the outset and was constructed by a German engineer. Enjoy the cooler temperatures at elevation (838m), and walk around the charming city. The main attraction is **Museu Imperial** *(@museu.imperial)*, Dom Pedro II's 19th-century palace, which includes his 1.95kg imperial crown and the feather-shaped gold pen Princess Isabel used to sign the Lei Aurea, which freed Brazil's remaining enslaved people in 1888. The princess' former home, **Palácio da Princesa Isabel**, is also in town, though it can be viewed from the outside only. Other Petropólis sites to visit include the 19th-century **Palácio de Cristal** and **Casa de Santos Dumont** *(@casasantosdumont, R$10)*, home to the Brazilian inventor of the airplane.

SUDS-ATIONAL BEER

Considering Petrópolis' German roots, it should be no surprise that the first brewery appeared shortly after the city's founding. Imperial Fábrica de Cerveja Nacional, opened by German immigrant Henrique Leiden, started brewing a beer branded Bohemia in 1853. The beer is still available today – though, like most mainstream beers in Brazil, is now owned by multinational brewer Ambev/Anheuser-Busch InBev.

The brewery, **Complexo Bohemia** (*bohemiapuromalte.com.br, 4/5/8 tastings R$48.40/82.50/137.50*), offers 1½-hour tours and tastings that include immersive exhibits on the history of beer-making.

Petrópolis is also blessed with several more breweries downtown and attracts tens of thousands for the free annual 10-day **Bauernfest** every June, which features lederhosen-clad bands, enormous mugs of beer, glühwein and sausages.

EATING IN NITERÓI: OUR PICKS

Mercado de Peixe São Pedro: Pick your fish or seafood and have it grilled or fried upstairs. *6am-5pm Tue-Sun, to 3pm Mon* $$

Botequim Arretado: Enormous restaurant and menu of northeastern specialties, cocktails with unique fruit from the north. Live music. *11am-midnight* $$

Seu Antônio: Big lineup on weekends for this destination restaurant and creamy shrimp served inside a coconut. *11:30am-7:30pm Tue-Sun* $$

Mocellin: A branch of one of Rio's finest all-you-can-eat *churrascaria* on the beach boardwalk. *noon-10pm* $$$

Where to Stay

It's tough to get both beach and culture without doing some moving around. Stays further from the beach tend to be more budget-friendly. Prices skyrocket in February and March for Carnaval.

There aren't enough accommodations in Gávea, Jardin Botânico and Lagoa for us to recommend staying in those neighborhoods.

Where to Stay If You Love ...

Beach, comfort and high-end shopping

Ipanema & Leblon (p78) Upper-class neighborhoods home to Rio's prettiest beach strip, international shopping and some solid restaurants. The health-focused atmosphere will want to make you want to get fitter.

Bars, beach and busy boardwalk

Copacabana & Leme (p98) Rio visitor hot-spot for the last century, with a busy boardwalk and beach as well as plenty of bars, restaurants and shopping.

Top restaurants, bars and hills

Botafogo, Urca & Humaitá (p116) Rio's best concentration of restaurants and bars in Botafogo, plus peaceful Urca surrounding Pão de Açúcar).

Markets and local life

Flamengo, Laranjeiras, Catete & Glória (p134) Experience life like a local in these quieter neighborhoods, with a long beach perfect for working out, several markets and an upstart bar scene.

Barhopping, street art and hilltop views

Santa Teresa & Lapa (p154) Bohemian neighborhoods with art around every corner, live music, bars and galleries. Great places to stay during Carnaval if you love to party.

Historic and business hub

Centro & Zona Norte (p174) Rio's crumbling downtown center has major corporate offices, some of the best parties, amazing architecture and museums, but it can be dangerous when quiet on the weekends.

Modern and beachy

Zona Oeste (p198) Long, 18km strip of beach with excellent surfing at the western end, along with modern US-style apartment buildings and malls.

Ipanema & Leblon

WATERFRONT

Sheraton $$$
MAP P95
Wake up to thrashing waves at this all-inclusive resort at the foot of Vidigal. There are tennis courts, bars, restaurants a happy-hour lounge, a nearly private beach and almost all balconies face the sea.

Hotel Arpoador $$$
MAP P89
Six-storey hotel in Ipanema steps from the best sunset spot in Rio, with freshly renovated rooms and a rooftop that has a small pool and free morning yoga. Beach service and bikes are also included.

SOCIAL

Mango Tree $
MAP P81
Hostel one block from Ipanema's Posto 9 in a cute 1930s house. It has a welcoming, social atmosphere without being a full-on party hostel. There are various dorms and privates available.

VIEWS

Varandas do Vidigal $
MAP P95
Spend the night in the popular Vidigal favela to get to know a Rio *comunidade*. It has some of the best views, as well as a friendly community vibe. Take a motorcycle up. Inherent favela risks apply.

L'Homme de Rio $$
MAP P81
Beautiful boutique hotel with huge rooms and an excellent view, especially from its outdoor pool. Find it on the road that leads up to the Cantagalo-Pavão-Pavãozinho favela above Ipanema.

Copacabana & Leme

CLASSICS

Copacabana Palace $$$
MAP P102
Stay where the brightest stars of the 20th century stayed at this iconic 1923 hotel owned by luxury hotel brand Belmond. The rooms are chic without being over the top, and there's a Michelin-star restaurant, a spa and a pool.

Hilton Rio $$$
MAP P113
Perfect location steps from Leme and Copacabana beaches, and comfortable, though dated rooms from the reliable international brand. Sunsets on the rooftop pool are the highlight.

SOCIAL

Aquarela do Leme $
MAP P113
Bright and clean hostel near the entrance to the favelas above Leme. Amazing views from its big windows, and there's a rooftop with a gym and bar. Very popular with French guests.

Pura Vida $
MAP P102
Party hostel in a multistory 1920s mansion on the Copacabana-facing street that leads to the Cantagalo-Pavão-Pavãozinho favela. Has dorms ranging from four to 12 people and a couple of privates. The terrace frequently hosts *churrascos* (barbecues).

Selina $$
MAP P102
Copacabana's Selina selfishly has incredible views from its tower over Copacabana, especially from the bar upstairs. Rooms and dorms are artistically decorated, and here's a huge shared kitchen.

HOW MUCH FOR A NIGHT?

Fancy beach-front hotel
from R$1200

Midrange hotel
from R$450

Pousada, guesthouse or B&B
from R$250

Hostel
dorms R$70-120

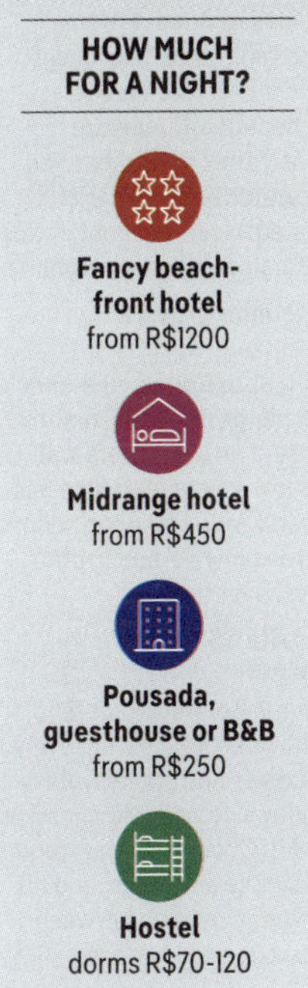

Botafogo, Urca & Humaitá

TRANQUIL

Urca Hotel $$
MAP P126
Feel like a star in this dreamy guesthouse set back from a residential street in Urca. The decor looks cut from a design magazine, with Brazilian art, tumbling plants and tile bathrooms.

O Veleiro Bed & Breakfast $$
Canadian and carioca-owned guesthouse that started as Rio'sfirst B&B in 1999. Located above Botafogo on a cobblestone road surrounded by Atlantic rainforest, with eight lovely rooms and a tranquil pool terrace.

CONVENIENT

Injoy $$
MAP P119
Business-y hotel with small suites and larger apartment-style rooms that include kitchenettes. Rooms are named after world cities and decorated as such. Perfectly located: close, but not too close, to Botafogo's famous nightlife.

Hotelinho Urca $$
MAP P126
Right above one of the bars that slings drinks for nightly sunsets on the *mureta* wall, this low-key guesthouse has several well-equipped rooms and a sunny veranda with views over the bay.

Farfalla $$
MAP P119
Historic Botafogo blue-and-white guesthouse with lovely balconies and stained-glass windows. Renovated ahead of the Rio Olympics, its six rooms are simple and clean, and it's in a great location between Botafogo and Humaitá.

Flamengo, Laranjeiras, Catete & Glória

IN THE TREES

Casa Caminho do Corcovado $$
MAP P141
Close to the Cosme Velho train station up to Cristo Redentor, this is the perfect place to enjoy the world's largest urban forest, Parque Nacional da Tijuca. The guesthouse itself is in a historic 1906 building and has peaceful outdoor areas.

ON A BUDGET

Jo & Joe $
MAP P141
West of of Laranjeiras in the neighborhood of Cosme Velho, this renovated mansion has cool dorms and private rooms and a terrace surrounded by Atlantic rainforest that includes a tree planted by Walt Disney.

Discovery Hostel $
MAP P149
A great place to meet fellow travelers and in a fine location next to Glória's hip bar, Fatchia, as well as the metro. The attractive converted house is also convenient for exploring Lapa.

Villa 25 $
MAP P137
Appealing to 'glampackers', this hostel is not the friendliest, nor is it very social, but the beautifully renovated 1889 building on Largo de Machado is exquisite and the mix of suites and dorms are modern and clean.

Santa Teresa & Lapa

HOSTEL

Castelo dos Tucanos $
MAP PP158-9
Social (but not party) hostel in a gorgeous mansion with views of Corcovado in Santa Teresa. There's a big pool with Sunday *churrasco*, and an inspiring coworking room with stained-glass windows.

LARISSA CARGNIN/SHUTTERSTOCK

Vila Galé, Centro

Mambembe $
MAP P167
You'll be busy at this hostel up the street from Lapa, and a staircase away from Santa Teresa. Its active WhatsApp group has invitations to events, both in-house and around Rio.

Selina $$
MAP P167
Upscale hostel chain that must be applauded for saving this gorgeous building facing the Lapa Arches and around the corner from the Selarón's Steps. Inside, the hostel is chic, with coworking and a rooftop bar.

BOUTIQUE

Casa Nova $$
MAP P167
Well-organized hotel with friendly staff and a lovely roof-top pool. Located down the street from the bar zone in Lapa.

Chez Georges $$$
MAP PP158-9
A work of art in Santa Teresa from modernist architect Wladimir Alves de Souza. Cool furniture in the common areas and seven rooms, plus 360-degree views from the balconies and poolside. Musicians such as Luedji Luna have recorded in the studio.

Casa Beleza $$$
MAP PP158-9
Enchanting former residence of the state governor in a 1930s mansion surrounded by lush forest. Owners are a Brazilian-French-Indian-Canadian-British family that plays music, produces documentaries and leads hiking tours around Tijuca Forest.

TOP TIP
If coming for Carnaval, stay close to the best *Blocos* and the Sambodrómo in the neighborhoods of Santa Teresa, Lapa, Glória, Flamengo or Centro. Alternatively, the beaches have fewer *Blocos* and offer a calmer respite.

Centro & Zona Norte

HISTORIC

Vila Galé $$$
MAP P177
High-end candy-pink hotel in a 19th-century building breathing new life into Centro. There's a peaceful pool, and rooms are quiet despite having the best of Rio's nightlife down the street in Lapa.

DOMESTIC AIRPORT

Prodigy Santos Dumont $$$
MAP P177
Located inside Rio's domestic airport in Centro, this stylish four-star hotel has superb views of Baía de Guanabara and Sugarloaf Mountain from its swanky rooftop patio and outdoor swimming pool.

Zona Oeste

BEACH

Longboard Paradise Hostel $
MAP P213
Surf hostel in front of Macumba Beach with thatched roofs that make it look like Southeast Asia. There's an on-site restaurant and lessons.

Pousada Barra Sol $
MAP P205
It's just a five-minute walk to the beach from this unfussy *pousada* (guesthouse) at the beginning of Barra de Tijuca. A night's stay includes a fresh and tasty breakfast.

ISLAND

Casanova Residence $$$
MAP P205
Spend the night on Gigóia Island. Room balconies look out on the water and Pedra da Gavéa overhead. Reserve ahead at the upscale in-house bistro.

RETREAT

Cliffside $$$
Take a break from all that partying at this extraordinary seaside boutique hotel in Joá built in 1968 by Brazilian architect Zanine Caldas. Stars such as Tom Jobim, Elis Regina, Steve McQueen and Jack Nicholson have stayed here.

Casa Guaiamum $$$
This holiday home in Barra de Guaratiba is a terrific place to recharge. Read a book in the net over the calm water in view of the mangroves and get some real R & R.

Sweet

TOOLKIT

The chapters in this section cover the most important topics you'll need to know about in Rio de Janeiero . They're full of nuts-and-bolts information and valuable insights to help you understand and navigate Rio and get the most out of your trip.

Carnaval (p46)
NURPHOTO SRL/ALAMY

Money

CURRENCY: BRAZILIAN REAL (R$)

Cards and Tap Payments

Cards and tap payments (Apple Pay, Samsung Pay and Google Wallet) are widely accepted. Even street vendors selling beer from a cooler should have a machine. Always run foreign cards as *crédito* (credit) even if it's debit. Paying with a card online becomes more difficult without a CPF (Brazilian tax ID).

Cash

It's a good idea to have cash when cards are not accepted, ie on buses or when vendors only accept Pix (local-only digital payment).

Taxes

Value-added tax (VAT) on purchases is 19% and always included in the given price. There's no system for VAT refunds on purchases made in Brazil.

Tipping

In restaurants, a 10% service charge is usually included in the bill and there is no expectation that anything be left beyond that. Taxis do not expect tips, though locals generally round up to the nearest *real*. Tour guides will appreciate a tip, especially on free walking tours.

HOW MUCH FOR A...

Public bus
R$4.30

Beach umbrella & chair
R$20-40

eSIM
from RS$29 for 1GB

Museum entry
free-R$30

HOW TO... Pay with Pix

The Brazilian digital transfer service Pix launched in 2020 and has taken off across the country, with many locals preferring it to carrying around wads of cash. But paying with Pix is very difficult for foreigners without a local bank account. If they ask for Pix, ask if you can pay with a card or online bank transfer. Otherwise, the Remitly app allows Pix if the minimum's above R$50.

LOCAL TIP

Bradesco's bank ATMs usually work with foreign cards and don't charge a transaction fee. While Banco24Horas ATMs should work, they charge a hefty withdrawal fee.

COST OF LIVING

Like pretty much everywhere, prices in Rio have spiked in recent years. Restaurants, hotel rooms and even produce at the grocery store aren't substantially less than in countries in the US and Europe – in some cases, prices are even higher.

This is especially tough on locals who earn salaries in *real*. Prices in Rio are particularly high for imported goods, due to Brazil's protectionist policies that levy high taxes. For example, an iPhone in Brazil is the second most expensive in the world after Türkiye.

FROM LEFT: GUSTAVOMELLOSSA/SHUTTERSTOCK, RAFASTOCKBR/SHUTTERSTOCK, DOROTTYA MATHE/SHUTTERSTOCK

Family Travel

Just as Rio's mixture of mountains, jungle and metropolis is marvelous for adults, it's awesome for kids, too. Parents bringing kids with them everywhere is part of the culture in Brazil, and nothing to be shy about. Take kids to see monkeys in the jungle and to play on the beach – just keep an eye out for sunstroke, as it gets hot.

Sights

Aside from the beach, Rio has plenty of fun activities for kids, including a zoo and an aquarium. It'll also spark their curiosity to look out for monkeys, birds and lizards at sites parents want to visit too, such as **Cristo Redentor** (kids love the train ride up) and **Pão de Açúcar** (particularly riding the *bondinho* up to the top).

Where to Eat

There are children's menus at almost every restaurant. They almost always include a simple protein ie chicken or beef with rice, beans and fries, so if your kid eats any of those, you can eat pretty much anywhere. Also, juice bars like **Bibi Sucos** (multiple locations) are perfect for eating out with kids because you can order as plain a sandwich as you want.

Facilities

Diaper-changing facilities are common in women's restrooms found in restaurants and malls in Zona Sul. Breastfeeding is acceptable everywhere.

Getting Around

Kids under six ride free on buses and metros. Ubers are quite affordable in Rio if you want to make things easier.

KID-FRIENDLY PICKS

AquaRio (p184) The largest aquarium in South America, with 8000 plus animals.

BioPark Rio (p193) Zoo inside Quinta da Boa Vista park, with lions, tigers and bears (oh my!).

Pão de Açúcar (p128) Ride the cable car up to the top and see fuzzy capuchin monkeys.

Bonde (p156) Take the cute yellow tram that travels up to Santa Teresa.

Museu do Amanhã (p182) Great for kids over seven, as it makes them think about the future of our planet.

DAY AT THE BEACH

Head to the beach before 10am for the quietest atmosphere and the freshest temperatures. Either way, you'll want to get an umbrella, chairs and possibly a table. Anywhere you go, keep your belongings with you, as beach bags can get snatched.

Look out for flags showing whether the water is safe to swim (red means it's not). For calmer water that's easier to swim in, visit **Praia Vermelha** (p125) or **Praia da Urca** (p125).

Join local families by walking strollers or riding bikes and scooters up and down beach avenues, such as Av Atlantica and **Aterro do Flamengo** (p136), which shut on Sundays to traffic.

Food, Drink & Nightlife

When to Eat

Café de manhã (breakfast, 8am to 10am) Generally a *cafezinho* (espresso) and piece of French bread.

Almoço (lunch, noon to 3pm) Heaviest meal of the day, *menu executivo* (plate of the day) or self-serve buffet. If there's no rice and beans, it's not *comida* (food).

Jantar (dinner, 8pm to 10pm) A lighter meal like a salad or sandwich or international cuisine like pizza.

Where to Eat

Lanchonete: Snack bar serving *salgados* (salty snacks), standard Brazilian plates, juices and coffee.

Por-kilo: Pay-by-weight self-serve buffets with highly varied options.

Quiosque: Permanent restaurants on the beach boardwalk.

Boteco/botequim: Neighborhood bars known for *petiscos* (snacks), *cervejas* (beer) and watching soccer games.

Rodízio: All-you-can-eat meals that don't stop until you say to.

Cafe: Baristas slinging specialty coffee and snacks is still a rarity in Rio, but there are a few spots.

MENU DECODER

açaí: Amazon berries

arroz: rice

bebida: drink

bolinho de bacalhau: fried codfish balls

brigadeiro: chocolate

camarão: shrimp

catupiry: cream cheese

carne: meat

chope: draft beer

churrasco: barbecue

coxinha: chicken-stuffed cornmeal balls

esfiha: Levantine savory pastry

farofa: crunchy cassava flour

feijão: beans

feijoada: beans and pork meat

frango: chicken

galeto: spring chicken

menu executivo: lunch special

milho: corn

molho: sauce

moqueca: seafood stew

pão de queijo: cassava and cheese ball

pastel: fried stuffed pastry

peixe: fish

picanha: fatty cut of steak

picante: spicy

sobremesa: dessert

tapioca: cassava flour pancake

HOW TO... Eat at a Por-Kilo Restaurant

Many restaurants in Rio are *por-kilo* buffets, meaning you pay for the weight of your food rather than the items you order. Kilo buffets usually have large buffets of salads, rice, beans, pasta and various meats. Remember, you're paying by weight, so be selective – carbs and meats tend to be heavier so you'll pay more. It's a good idea to scope things out before filling up your plate. After carefully selecting your food, place your plate on the scale before paying. You may then order drinks. For many, the advantage of kilo restaurants is that you can try many things. They're also often healthier, as you can choose larger portions of veggies. An especially beloved kind of kilo place is the type that serves *açaí*. At those, you can add as many toppings as you like before weighing and paying.

FROM LEFT: DUMPSTOCK/SHUTTERSTOCK, IMAGENSSTOCKBR/SHUTTERSTOCK RODRIGOBARK/SHUTTERSTOCK, ARTBYPIXEL/SHUTTERSTOCK

HOW MUCH FOR A...

coffee
R$5–10

coconut water
R$10

salgado
R$5–12

beer (600ml)
R$12–20

caipirinha
R$10–35

menu executivo
R$20–50

feijoada
R$45+

churrascaria
R$200+

HOW TO... Tackle a Churrascaria

One of the top things to do on any Rio itinerary is to eat at a *churrascaria*, a type of *rodízio* (all-you-can-eat) extravaganza where the food doesn't stop coming until you say so. The first word of wisdom is to not eat very much for a solid 24 hours before eating, as this is going to be a feast.

When it comes time to dine, you'll likely be given a card to signal to the waiter to bring more food or stop. If you want more, cuts of various types of meat will be brought to your table. Among them will surely be *picanha*, Brazil's favorite steak cut, which comes from the top of the cow's rump and is recognizable by its thick strip of fat. Your waiter will slice it off a spit and ask you to pull off a piece with supplied tongs.

Other cuts of beef will come to your table, as will other meats, most likely chicken hearts and fish. But that's not all. *Churrascarias* usually have a full buffet, complete with sushi, pasta and other typical Brazilian dishes. You can also often order side dishes, including grilled bananas and *pão d'alho* (garlic bread). Be careful not to fill up on carbs to get the most value from the high cost of the meal. If steak isn't your thing, you can also find *rodízios* for pizza, sushi and *petiscos*.

Backyard Churrasco

The best way to eat *churrasco* is with locals who grill expertly seasoned meat on backyard barbecues until you can't eat anymore – then they bring more. *Churrascos* are common for celebrations and birthdays.

DRINKING AT A BOTECO

In Rio, *botecos* or *botequim* are small bars where locals hang out to sip beer and watch soccer games, usually while seated on plastic stools or chairs situated shakily on the sidewalk.

When you arrive, you'll be asked if you want a beer. You can choose from either a *chopp* (pint), longneck (traditional beer bottle) or the default *seiscentos* (600ml beer).

Beers always come *estupidamente geladinha* (stupidly cold), never warm. Sometimes, beer may even be partially frozen when they come to your table. If you opt for a 600ml beer, it'll be placed in a *camisinha* (plastic holder) to keep the beer cold (comically, *camisinha* is also the Brazilian Portuguese word for condom). Now pour the beer into one of the small glass or plastic cups provided. If you're with friends, keep pouring the beer so no one's glass is empty. *Tim Tim* (pronounced 'chin chin') is the expression for cheers.

When it comes to choosing which local beer to drink, most are made by the same multinational brewer, Ambev (Anheuser-Busch InBev), despite the different labels. The most common (and best) options are Antarctica and Original, light pilsners that go down like water; and Brahma, a slightly thicker lager. Craft beer is rare in *botecos*, though it is catching on elsewhere.

If you're not a beer drinker, there's a good chance the *boteco* can whip you up a *caipirinha* – a potent cocktail made with sugarcane spirit *cachaça*, sugar and limes or other fruit like *maracujá* (passion fruit), *manga* (mango) or *abacaxi* (pineapple).

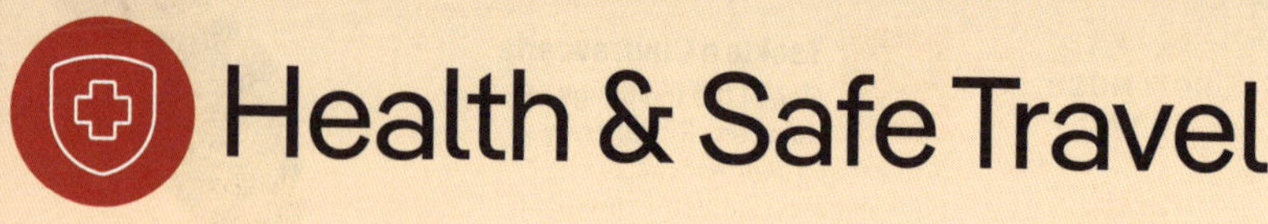

Health & Safe Travel

MOSQUITOS & INFECTIOUS DISEASES

In 2024, Rio experienced alarmingly high levels of dengue fever, a mosquito-transmitted virus that, while not usually deadly, can be extremely painful. Even though Rio has been fighting the disease, including by releasing dengue-fighting mosquitos, wear mosquito repellant if this is a concern. Pregnant mothers and those trying for a baby may also want to keep an eye out for Zika flare-ups.

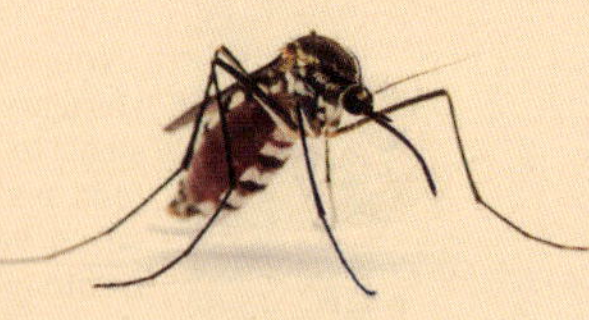

Healthcare

Public healthcare is free to anyone in Brazil, resident or not. However, public hospitals usually have long wait times and the experience can be chaotic. Buy a travel insurance policy that gives you access to Rio's excellent private health care instead.

Petty Theft

It's no secret that Rio has a reputation as an unsafe destination, but while crime rates are high, the largest threat to travelers is petty theft. Thieves on motorbikes commonly snatch phones out of hands and can hold people up at gunpoint or knife point. Pickpocketing and bag snatching are also common. Don't risk resisting, just hand over your stuff.

CARD CLONING

Card cloning is Brazil's most common form of scam. Cut your odds by using ATMs inside banks during banking hours.

SWIM SAFETY

Green flag: Safe to swim.

Yellow flag: Be cautious – non-expert swimmers shouldn't swim alone.

Red flag: Do not swim.

Sunburns & Heat Exhaustion

Bright red or peeling skin is a sign of an unprepared visitor. Always wear sunscreen on the beach, even on cloudy days (locals do, too). Heat is another challenge in Rio. A heatwave in 2024 hit 62.3°C (144.1°F). Look out for symptoms of heat exhaustion, including headaches, fatigue, nausea and a rapid pulse.

PRECAUTIONS TO PREVENT THEFT

Carry only the minimum cash needed and avoid using your phone on the street. Wear a money pouch in crowds and don't wear flashy jewelry. Walk purposely and avoid dark, empty streets.

Only use ATMs inside banks during the day. Keep an eye on your belongings on the beach and avoid the sand at night.

CLOCKWISE FROM TOP LEFT: KHLUNGCENTER/SHUTTERSTOCK, NITO/SHUTTERSTOCK, DI3MA/SHUTTERSTOCK

LGBTIQ+ Travelers

Rio de Janeiro is one of the top gay destinations in Latin America, if not the world. Festivals like Carnaval, Réveillon and Rio Pride are an outpouring of affection for all. However, Brazil as a country is not Shangri-la, particularly for trans people. Brazil has shockingly high numbers of trans murders, and recently passed at least 77 anti-trans laws.

Réveillon, Carnaval & Pride

Dressed in white for the fireworks, **Réveillon** (p100; New Year's Eve) on **Copacabana Beach** is one of the top events on the world gay travel calendar – and the biggest bucket-list item for Rio. Not to be outdone, Rio's **Carnaval** in February or March showcases the city's tolerance, with public displays of affection unlikely to draw an eye – everyone's too busy looking for their own person to kiss. **Rio Pride** is in November, but São Paulo's parade is bigger, reaching four million people in 2024 – the world's largest.

BARS & NIGHTCLUBS

While Rio's tolerance makes it so LGBTIQ+ people are welcome everywhere, there are a few neighborhoods particularly known for their gay nightlife. Botafogo has a few gay bars, some of which have dancing the later it gets, and Copacabana has a couple of well-known nightclubs staying open into the wee hours. There are also a few spots in Centro, and many DJ shows are gay-friendly.

Beach Hangouts

Rio's beaches maintain a permanent welcoming presence for LGBTIQ+ people. **Ipanema Beach**'s Posto 9 has long been a hub for queer sunbathers. Another popular spot is **Praia do Leme's**'s **Barraca Ponto G**, meaning the G spot, at *barraca* (tent) 26. There's a nude beach west of the city at Abricó (Praia de Grumari).

FILM FESTIVAL

Starting in 2011, Rio has hosted an annual **LGBTIQ+ International Film Festival** at venues across the city. The July festival featured a total of 90 films in 2024, with both Brazilian and international films shown. Aside from screenings, the festival has panel discussions and an art fair.

RESOURCES

Mix Brasil *(mixbrasil.org.br)* Largest Brazilian LGBTIQ+ site.

ABGLT *(abglt.org)* Nonprofit network of more than 300 LGBTIQ+ and similar groups.

Aliança Nacional LGBTI+ *(aliancalgbti.org.br)* Defends LGBTIQ+ human rights.

Antra *(antrabrasil.org)* Brazil's largest transgender network.

Brazil Ecojourneys *(brazilecojourneys.com)* Brazilian LGBTIQ+ tour operator with trips like gay surf camp.

Rio Queer *(@rioqueer)* Weekly list of queer-friendly events.

Trans Murders

Every three days, a trans person is murdered in Brazil, according a study by the National Association of Transvestite and Transgender People (Antra). These shocking numbers make Brazil the deadliest country in the world for total trans people killed annually.

Responsible Travel

Climate Change & Travel

It's impossible to ignore the impact we have when travelling; Lonely Planet urges all travellers to engage with their travel carbon footprint, which will mainly come from air travel. While there often isn't an alternative, travellers can look to minimise the number of flights they take, opt for newer aircrafts and use cleaner ground transport, such as trains. One proposed solution—purchasing carbon offsets—unfortunately does not cancel out the impact of individual flights. While most destinations will depend on air travel for the foreseeable future, for now, pursuing ground-based travel where possible is the best course of action.

The **UN Carbon Offset Calculator** shows how flying impacts a household's emissions.

The **ICAO's carbon emissions calculator** allows visitors to analyse the CO2 generated by point-to-point journeys.

75.7%

According to a 2021 survey by Brazil's official statistics agency, citizens who identify as White earn R$3099, or 75.7% more per month than those who identify as Black (R$1764).

Food for the Houseless

When you eat a 3-course lunch at **Refeittorio Gastromotiva** *(p171; 11am-3pm, Mon-Fri, R$45)* in Lapa, you're supporting a project that feeds 72 houseless people five days per week. The nonprofit also supports up-and-coming chefs.

Shop Local

Support local clothing brands like **FARM Rio** (p84). They're not only stylish, but cheaper than international products, due to Brazil's protectionist policies. Better yet, shop at **Oficina Muda** (p109), which upcycles clothing from top local brands.

Visit a *quilombo* (communities founded by fugitive enslaved people) such as **Quilombo Ferreira Diniz** *(p153; @quilomboferreiradiniz)* in Glória for its Friday *feijoada*. In doing so, you're supporting a self-sustaining community with strong egalitarian values.

Carnaval glitter is made out of the same kind of plastic as water bottles, only smaller, so they seep easier into waterways. Instead, buy biodegradable glitter from local businesses like **Purpine** *(@ppurpurine)* and **Pura Color Beauty** *(@pura.colorbeauty)*.

It's tempting to want to see favelas on a jeep tour, but you should resist the urge. These tours often don't support these communities and stereotype them as permanent war zones.

Project Refauna *(refauna.org.br)* is hoping to save the world's largest urban rainforest, **Parque Nacional da Tijuca** (p74), by reintroducing endemic species. By visiting the park, you're proving that their work to rewild the area is worthwhile.

Skip Taxis

Ubers and taxis are tempting, but do your part by taking the metro, buses or the electric **Bonde** (p100) tram up to Santa Teresa. Itaú bikes or electric Whoosh scooters are also more carbon-conscious – and fun.

Museum of Tomorrow

Reflect on climate change, and our effect on it, by visiting **Museu do Amanhã** *(p182; museudoamanha.org.br)*. The museum for future technology is LEED-certified and provides fascinating, chilling, facts about the environment.

Shop at Junta Local *(juntalocal.com)* street markets that showcase small businesses selling sustainable food and clothing.

Fill reusable bottles with filtered water and bring a reusable mug to the beach for drinks.

Support Nonprofits

Support favela nonprofits, such as **Yoga On High** *(p94; ameviva.org)*, which teaches healthy living; **Nós do Morro** *(p96; @gruposnosdomorrooficial)*, which provides access to art; and **Favela Orgânica** *(112; favelaorganica.com.br)*, which teaches urban agriculture and composting.

Humpback Conservation

Go on a whale-watching tour with Projeto Baleia Jubarte *(baleiajubarte.org.br)* on its partner ship **Valeiro Sagarana** *(veleirosagarana.com)*. The conservation organization has helped migrating humpback whale populations bounce back.

Go Vegan or Veggie

Brazilians love their *churrasco* (barbecue meat), but vegetarian and vegan options are starting to catch on. Consider Brazilian dishes made vegan, like cashew cream *moqueca* (Bahian stew) and mushroom ***feijoada*** (black bean stew).

RESOURCES

ipe.org.br
Nationwide biodiversity conservation specialist

iis-rio.org
Brazilian sustainability nonprofit

bvrio.org
City nonprofit for economic, environmental and social sustainability

CLOCKWISE FROM TOP LEFT: SIDNEY DE ALMEIDA/SHUTTERSTOCK, MARINA JOSAN/ALAMY, JEFFREY ISAAC GREENBERG 9+/ALAMY

Accessible Travel

Rio de Janeiro has been making a concerted effort to become more accessible, and seeing its primary attractions are doable with limited mobility. There are also accessibility services in place from private taxi and tour companies. Still, it's a good idea to consult with relevant experts and plan ahead.

Fast Pass

At certain attractions like the *bondinho* (aerial cable car) at **Pão de Açúcar** (p128), those with accessibility issues (ie wheelchairs, pregnant, seniors or people with mobility issues) can cut the line.

Airport

Both **Galeão International** (GIG) and **Santos Dumont** (SDU) airports offer assistance for wheelchair users and travelers with visual impairments. Request it through your airline in advance. Both airports also have accessible bathrooms, ramps and elevators.

Accommodations

By law, hotels built, expanded or renovated since 2004 must have at least 10% of their rooms adapted for accessibility. Major hotels on the beachfront, such as **Hilton Rio** (p223) and the **Sheraton** (p223) are your best bet.

BEACH FOR ALL

Operating on six Rio beaches, Praia por Todos *(praiaparatodos.com)*, offers physical assistance and materials, including mats for wheelchairs, sound signaling for people with visual/hearing impairments, accessible toilets and adapted surfing. Main beaches also have wheelchair-accessible curb cuts.

Cristo Redentor

Wheelchair users can ride the train up Corcovado and take an elevator to the upper level, but the statue itself is only accessible via an escalator (manual wheelchairs only).

Public Transport

Municipal buses have electronic wheelchair lifts, and both the metro and light-rail entries are flat. Most metro stations have elevators from street level, but some close on weekends. Wheelchair users usually ride the metro for free.

Football & Future

Legendary football stadium **Maracanã** (p194) is accessible for wheelchair users in its museum and has special seating during matches. **Museu do Amanhã** *(p182; museudoamanha.org.br)* is also fully accessible.

TOURS

Rio Accessible Tour *(rioaccessibletour.com.br)* Accessible tour company that can tailor itineraries.

Praia para Todos *(praiaparatodos.com)* Assistance and accessibility support on six beaches.

Especial Coop Taxi *(02132959606)* Taxi service for wheelchair users and two companions.

Programa Turismo Acessível *(turismoacessivel.gov.br)* Government accessible-travel initiative.

SATH *(Society for Accessible Travel & Hospitality; sath.org)* Resource for travelers with disabilities.

Wheel the World *(wheeltheworld.com)* Search engine for accessible stays and experiences.

BENJAMIN CONSTANT

One of the fathers of the Brazilian republic taught at a Rio school for the visually impaired that still exists today. Visit his former residence, Museu Benjamin Constant *(p163; museucasabenjaminconstant.museus.gov.br)*, which includes sensory textiles and pottery you can touch.

How To Wear Havaianas

No clothing brand, and certainly no article of clothing, is more ubiquitous to a country than Havaianas are to Brazil. Everyone owns a pair (or five) of these comfortable rubber flip-flops. Havaianas are so essential that during the 1980s inflation crisis, the Brazilian government added them to the list of fixed-price goods – alongside staples like rice and beans. Of course, Havaianas are now sold in more than 100 countries and worn on beach boardwalks everywhere.

History of Havaianas

Havaianas were created in 1962 in Brazil after Scottish businessperson Robert Fraser fell in love with a Japanese thong sandal called a Zori, which had fabric straps and soles made from rice straw. Wanting a sturdier version suitable for Brazilian beach life, he took some high-quality rubber and molded his own Zori-like sandals – the first pair of Havaianas, named after Hawai'i (Havaí, in Portuguese).

World's Most Expensive Havaianas

Some Havaianas have impressive price tags, like H. Stern's 2003 collaborative pair, decorated with 1636 gold feathers and adorned with diamonds, which clocked in at R$58,500. In 2021, João Canhada, president of the cryptocurrency brokerage Foxbit bought the most expensive pair of Havaianas that you can't wear – a Havaianas NFT titled Happy Feet. At the time, the NFT in the metaverse cost 0.28 ETH (Ethereum), equivalent to R$5600. Part of the proceeds from the sale (7% of the net profit) were promised to Favela Galeria, an open-air art museum in São Paulo.

Where to Buy Havaianas

You can buy Havaianas anywhere in Rio, from pharmacies to street kiosks. But there are also official Havaianas *(havaianas.com.br)* shops offering an almost absurd range of colors, styles and sizes. You can even customize your own pair. Depending on where you buy them and the style you purchase, Havaianas generally cost between R$15–$50.

How to Wear Them

Havaianas are the most popular and versatile footwear in Rio. You can wear them to the beach, the shops, dinner, or even to a party. Havaianas are also a great substitute for slippers and make perfect goalposts for beach football. They are the solution for a wobbly bar table and even make good doorstops and mosquito killers. When you hit the beach, wear your Havaianas on your arms to carry them across the sand.

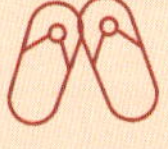

How to Fix a Broken Pair

While long-lasting considering the amount of use they get, the nub that holds the straps to the soles will inevitably break off. Save yourself from buying a new pair by poking a paper clip through the toe post and folding it back so it's flush with the sole.

SERGIO AZENHA/ALAMY

Digital Nomading

So you love Rio and want to stay longer – who can blame you? This marvelous city is a popular destination for remote workers who live and travel outside their country of residence, aka digital nomads. Brazil has actively attracted digital nomads by introducing a special visa that permits temporary stays of a year or two. Here's what you need to know if you'd like to be a digital nomad in Rio.

Digital Nomad Visa

Many European and North American passport holders may stay in Brazil for up to 90 days on a Brazilian tourist visa. Some, like Canadians and Americans, may extend for 90 more for a total of 180 days a year. To stay a year or two, you may apply for a digital nomad visa. To qualify, applicants must earn more than US$1500 monthly from outside the country or have US$18,000 in savings. Instructions for the considerably complicated process can be found at the QR code on the right.

Meeting Other Nomads

Rio is a social city and cariocas are some of the friendliest on the planet, but if you're looking for people with similar careers and who speak your language, there are plenty of ways to meet other digital nomads. Rio Digital Nomads (riodigitalnomads.org) facilitates an array of WhatsApp groups that share everything from short-term stays to parties on the weekend to volunteering opportunities. It also has a helpful guide that goes into the nitty gritty of life in Rio. Rio Digital Nomads commonly shares info about happy hours, comedy nights, and language exchanges.

Student Visas

An option with less paperwork is to apply for a student visa (QR code below), which can last a year and is extendable as long as you're still studying. To qualify, applicants must enroll in studies that last 100+ hours.

This could include Portuguese classes or a program at a university. Language schools in Rio are familiar with the visa and can provide an enrollment form. It's usually easier to apply before you arrive in Brazil.

CPF

First, you'll need a Cadastro de Pessoas Físicas (CPF). CPFs are similar to social-security numbers and are necessary for everything in Brazil, from getting a SIM card to booking local flights to filling in visa documents. Nonresidents can get a CPF by filling out the form at the QR code below and going to the Receita Federal office in Ipanema before 9am with printed copies of the form and confirmation. Bring your passport, a photocopy, and proof of where you're staying. After filling out some paperwork you should receive your CPF by email in a couple of weeks.

BE ONE OF THE GOOD ONES

Digital nomads have earned a reputation as hedonists who travel for sunshine, avoid taxes and raise rent wherever they are. But working remotely isn't necessarily bad if you do so as ethically as possible. If you stay, study Portuguese and make Brazilian friends. Brazilian history and culture are fascinating – learn about them. Rent accommodation directly from locals – subletting a room while a local is traveling can be a win-win for everyone. Volunteer, support local businesses and give back as much as you can.

FLAG: MINI ONION/SHUTTERSTOCK, LAPTOP: VELISHCHUK YEVHEN/SHUTTERSTOCK

Nuts & Bolts

OPENING HOURS

Banks 10am–4pm, Monday–Friday

Cafes 7am–11pm

Nightclubs 10pm–4am, Thursday–Saturday

Bars 11am–2am

Post offices 9am–5pm, Monday–Friday

Restaurants Noon–10pm

Shops 10am–6pm, Monday–Saturday

Tap Water

Municipal tap water is safe to drink, though it doesn't taste great. Most locals drink filtered water, as it tastes better and limits risks.

Toilets
Due to poor plumbing in many of Rio de Janeiro's buildings, you'll have to toss used toilet paper in the trash instead of flushing it.

Smoking
Smoking is banned in restaurants and bars; and cannabis is illegal, though decriminalized.

GOOD TO KNOW

Time Zone
Brasilia Time (GMT/UTC minus 3 hours)

Country Code
+55

Emergency number
190

Population
6.7 million

PUBLIC HOLIDAYS

New Year's Day January 1

Saint Sebastian's Day January 20

Carnaval February/March (the two days before Ash Wednesday)

Good Friday & Easter Sunday March/April

Tiradentes Day April 21

Saint George's Day April 23

May Day/Labor Day May 1

Corpus Christi Late May/June (60 days after Easter Sunday)

Independence Day September 7

Day of NS de Aparecida October 12

All Souls' Day November 2

Proclamation of the Republic November 15

Zumbi dos Palmares (Black Awareness) Day November 20

Christmas Day December 25

Electricity

Types C 220V/50Hz and N 127/220V/60Hz

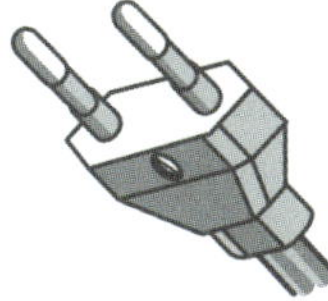

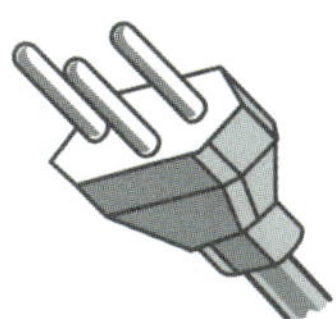

Type C

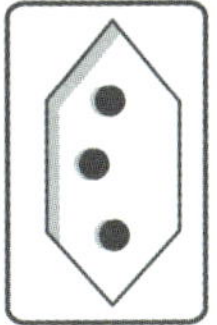

Type N

Language

Learning some Brazilian Portuguese – with its distinct spelling, pronunciation and vocabulary – will open the door to local knowledge, new relationships and a unique travel experience.

Basics

Hello. Olá. o·*laa*

Goodbye. Tchau. tee·*show*

How are you? Como vai? *ko*·mo vai

Fine, and you? Bem, e você? beng e vo·*se*

Excuse me. Com licença. kong lee·*seng*·sa

Sorry. Desculpa. des·*kool*·paa

Yes./No. Sim./Não. seeng/nowng

Please. Por favor. por faa·*vorr*

Thank you.

Obrigado. o·bree·*gaa*·do **(m)**

Obrigada. o·bree·*gaa*·daa **(f)**

You're welcome. De nada.. de *naa*·daa

What's your name? Qual é o seu nome? kwow e o se·oo *no*·me

My name is ... Meu nome é ... *me*·oo *no*·me e ...

Do you speak English? Você fala inglês? vo·se *faa*·laa eeng·*gles*

I don't understand. Não entendo. nowng eng·*teng*·do

Eating & Drinking

What would you recommend? O que você recomenda? oo ke vo·*se* he·ko·*meng*·daa

What's in that dish? O que tem neste prato? o ke teng *nes*·te *praa*·to

Cheers! Saúde! sa·*oo*·de

That was delicious. Estava delicioso. es·*taa*·vaa de·lee·see·*o*·zo

Bring the bill/check, please. Por favor traga a conta. porr faa·*vorr* *traa*·gaa aa *kong*·taa

Emergencies

Help! Socorro! so·*ko*·ho

Leave me alone! Me deixe em paz! me *day*·she eng paas

Call ...! Chame ...! *sha*·me ...

a doctor um médico oom *me*·dee·ko

the police a polícia aa po·*lee*·syaa

It's an emergency. É uma emergência. e *oo*·maa e·merr·*zheng*·see·aa

I'm lost.

Estou perdido. es·*to* perr·*dee*·do **(m)**

Estou perdida. es·*to* perr·*dee*·daa **(f)**

I'm ill. Estou doente.. es·*to* do·*eng*·te

Where are the bathrooms? Onde tem um banheiro? *on*·de teng oom ba·*nyay*·ro

Time

What time is it? Que horas são? kee *aw*·raas sowng

morning manhã ma·*nyang*

afternoon tarde *taar*·de

evening noite *noy*·te

yesterday ontem *ong*·teng

today hoje *o*·zhe

tomorrow amanhã aa·ma·*nyang*

Signs

Banheiro Toilet

Entrada Entrance

Não Tem Vaga No Vacancy

Pronto Socorro Emergency Department

Saída Exit

Tem Vaga Vacancy

NUMBERS

0 **zero** zerro

1 **um** oom

2 **dois** doys

3 **três** tres

4 **quatro** *kwaa*·tro

5 **cinco** *seeng*·ko

6 **seis** says

7 **sete** *se*·te

8 **oito** *oy*·to

9 **nove** *naw*·ve

10 **dez** dez

GRINGO, GRINGA

In Brazilian Portuguese, this term refers to almost anyone who is not Brazilian. It's generally not an insult.

ADDRESSING BRAZILIANS

It's always best to address older people using Senhor or Senhora. You'll notice that first names are used with titles, often more so than family names.

Word Stress

Stress generally occurs on the second-to-last syllable of a word, though there are exceptions. When a word ends in a written -r or is pronounced with a nasalised vowel, the stress falls on the last syllable. Another exception: if a written vowel has an accent marked on it, the stress falls on the syllable containing that vowel.

Street Talk

Foi legal

It was cool.

'Legal' means 'good' or 'cool.' It's one of the most popular slang expressions in Brazil.

Nossa!

Wow!

Short for 'Nossa Senhora' (meaning 'Our Lady' or 'Our Maddona'), this expression conveys surprise. Note that 'nossa' is also used in conversation for its formal meaning, the word for the possessive first person plural feminine pronoun 'our.'

Tudo bom?

All good.

Can be made into a question as a common greeting or a declarative sentence as the standard answer to many questions.

De onde você é? / Eu sou de...

Where are you from?/ I'm from...

This will undoubtedly be one of the first questions you're asked, especially if you're trying to speak Portuguese.

Como você diz...?

How do you say...?

If you want to learn how to say something, just ask. People are generally happy to help you learn their language in Brazil.

NASAL VOWELS

A characteristic feature of Brazilian Portuguese is the use of nasal vowels. Nasal vowels are pronounced as if you're trying to force the sound out of your nose rather than your mouth. It's easier than it sounds. English also has nasal vowels to some extent – when you say 'sing' in English, the 'i' is nasalised by the 'ng'.

STORYBOOK

Our writers delve deep into different aspects of Rio life

***Blocos da Rua*, Carnaval (p46)**

A.RICARDO/SHUTTERSTOCK

HISTORY OF RIO DE JANEIRO IN 15 PLACES

Rio de Janeiro might just be the world's most beautiful city. But beneath its sun-kissed sand, pointed peaks and busy cityscape is a tumultuous history of genocide, slavery, military dictatorships and popular resistance. Visit these 15 sites to better understand the history that shaped this marvelous city. By Joel Balsam

OF COURSE, RIO de Janeiro wasn't 'discovered' by Portuguese colonists – there were as many as 80 indigenous villages in the area. But it was first seen by European eyes on January 1, 1502, when a Portuguese ship first entered Baía de Guanabara. On board was Italian navigator Amerigo Vespucci (1454–1512), who misnamed the bay Rio de Janeiro (River of January). The name stuck, as did America (after Amerigo) for the so-called New World.

In more than half a millennium, Rio has undergone massive transformations, both politically and physically. Built by millions of enslaved Africans and indigenous people, Rio became the capital of the Brazilian colony in 1763 and seat of the Portuguese kingdom (1808–21). From Rio, Brazil was declared independent (1822) and a Republic (1889), a year after slavery was finally abolished.

The 20th century saw more changes, as Rio aimed to be a world-class capital, with grand theaters and boulevards along with spectacular beaches, parks and neighborhoods crafted by human hands. The capital moving to Brasília in 1960 and a 21-year military dictatorship stifled Rio, but a counterculture movement marched the city through. The 2014 World Cup and 2016 Summer Olympics transformed the city again – what's next is to be determined.

1. Fortaleza de São João

RIO'S FIRST BUILDING

It wasn't the Portuguese but the French who were the first Europeans to settle around Baía de Guanabara in 1555. The two European kingdoms battled for the bay while fending off indigenous inhabitants (though disease did most of the fighting for them). In 1565, the Portuguese declared victory and named its settlement São Sebastião do Rio de Janeiro. That year, it set up Forte de São José, the city's first building, which was swallowed by a larger military fort, Fortaleza de São João. Visit the private military base on a free guided tour.

For more on Fortaleza de São João, see p127

2. Igreja de Nossa Senhora da Glória do Outeiro

SYMBOL OF PORTUGUESE CONQUERING

In the 16th century, there was a Tupinambá village at the base of Glória Hill called kari'oka in the Tupi-Guarani language (the origin of carioca, meaning someone from Rio). After the Portuguese almost eliminated the Tupinambá, a small chapel was built on Glória Hill in 1671, and the current church, Igreja de Nossa Senhora da Glória do Outeiro (Church of Our Lady of the Glory of the Hill) was constructed in 1739. The church was beloved by the royal family, including Emperor Pedro II (1825–91), who baptized his daughter Isabel (1846–1921) there on November 15, 1846.

For more on Igreja de Nossa Senhora da Glória do Outeiro, see p152

3. Cais do Valongo

INFAMOUS PORT

The enslavement of indigenous people wasn't enough to rob Brazil of its resources – the Portuguese needed more laborers. Quickly after settling in Brazil, Portugal started to bring enslaved Africans, mostly from western and central Africa, on ships.

Over more than four centuries, four million enslaved people were brought to Brazil, and 1 million of them came through Rio's Cais do Valongo (Valongo Wharf) in just 20 years (1811–31). Today, the UNESCO-recognized former port is little but stone ruins in a square, but its significance weighs heavy.

For more on Cais do Valongo, see p185

Cais do Valongo

FOCUS PIX/SHUTTERSTOCK

4. Pedra do Sal

BIRTH OF SAMBA

In 1831, Brazil outlawed the international slave trade and ordered the liberation of enslaved people entering the country. Without reparations and facing ongoing discrimination, freed and fugitive enslaved people formed tight-knit communities called quilombos, including one located steps from Cais do Valongo at Pedra do Sal. The Pedra do Sal Quilombo became a meeting point to practice repressed African culture, including the Candomblé religion and capoeira, a martial art disguised as a dance. It also gave birth to a new genre of music: samba.

For more on Pedra do Sal, see p186

5. Parque Nacional da Tijuca

REPLANTED FOREST LANDSCAPE

Brazil's coastline was covered with 1,000,000 sq km of Atlantic Forest when the Portuguese arrived, but centuries of relentless agriculture crushed it to just 15% of its original size. The destruction of Atlantic Forest had particularly dire consequences for Rio, which faced impending drought in the 19th century. In the 1860s, emperor Dom Pedro II ordered the planting of 100,000 trees to create what's now Parque Nacional da Tijuca (Tijuca National Park). The park is the world's largest urban rainforest and includes some of Rio's most remarkable mountain hikes, as well as its world wonder, Cristo Redentor.

For more on Parque Nacional da Tijuca, see p74

6. Praça XV (Quinze) de Novembro

HONORING THE NEW REPUBLIC

In Brazil, the trade of enslaved people was finally abolished when Princess Isabel signed the Lei Áurea (Golden Law) on May 13, 1888 – making it the last country in the world to do so. On November 15, 1898, 43 years to the day after Princess Isabel was baptized in Glória, the military decided to abolish the monarchy and the royal family was exiled in favor of a republic. Praça XV (Quinze) de Novembro celebrates Brazilian independence with a square at the foot of Paço Imperial, the former Royal Palace.

For more on Praça XV (Quinze) de Novembro, see p181

7. Theatro Municipal

SHOWCASING RIO AS A NEW PARIS

As a fresh republic, Brazil's leaders wanted Rio to match the opulence of capitals in Europe, such as Paris. A 1902–05 urban reform project transformed the city center, with grand boulevards like Av Central (now Rio Branco), new sewage and water systems, as well as European-style architecture, such as Theatro Municipal. Opened in 1909, Theatro Municipal remains a landmark for Brazilian performing arts, and was where Brazil's first Black ballerina, Mercedes Baptista (1921–2014), got her start.

For more on Theatro Municipal, see p179

8. Copacabana Palace

BIRTH OF A BEACH CITY

Copacabana Beach was a humble fishing village for much of the 19th century, but that changed with the digging of Túnel Velho (Old Tunnel) in 1892, which connected the neighborhoods of Botafogo and Copacabana. The tunnel allowed Brazilian elites to escape the hectic, disease-ridden center in favor of sunbathing on the beach, but the neighborhood really took off in 1923 with the opening of luxury hotel: Copacabana Palace. Built by the wealthy Guinle family for Brazil's centenary, Copacabana Palace attracted the world's top stars and kick-started Rio's tourism industry.

For more on Copacabana Palace, see p101

9. Maracanã Football Stadium

LEGENDARY FOOTBALL STADIUM

The first half of the 20th century saw the game of football, or soccer, explode in Rio de Janeiro. To suit the appetite, the city constructed the Maracanã in 1950, the world's largest football stadium at the time, which was capable of holding more than 200,000 people. The stadium in the Zona Norte (North Zone) got its first workout at the 1950 FIFA World Cup – the first tournament in 12 years, due to WWII. Brazil lost to Uruguay in the final, but there have been many successes since then, as the stadium still hosts local and international matches.

For more on Maracanã Football Stadium, see p194

10. Museu da República

DICTATOR'S PALACE

Few individuals have had more of an effect on Brazilian politics than Getúlio Vargas (1882–1954). After losing in Brazil's 1930 election, Vargas rallied the military to take over in a coup. Vargas went on to rule, both as dictator and democratically-elected president, from 1930 to 1945 and again in 1954. Throughout his rule, Vargas reigned from Palácio do Catete, now known as Museu da República, a free museum and public garden. Facing political upheaval, Vargas shot himself in the palace in 1954.

For more on Museu da República, see p145

11. Aterro do Flamengo

WOMAN-MADE PARK & BEACH

To better connect downtown to the beaches in the growing Zona Sul (South Zone), Rio de Janeiro destroyed a series of hills, including Morro de Santo Antônio. With the empty space, female architect Lota de Macedo Soares (1910–57) carried out an ambitious plan in 1952 to create a 1,300,000-sq-meter urban park in the neighborhood of Flamengo. The ensuing Aterro do Flamengo (Flamengo Landfill), aka Parque do Flamengo, contained a beach, museums and monuments and was recognized by UNESCO for urban landscape design in 2012.

For more on Aterro do Flamengo, see p136

12. Teatro Rival

DRAG RESISTANCE VENUE

In 1960, then-President Juscelino Kubitschek (1902–76) decided to move the capital to Brasília, devastating Rio's economy. A year later, Brazil elected left-leaning President João Goulart (1909–76). Fearing a turn towards communism, a US-backed military coup deposed Goulart in 1964 and the military dictatorship cracked down on forms of artistic expression. In Rio, the Cinelândia area was the cultural center of the city during the dictatorship, and artists there defiantly resisted its puritanism, including by hosting drag shows at Teatro Rival.

For more on Teatro Rival, see p179

Igreja de Nossa Senhora da Candelária

13. Igreja de Nossa Senhora da Candelária

PROTEST SITE AGAINST THE DICTATORSHIP

As soon as the military dictatorship began, it was met with student protests in major Brazilian cities. A particularly bloody protest occurred in Rio de Janeiro on June 21, 1968, coming to be known as 'Bloody Friday' when 28 were killed and 1000 arrested. Five days later, March of the 100,000 filled Rio's streets and the protest's student leader gave a passionate speech in front of Candelária church Igreja de Nossa Senhora da Candelária.

In 1993, Igreja de Nossa Senhora da Candelária was also the site of a massacre in 1993 where eight houseless people, including six minors, were shot by a group of men that included three members of the military police.

For more on Igreja de Nossa Senhora da Candelária, see p181

14. Circo Voador

MUSIC LAUNCHPAD

In 1982, a group of artists erected a blue-and-white tent on Arpoador called Circo Voador. In was supposed to be up for a month but stayed for three, becoming a hot spot for budding musicians and performing artists. Circo Voador convinced the city to give it a new home near the Arcos da Lapa (Lapa Arches) and it became one of the city's most cherished venues. Without the influence of Circo Voador, major festival Rock in Rio, which started in 1985, probably wouldn't have happened.

For more on Circo Voador, see p169

15. Museu do Amanhã

WORLD CUP & OLYMPICS REMNANT

Following the election of Luiz Inácio Lula da Silva (1945–) in 2002, Brazil entered a boom period that saw 20 million people rise out of poverty. Riding high, Rio de Janeiro managed to win bids for the 2014 FIFA World Cup and 2016 Summer Olympics and put together funding for impressive new infrastructure projects, including the future technology museum Museu do Amanhã (Museum of Tomorrow). Reflect on the future, and Rio's place in it, when you visit.

For more on Museu do Amanhã, see p182

MEET THE CARIOCAS

Charismatic and quick to charm, cariocas – the affectionate name for residents of Rio de Janeiro – are easy to connect with. Ana Duék introduces her people.

'WE LIVE WHERE you vacation.' This playful mantra perfectly captures the pride of cariocas, who call Rio de Janeiro – one of the world's most coveted cities – home. While many imagine cariocas spending their days lounging at the beach or dancing at samba parties, the truth is that we are as diverse and eclectic as Brazil itself. The iconic samba-loving trickster who inspired Disney's José Carioca is just one facet of a Rio resident: a dedicated worker, athlete, soccer enthusiast, gourmet, rocker, funk lover, traveler, and, above all, a warm, cheerful, and welcoming host.

Who & How Many?

Rio de Janeiro is home to over 6.2 million residents, with 54.3% identifying as Black. The city also hosts nearly 7000 Indigenous people.

Cariocas are sun worshippers, to the point where we applaud the sunset, and cold or rainy days simply don't suit the city, or its people. When temperatures dip below 22°C, we're quick to grab our winter outfits. On typical days, though, our wardrobe revolves around shorts, flip-flops, tank tops, and breezy dresses. Completing the scene is a classic iced *maté* (unlike the warm version popular in the South), a cold beer, or a frosty *caipirinha*. And when the heat soars above 40°C, *cariocas* always find creative ways to stay cool.

Known for our informality, cariocas will likely call you by your nickname right away and invite you to enjoy live music in a cozy Rio spot. Charismatic and quick to charm, we're easy to connect with, though relationships often rely on chance encounters. You'll hear us say, 'Let's talk' or 'We'll catch up,' and sometimes that's where it ends. But give us a chance, and we can become loyal, lifelong friends.

The word carioca has Indigenous Tupi roots, derived from *kara'iwa* (white man) and *oka* (house), reflecting the region's first inhabitants. Today, this 'house of the white man' is a vibrant blend of indigenous, Afro-Brazilian, and European influences, with 54.3% of the population identifying as black. While known globally for bossa nova and the song 'The Girl from Ipanema', Rio's true spirit thrives in Afro-centered cultural expressions like samba, funk, charme, and passinho.

From 1763 to 1960, Rio was Brazil's capital, flourishing under Portuguese rule while becoming the country's largest entry port for enslaved Africans. Over 1 million Africans passed through Cais do Valongo (p185), now a UNESCO World Heritage Site. Like much of Brazil, Rio took years to acknowledge the profound influence of its indigenous and African roots. Today, we proudly honor and celebrate this unique identity, sharing it with visitors from around the world.

MY RIO STORY

Perhaps I'm not a typical carioca, with roots that stretch to Syria, Egypt, Austria, and Bessarabia. Four of my great-grandparents, from distant corners of the world, found their way to Rio de Janeiro in the early 20th century – a testament to the city's diversity. Since my grandparents' generation, we've proudly called ourselves *cariocas da gema* (true *Cariocas*).

I'm a privileged *carioca*, born near the ocean with the freedom to chart my own course. I earned a degree in journalism and traveled across Brazil and the world, collecting stories to share. While visitors often imagine the sea as central to every *carioca*'s life, only a lucky few live close to the beaches – privileges that come at a steep cost.

I have a conflicted relationship with my hometown, fully aware of the inequalities and struggles we face. Yet, I'll always feel honored to be a carioca – proud of Rio's unparalleled beauty, my lilting accent, my samba school Mangueira, and the simple pleasure of saying, 'Meet me in Ipanema for some coconut water!'

Beach football, Ipanema Beach (p82)
LAZYLLAMA/SHUTTERSTOCK

JOGO BONITO THE BEAUTIFUL GAME

There are few things *cariocas* (residents of Rio) care more about than *futebol* (football, aka soccer). By Joel Balsam

JOGO BONITO (the beautiful game) is an obsession in Rio de Janeiro, more so even than Carnaval. Games from the city's four local teams – Flamengo, Fluminense, Botafogo and Vasco da Gama – are played year-round and watched with undivided fervor from neighborhood *botecos* (small, open-air bars), cell phones and virtually every establishment with a TV. Matches at its three major stadiums, all in Zona Norte (North Zone), are electric, especially when local teams play each other, known as a *clássico*. Seeing a game at the Maracanã, probably the world's most legendary *futebol* stadium, is an experience worthy of telling your grandkids. The energy in the city becomes even more palpable when Seleção Brasileira (Brazil's national team) takes the pitch in its proud yellow-and-green jerseys for international competitions such as the World Cup, the Olympics and Copa America. Here's what to know about Rio's love for *futebol* and how to get tickets for a game.

History of Futebol in Rio

Futebol arrived in Rio de Janeiro from England at the end of the 19th century. Oscar Cox, a Rio-born son of a British diplomat, learned about *futebol* while studying in Europe and returned to start the city's first club team, Fluminense, in 1902. Rio's other three teams started as rowing clubs before picking up *futebol:* Botafogo in 1904, Flamengo in 1911 and Vasco da Gama in 1915.

In 1914, British club Exeter City was traveling to Argentina for a *futebol* match and decided to stop and play a game at Fluminense's home stadium in Laranjeiras. Brazil selected its best players from around the country (the first iteration of Seleção), and managed to defeat the English side in a violent match 2–0. Rio was officially obsessed.

Brazil took to the pitch in Uruguay for the first World Cup and won the right to host the international tournament in 1950. Rio built a brand new stadium for the occasion: the Maracanã, then the world's largest. The team made it to the final against Uruguay and managed to take the lead but ended up losing 2–1 in front of 200,000 fans (games aren't played at that size anymore for safety reasons).

After the devastating defeat, Brazil changed from playing in white to the *Canarinho* yellow, green and blue jersey to

match the country's flag. At the 1958 World Cup, Brazil brought a 17-year-old phenom named Edson Arantes do Nascimento, aka Pelé, and won. Pelé became the greatest to play the game, and Brazil went on to win five World Cups with legendary players like Didi, Ronaldo and Ronaldinho – the most of any country to this day. However, since winning in 2002, the Brazilian national team has struggled to regain its former glory. A 7–1 loss to Germany at the 2014 World Cup in Brazil was a low point that locals won't soon forget.

On the women's side, Brazil has also cast legendary players, including Marta, who has been voted the best in the world six times. While Brazilian women haven't managed to win any World Cups, it hopes its fortunes can change when Brazil hosts the tournament in 2027.

Leagues & Teams

Futebol in Rio isn't just an event every two or four years when Brazil plays in international competitions. *Cariocas* passionately support their local clubs throughout the year in national and regional tournaments.

Campeonato Brasileiro (Brazilian Championship) is the top national league and is played between July and November. Copa Libertadores is South America's top competition and runs from February to August. The oldest league is Campeonato Carioca, the Rio de Janeiro state championship played between January and April.

Flamengo, which plays in red and black from its headquarters in Leblon, is Rio's most popular club, with millions of supporters worldwide. A fan is called a Flamenguista and the team plays its home

ANDRE_MA/SHUTTERSTOCK

Fluminense fans, Maracanã Stadium (p194)

games at the Maracanã, which can fit just under 79,000 fans.

Fluminense sports maroon, green and white stripes, giving its fans the nickname Tricolor. The Laranjeiras-born team now plays out of the Maracanã.

Botafogo wears white and black stripes and is named after the neighborhood where it's based. A fan is a Botafoguense. Botafogo plays its home games at Estádio Nilton Santos (also known as Engenhão or the Olympic Stadium), which can fit about 45,000 spectators. Botafogo plays at the Maracanã for major matches.

Vasco da Gama is credited with being the first team to champion black and multiracial players in the 1920s. Fans are called Vascaíno and the team plays at the 18,000-person stadium Estadio São Januário. Like Botafogo, big matches are played at the Maracanã.

How to Buy Tickets

Buying tickets for matches can be a headache without a CPF (Brazilian ID number). Most tickets are reserved for club members and only go on sale to the public two or three days before game time. Wherever you buy tickets, you'll need your physical passport and will have to get your face scanned.

Buy tickets for Flamengo home games at Maracanã (p194) from the team's official *loja* (store) in Copacabana or at its club headquarters in Leblon, Clube de Regatas do Flamengo. Tickets can also be purchased with a passport at *flamengo.superingresso.com.br* or at the stadium on game day. Fluminense sells tickets to passport holders from its official store in Copacabana and at Maracanã. Tickets for Botafogo home games at Nilton Santos (p123) are sold online through *ingresse.com,* as well as at the stadium. Vasco da Gama sells online at *sociogigante.com/ingressos,* but tickets almost always sell out to club members unless they play at Maracanã.

Local tour operators, accommodations and probably a friend of a friend of a Brazilian you know who's a club member may also be able to get you tickets, and can sometimes escort you to the game. However, be prepared to pay a premium for these tickets.

THE SOUNDS OF RIO
MUSIC OF THE CARIOCAS

Music is as integral to Rio de Janeiro as its beaches and mountains. By Joel Balsam

BRAZILIAN PORTUGUESE SPEAKERS rarely use the word for song, *canção*. A track is simply *a música* (the music) or *o som* (the sound). There's no need for song, since music doesn't stop in Rio de Janeiro, one after the next, all day and night long. You'll hear music blasting from the beach to the hilltop favelas, from tiny bars to shoddy car speakers, and everywhere in between. International chart toppers like American pop or even reggaeton aren't common. Instead, *choro,* samba, *pagode, música popular brasileira* (MPB) and *funk carioca* dominate the airwaves and are a pivotal component of *Brazilidade* (Brazilian identity and pride).

Every popular Brazilian musical genre is rooted in some way or another by African rhythms, which were brought over by the nearly four million enslaved people who came to this country in more than three centuries of slavery. Drumbeats from Afro-Brazilian religions like Candomblé laid the groundwork for the first samba songs, which went on to influence a few middle-class cariocas to slow down the rhythm and sing about a pretty girl on a beach in Rio. The *tropicália* movement of the late 1960s proved that Brazilian music is more than just love songs, and funk *carioca* put and Rio's favelas, and their daily struggles with violence, on full display.

Here are the most popular sounds of Rio, and where to hear them.

Choro

In the middle of the 19th century, polka and the waltz were all the rage in Europe. In Rio de Janeiro, African rhythms like lundu, a Bantu song and dance, were popular on the streets. In the 1870s, Brazilian composer and flutist Joaquim Antônio da Silva Callado fused these genres to create an instrumental music genre played with European string and brass instruments that came to be known as *choro*, or *chorinho.*

In the early 20th century, Alfredo da Rocha Viana Filho, aka Pixinguinha, took choro and mixed it with another African-inspired rhythm: jazz, which spawned from New Orleans around the same time.

Hear Pixinguinha's style of *choro* on Mondays at Bar do Serginho, Wednesdays at Bip Bip and Saturdays at Feira de Laranjeiras.

Forró

Another Brazilian genre born in the 19th century was *forró,* though it was popularized by Luiz Gonzaga in the 20th century. Stemming from popular dance parties in the country's northeast that were 'for all', *forró* is a fast-paced genre played with a *zabumba* (drum), a triangle and an accordion. *Forró* is also a popular couples' dance with a leader and a follower.

Hear and dance *forró* on Fridays at Clube dos Democraticos.

CAR
NA
VAL
53

Brass band, Banda de Ipanema Carnaval

LAZYLLAMA/ALAMY

Samba

The late 19th century brought the end of slavery and the birth of Rio de Janeiro's most well-known genre: samba. Samba's matriarch was Bahia-born Hilária Batista de Almeida, aka Tia (Aunt) Ciata. By day, Tia Ciata would sell *acarajé* (fried bean, fish and palm oil snack) in a downtown Rio square. At night, she'd host *Candomblé* (an Afro-Brazilian religion) ceremonies and musicians at her home, Casa da Tia Ciata in Paquena África (Little Africa). Since practicing *Candomblé* was banned, Tia Ciata cleverly invited musicians like Pixinguinha to play in the front of the house to throw off the police. In the backyard, musicians would be playing samba, which was influenced by *Candomblé* drum rhythms and often played in a *roda* (circle) with instruments like a *pandeiro* (tambourine), a *cuíca* (pull drum) and *xequerê* (rattling beads on a gourd).

The first samba song, Pelo Telefone (1916), was recorded in Tia Ciata's backyard, and while the song is credited to Donga, Tia Ciata herself is believed to have helped compose it. Samba caught on with Carnaval *ranchos,* later called *Blocos,* that would pass Tia Ciata's house on their parade route. Ranchos took samba and turned them into parade anthems played on brass and percussion instruments (called *fanfarra*), and in 1926, the first Carnaval samba school, Deixa Falar, was born.

Samba went global in the 1930s when a young Portuguese-born singer named Maria do Carmo Miranda da Cunha, or Carmen Miranda, was spotted in a Rio casino and invited to perform in the US. Miranda's version of samba, which involved hip-notizing dancing and extravagant clothing, such as her famous fruit hat, took the US by storm. She appeared in 14 Hollywood films and was the highest female US taxpayer in 1945. In Brazil, Miranda didn't have as warm a reception, with many critical that she embellished Brazilian stereotypes and appropriated the Afro-Brazilian genre.

Hear samba steps from Tia Ciata's house at Pedra do Sal on Mondays and Fridays. Other authentic samba venues include Renascença Clube and Cacique de Ramos in Zona Norte as well as Vaca Atolada in Lapa.

Bossa Nova

In the late 1950s, songwriter and composer Antônio Carlos (Tom) Jobim along with lyricist-poet Vinícius de Moraes and guitarist João Gilberto slowed down and altered the basic samba rhythm to create a more intimate, harmonic style. Their new genre, bossa nova ('new wave'), was influenced by US blues music and first recorded on the 1957 song 'Chega de Saudade' ('No More Blues') by Brazilian singer Elizete Cardoso. Bossa nova took off in 1962 when Jobim and Moraes wrote a song about a cute girl walking to Rio de Janeiro's Ipanema Beach called 'Garota de Ipanema' ('The Girl from Ipanema').

The second version of the song by Frank Getz and Astrud Gilberto (João's then-wife) became an international sensation, and it was recorded in English by Jobim and Frank Sinatra in 1967. It's believed that 'The Girl from Ipanema' is the second-most recorded song ever after The Beatles' 'Yesterday'. Other bossa nova performers include the great singer Elis Regina and Sérgio Mendes, who made a bossa-nova version of the Jorge Ben (Jor) song 'Mas Que Nada' in 1963 that became a huge hit in the US.

Hear bossa nova where it was first played live by its original founders at Copacabana's Beco das Garrafas. Nearby Blue Note is another terrific venue.

Tropicália & MPB

As bossa nova dominated the airwaves in the early 1960s, the tone in Brazilian politics was much less chill. The capital moved from Rio de Janeiro to Brasília in 1960, and a military coup unseated a left-leaning present in 1964. Four years later, 100,000 people took to the streets to protest the dictatorship and demand an end to police brutality. At the protest were two rebellious musicians from Bahia: Caetano Veloso and Gilberto Gil. That same year, Veloso and Gil released an album in

LAZYLLAMA/ALAMY

Bossa nova musician, Ipanema Beach (p82)

collaboration with fellow musicians Tom Zé, Nara Leão, Os Mutantes and Gal Costa called *Tropicália – Ou Panis et Circenses*. The album, which is classified under the genre *música popular brasileira* (MPB), ridiculed the consumerism of the US-backed dictatorship and was censored along with other forms of artistic expression. Veloso and Gil were arrested in 1969 and fled to Europe in exile, but the tropicália movement could not be stopped. Other MPB artists to carry on tropicália's sound and critical lyrics include Jorge Ben Jor, Chico Buarque, Milton Nascimento, Maria Bethânia and Djavan. Recently, MPB has been making a comeback with a new generation that includes Luedji Luna and Gilberto Gil's sons and grandson, Gilsons.

There is no specific place to go to hear MPB in Rio, but it's often played in bars, restaurants and shops all over the city.

Pagode, Rock, Pop & Funk

Technically, MPB includes all Brazilian popular music, which means MPB is also *pagode,* rock, hip-hop, pop and *funk carioca. Pagode* evolved in the late 1970s as a subgenre of samba and is known for its simple, catchy lyrics. Hear it at the bar named after the genre's most well-known composer, Bar do Zeca Pagodinho.

Rock music grew in popularity in Rio de Janeiro, thanks in part to Circo Voador, formerly a concert tent on the beach that moved to Lapa, becoming one of the city's most popular venues to this day. You can also hear the genre at the city's biggest music festival, Rock in Rio *(rockinrio.com)*, though it plays much more than rock these days.

Funk, as the genre is known in the US, made its way to Brazil in the 1970s, with artists like Tim Maia – but that's not the same thing as *funk carioca*. Also known as *favela funk*, Brazilian funk or simply funk (pronounced funk-ee), the hugely popular genre started in Rio's favelas, similar to how hip-hop and house began in New York and Chicago – electronic DJs mixed funk and soul to create a new counterculture sound. Also influenced by Afrobeat and Miami bass, funk carioca has a distinctive cha-cha-chacha beat and, like modern rap, usually features raunchy lyrics about sex, drugs and guns – realities of life in Rio's poorest neighborhoods. *Funk carioca*'s biggest name is Anitta, born Larissa de Macedo Machado in a Rio favela, who fused the genre with pop and became Brazil's most popular international female singer since Carmen Miranda. Outside of Brazil, the genre is called baile funk; though in Rio, that term refers to gang-led favela parties, where guns are carried in the open.

Hear *funk carioca* anywhere people like to shake it, though especially at clubs in Lapa and Centro.

FAVELAS
ALL SIDES OF RIO

Tourists are increasingly drawn to favelas for their samba schools, creative energies, excellent parties and unique cultural experiences. However, it's worth noting that drug trafficking is an issue, and while it may be unlikely you'll be drawn into anything as dramatic as a gang war, it's important to be mindful of the risks. By Marisa Megan Paska

FAVELAS ARE SUB-TERRITORIES of Brazilian cities, with less government support and access to services than normal areas. Favelas don't have post offices or sewage systems; health centers are few and under-resourced, and even ambulances frequently won't enter, due to safety concerns.

There have been attempts to integrate favelas into greater metropolises. In 2008, Rio de Janeiro began a program to 'pacify' the favelas around the city. A special task force, called the UPP, trained both in combat and community relations, drove the gangs out of the neighborhoods, installed security forces and set up social programs for the local residents. The aim of the program was to bring peace and infrastructure into these zones, with the long-term goal to integrate favelas into the city.

Pacification allowed for the government to improve their actions within the favelas, and for social projects and small businesses to begin to fill in the gaps where government offerings fell short. It also set the stage for tourism to take root.

Should You Visit?

Some middle- or upper-class Brazilians may warn you off visiting favelas. They're too dangerous, they'll tell you. It's too risky. Then, the question will inevitably follow: why would you want to go to one?

It's a tricky subject. Visiting neighborhoods to gape at or judge a different way of life is akin to visiting a human zoo. It's not a great idea.

Visiting a community to better understand the lives of the people who live there, or to interact and exchange with them, to celebrate their unique culture and economically support local ventures or social projects is the sort of positive effect tourism is supposed to have on the world.

If you are considering visiting a favela in Brazil, it's best to do your research and be prepared.

Understand the Culture

Tourism can be an enriching exchange that valorizes the unique cultures that have grown out of socially marginalized zones, but the tendency to focus on the risks can

Vidigal favela

MATTHIAS KESTEL/ALAMY

easily diminish the importance of an area's contribution to society.

Favelas might be more dangerous than the rest of the city, but they're also creative and cultural hubs of the country, which produce the best sambistas, rappers and funkeiros, along with top artists, athletes and entrepreneurs.

'Easily the most relevant culture in Brazil today is favela culture,' says Micael Amarante, who worked for the city of Rio as part of the UPP favela pacification project when it was first introduced in 2008. Creativity is often born of necessity, and it's true that life in favelas can be quite difficult.

'If a foreigner brings money into the favela, it's going directly into the hands of the residents there. That's positive,' concedes Amarante. 'The problem is that if you want to enter a favela, you are never going to be completely safe, because you're never going to know if there are any problems between the three factions, or the police, at that exact moment.'

Carolina Maria de Jesus' celebrated autobiography Quarto de Despejo - Diário de Uma Favelada (1960) gives a detailed account of Jesus' day-to-day life in a favela in São Paulo. Although the book (which has been translated into 13 languages) is from the 1950's, Jesus' account of the realities of favela life is still very true today.

A better understanding of both the positive and negative aspects of life in a favela will only serve to enrich your visit, should you choose to do so.

Know the Rules

There are a few rules you should follow if you decide to visit a favela. First off: know where you can and can't go. Some streets, for example, are to be avoided, as they're where trafficking takes place. If you're told to stay away from somewhere, follow these instructions to the letter.

The second rule is to always go with someone who knows the area. It's easy to get confused in the labyrinth-like streets, so make sure you arrive with a guide, be they a local tour guide or a friend who works at a social project. If you ever get lost or are unsure where to go, tell a resident who you are, who you're with and why you're in the neighborhood. Once the locals know your purpose, they'll be better placed to help you get where you're going without incurring any hassle.

Rule three: ask before you click. It's generally okay to take pictures in favelas, but avoid taking pictures that show someone's face unless you've previously asked for, and received permission to. In some favelas, the controlling gangs don't want any photos taken; in others, residents can be prosecuted by the police if even a minor discretion – such as smoking weed or underage drinking – is caught on film.

With these rules firmly in mind, we've compiled a short list of some Rio favelas.

Vidigal e Chácara do Céu

Sandwiched in between the absurdly expensive neighborhoods of Leblon and São Conrado in Rio de Janeiro sits the well known favela Vidigal and its little brother Chácara do Céu. Their brick and concrete-block houses creep up the side of the renowned Dois Irmãos (Two Brothers) mountain, offering expansive views of Ipanema, Leblon, the Lagoa and of the Cagarras Islands.

Its privileged location made Vidigal a magnet for tourism, with bars, party spots, restaurants, and hostels popping up across the hillside. Foreigners – including David Beckham and Madonna – bought property, and a luxury hotel was even built on high.

Some of the top attractions are Alto Vidigal, a party space situated at the top of the hillside with breathtaking views; its neighbor Bar do Lage, a bar and restaurant with the same spectacular view; the Italian-South American restaurante Flor do Céu in Chácara do Céu (reservations only); the theater group Nós do Morro (We of the Hillside); Sitiê Parque Ecológico (Sitiê Ecological Park); and the trail to the top of Dois Irmãos mountain.

Morro da Mangueira

Just behind the small residential neighborhood of Leme, at the far end of Copacabana Beach, sit the favelas Morro da Babilônia and Chapéu Mangueira: two

BRAZILPHOTOS/ALAMY

Estrelas da Babilônia

relatively safe communities blessed with peaceful ocean views, Atlantic rainforest hiking and some of the best bar food in the city.

The tourist itinerary in the Morro da Babilônia and Chapéu Mangueira includes a stop at the 140m mosaic Mural Babilonia, guided hiking through the rainforest through the Circuito do Morro da Babilônia, a sunset drink at the ocean-view terrace of Estrelas da Babilônia (if you don't mind climbing the stairs to get there), and finally a stop at Bar do David, twice-voted the second-best bar food in the city in the *Comida di Buteco* competition.

Cultural Immersion

While tourism can be an enriching exchange that valorizes the unique culture that has grown out of these socially marginalized zones, favela culture doesn't just exist in favelas.

If you want to know more, head to Lapa in Rio and check out a Carioca Funk show at the Fundição Progresso, visit an exposição of favela-inspired art at the MAR, stop by a samba school or visit a traditional roda de samba at Pedra do Sal, just below the Morro da Conceição to get an insight in the rich, unique culture that's grown from Rio's hilltops.

INDEX

Map Pages **000**

D

G

Map Pages **000**

Map Pages **000**

"Praia do Leme (p112), where I grew up, has a tranquil, authentic vibe. With its warm, local atmosphere, it is the perfect spot to experience the genuine essence of Rio."

ANA DUÉK

"Praia do Arpoador (p88) is my favorite place to start the day. It's where I go for a early-morning swim or surf, take my dogs for a run, or simply sit on Pedra do Arpoador and watch the city wake up."

MARISA MEGAN PASKA

"That time I was sipping Original in Urca and saw a penguin swim by. A sign that you never really know what to expect in Rio!"

JOEL BALSAM

Mapping data sources:
© Lonely Planet
© OpenStreetMap http://openstreetmap.org/copyright

FROM LEFT: THOMAS ROUSSEL/ALAMY, JOHN MICHAELS/ALAMY

THIS BOOK

Destination Editor
Alicia Johnson

Coordinating Editor
Tasmin Waby

Assisting Editors
Soo Hamilton, Maura Murphy, Karyn Noble

Production Editor
Claire Rourke

Image Editor
Norma Brewer

Cartographer
Eve Kelly

Assistant Cartographer
Daniela Machová

Cover Researcher
Giada de Agostinis

Thanks Ronan Abayawickrema, James Appleton, Imogen Bannister, Charlotte Orr, Clifton Wilkinson

Paper in this book is certified against the Forest Stewardship Council™ standards. FSC™ promotes environmentally responsible, socially beneficial and economically viable management of the world's forests.

Published by Lonely Planet Global Limited
CRN 554153
11th edition – Oct 2025
ISBN 978 1 78868 427 9

10 9 8 7 6 5 4 3 2 1
Printed in Malaysia